Unlocking the Files of the FBI

A Guide to Its Records and Classification System

Unlocking the Files of the FBI

A Guide to Its Records and Classification System

Gerald K. Haines
and
David A. Langbart

SR *Scholarly Resources Inc.*
Wilmington, Delaware

The paper used in this publication meets the minimum requirements of the American National Standard for permanence of paper for printed library materials, Z39.48, 1984.

© 1993 by Scholarly Resources Inc.
All rights reserved
First published 1993
Printed and bound in the United States of America

Scholarly Resources Inc.
104 Greenhill Avenue
Wilmington, DE 19805-1897

Library of Congress Cataloging-in-Publication Data

Haines, Gerald K., 1943–
   Unlocking the files of the FBI : a guide to its records and classification system / Gerald K. Haines and David A. Langbart.
      p. cm.
  Includes index.
  ISBN 0-8420-2338-0
  1. United States. Federal Bureau of Investigation—Archives. 2. Law enforcement—United States—Archival resources. I. Langbart, David A., 1956– . II. Title.
HV8144.F43H35 1993
026'.3530074—dc20
                             92-16728
                                CIP

Gerald K. Haines is a senior historian on the DCI History staff of the Central Intelligence Agency and was a member of the NARA/FBI Task Force that evaluated preservation options for FBI records. He is the author of *A Reference Guide to United States Department of State Special Files* (Westport, CT, 1985), which received the 1988 Thomas Jefferson Prize from the Society for History in the Federal Government, and *The Americanization of Brazil: A Study of U.S. Cold War Diplomacy in the Third World, 1945–1954* (Wilmington, DE, 1989).

David A. Langbart is an archivist on the staff of the Records Appraisal and Disposition Division of the National Archives.

Contents

Introduction

Background

The Federal Bureau of Investigation (FBI) is one of the best-known and, at times, most controversial law enforcement agencies in the world. From its humble beginnings in 1909 as the Bureau of Investigation (BOI), to its vast expansion under J. Edgar Hoover, to the modern-day FBI under William Sessions, the Bureau has played an important role in American society. Over the years it has gathered information on and investigated not only criminal activities in the United States, such as organized crime, bank robbery, kidnapping, murder, and white-collar crimes, but also has become intimately involved in intelligence matters ranging from counterintelligence activities and domestic security concerns to terrorist and narcotics problems.

The Bureau's records touch on all aspects of American society from prostitution and auto theft to espionage and subversion. During 1919 and 1920 it was deeply involved in the controversial Palmer Raids. In the 1930s it gained notoriety under Director Hoover as a tough, honest Federal law enforcement agency leading the fight against corruption and organized crime. During the late 1930s and 1940s, in response to the growing world crisis and President Franklin D. Roosevelt's urging, it expanded its responsibilities in the foreign intelligence arena. It monitored Nazi, Fascist, and Communist activities in the United States and conducted an extensive intelligence operation abroad, especially in Latin America. Deeply committed to the Cold War in the late 1940s and early 1950s, the Bureau launched an intensive anti-Communist crusade that brought it into direct contact with American citizens. The 1960s and 1970s saw Hoover and the FBI embroiled in domestic social, political, and economic matters as the Bureau sought not only to monitor but also to disrupt the civil rights movement, anti-Vietnam War protest groups, and black activist organizations. The Bureau's use of "black bag" techniques—wiretaps and electronic surveillance as well as official break-ins—and its Counterintelligence Program

(COINTELPRO) entangled it in massive legal and social questions regarding its mission, authority, and responsibilities in domestic intelligence. In the 1980s the drug war dominated Bureau activities.

The information gathered and produced by the Bureau in the course of developing its investigations is massive. Its records, for the most part carefully maintained, constitute a valuable source for scholars and others interested in almost every aspect of American development in the twentieth century. The social historian investigating changing mores and attitudes in the United States relating to civil rights, racial matters, and minority concerns; the foreign policy specialist delving into U.S. intelligence activities or the intense U.S. focus on communism and the Soviet threat; the political scientist examining the operation and structure of the bureaucracy; the criminologist studying law enforcement techniques and federal, state, and local cooperation; or the social scientist hoping to develop a profile of conscientious objectors or white-collar criminals will all find a wealth of primary source material within the FBI files. These FBI files contain classifications for all cases investigated and cover diverse topics from kidnapping to bank fraud to cattle rustling, civil rights violations to espionage. They include raw data and initial interviews as well as finished reports, internal Bureau memorandums, directives, guidelines, agent interviews, surveillance logs, phone logs, photographs, and related court and other agency records.

Unfortunately, until recently most of the FBI's records have been unavailable for research purposes. The Bureau itself retained almost all of the records it generated; they were not transferred to the National Archives and Records Administration (NARA), nor was there an informative guide to their content. The publication of this *Guide* offers the first comprehensive attempt to provide the researcher with a tool with which to unlock this valuable source. The intent of the *Guide* is to provide the reader with a brief overview of the FBI's record-keeping organization and procedures; a profile of each of the classifications, containing information on when the Bureau established it, what types of information may be found within it, and descriptions of some of the cases; information concerning where the records are currently located, how to obtain access to them, and what their legal status is as far as their disposition is concerned (whether they will be preserved and transferred to the National Archives as permanently valuable records or scheduled for destruction); and a listing of related records that might be helpful to the researcher, including those FBI records released under the Freedom of Information Act (FOIA).

This *Guide* is based not only on the extensive National Archives and Records Service and the Federal Bureau of Investigation 1981 report submitted to Judge Harold H. Greene, *Appraisal of the Records of the Federal Bureau of Investigation,*[1] and the National Archives 1986 *Update to the FBI Records*

---

[1]Under a court order issued by Federal District Court Judge Harold H. Greene, experts from the National Archives in 1980–81, for the first time, examined in detail the existing records and record-keeping practices of the FBI. They studied not only records

Schedule,[2] but also on the extensive and unique materials gathered by the NARA/FBI Task Force itself.[3] The task force records were extremely useful and included draft historical profiles of each classification, preliminary appraisal write-ups on each classification by the members of the task force, overall impressions of each classification, and comments concerning specific case files compiled on individual data collection sheets, which provided both the basic characteristics of each classification and a detailed look at individual cases. These records also contained detailed special studies of particular FBI records and files.

The FBI Record-keeping System

Charles J. Bonaparte, attorney general under President Theodore Roosevelt, created a force of special agents in the Department of Justice in July 1908. This investigative service became the Bureau of Investigation under Stanley W. Finch in 1909. After several name changes, in 1935 it became the Federal Bureau of Investigation.

From its inception the Bureau established and relied upon an extensive record-keeping system to help it perform its mission. The first filing system created in 1909 consisted of cases numbered from 1 to 42,975. This system, eventually known as the Miscellaneous File, remained in use until 1922. A

---

in FBI headquarters but field office, auxiliary office, and legation records as well. Their report, which included recommendations for the permanent retention of certain FBI records and suggested dates for their transfer to the National Archives, provided the first full review of the potential of these materials for scholarly research. See National Archives and Records Administration and Federal Bureau of Investigation, *Appraisal of the Records of the Federal Bureau of Investigation: A Report to Honorable Harold H. Greene, United States District Court for the District of Columbia* (Washington, DC, November 9, 1981). The report is presently available on microfiche from the Publications Services Branch of the National Archives. At the time of the task force review the Bureau had established 214 separate classifications. Today there are 278 classifications.

[2] In 1984 NARA and the FBI entered into a memorandum of agreement regarding future modifications of the comprehensive records control schedule developed in 1981. This memorandum called for NARA to review the FBI's records management program and records schedule every five years. NARA carried out the first review in 1986. The NARA review team attempted to appraise each classification for which records retention criteria could not be established in 1981 and to appraise each of the new records classifications established since 1981. By the time of this NARA review there were 258 FBI classifications. See National Archives and Records Administration, "Report on the 1986 Update to the FBI Records Schedule " (National Archives, February 18, 1987). Another NARA review of FBI records occurred in 1991.

[3] Most of the records of the FBI task force are unaccessioned and scheduled for disposal. The authors gained access to the material by filing an FOIA request with the National Archives before the records were destroyed. The material we received was heavily sanitized by the FBI. Those records deemed permanent will eventually be accessioned into Records of the National Archives and Records Administration, Record Group 64.

"case" file did not necessarily correspond to an investigation or to a court case per se but rather referred to a particular subject matter. Even today, FBI classifications contain such cases.

In 1910 the Bureau added a set of numerical files for cases evolving from investigations relating to the Mann Act (the White Slave Traffic Act). In 1916 the Bureau created two additional categories: the Mexican File, for investigations involving Bureau intelligence activities in Mexico during and after the Mexican Revolution, and the Old German File for investigations of enemy aliens and World War I matters. The Old German File eventually contained cases relating to "radicals" as well. In 1918 the Bureau created an additional file for cases generated by the Lever Act on wartime profiteering.

In 1920 the BOI experimented with a new filing system based on the source of the documents. It quickly proved unsatisfactory and in September 1920 the Bureau integrated its records into those of the Department of Justice. This move too proved unworkable. After the Department of Justice returned all BOI files, the Bureau in October 1921 set up a classified filing system in which each classification related to a specific violation of law. To start, it borrowed classification numbers 5 to 60 (with gaps) from the Department of Justice system. Under this system each classification corresponded to a specific Federal crime, Bureau investigative responsibility, or subject. For example, under the system a kidnapping case file might carry the number 7-12, indicating that it was a case in Classification 7 Kidnapping and that it was the twelfth kidnapping case opened. Each document in the case would carry its own numerical designation or serial number as well. Hence, 7-12-4 would refer to the fourth document or "serial" in the twelfth case conducted under Classification 7. The serials are numbered consecutively in chronological order. This system gave the Bureau item control over its records, a facility it retains today.

The present FBI Central Records System is based on the early system and remains essentially unchanged from 1921, although many additional classifications have been added. Each classification begins with a zero (0) file and a double zero (00) file. These are used for documents that relate to the classification but do not warrant a separate case designation. Most of the 00 files, for example, contain material relating to the administrative history of the classification and document why the Bureau initiated it, changes in legislation affecting it and Bureau responsibilities, investigative policies and procedures, and the relationships of the Bureau with other Federal agencies, including jurisdictional disputes. The 0 files predate the establishment of the 00 files and were sometimes used for policy documentation as well. The 0 files, however, principally contain citizen complaints, routine requests for information, general reference material, and newspaper clippings relating to the classification.

Bureau investigations involving more than one violation are routinely classified under the more serious crime. For example, if a stolen vehicle (Classification 26) is used to transport a kidnapped person (Classification 7) across state lines, the case would normally be found in the Kidnapping classification. In security cases, it is Bureau policy to use only one file for an individual or an organization. For example, the Alger Hiss file is found in Classification 101 Hatch Act even though he subsequently was prosecuted and convicted of perjury (Classification 74).

The Bureau established two classifications, 62 Administrative Inquiry and 66 Administrative Matters, in 1921 as repositories for miscellaneous administrative files. As the classifications evolved, however, they became increasingly heterogenous in content. For example, Classification 62 combines routine public correspondence files with sensitive informant control files.

In order to maintain intellectual control of these massive files, the Bureau developed an extensive series of indexes. The most important is the General Index, consisting (in 1981) of approximately 65,500,000 3" x 5" cards arranged alphabetically. The Bureau prepared two types of cards for its General Index: (1) main cards for individuals, organizations, and general subjects that are the primary focus of an investigation, and (2) cross-reference or "see" cards for secondary subjects. In 1979, Bureau officials divided the General Index into two sections—active and inactive. Criminal subject cards dated before 1973 and security cards dated prior to 1958 were put into the inactive section in preparation for computerization of the entire system.

In general, the field offices adopted the same procedures that Bureau headquarters maintained. Some variations, however, exist. For example, the field offices separate their closed and pending investigation files, and Classification 80 Laboratory Research Matters is used differently in the field than at headquarters. Because the files are numbered consecutively in each classification, the same case will not have the same number at headquarters as in the field offices. In some instances the case may even be filed in an entirely different classification in the field than at headquarters.

In addition to the Central File the Bureau has maintained some headquarters records separately. These included records in the Special File Rooms, electronic surveillance (ELSUR) materials, personnel and budget records, FBI National Academy records, public inquiries, computer records, and audiovisual materials.

In 1948, Hoover established at FBI headquarters Special File Rooms to hold "all Files that have an unusually confidential or peculiar background . . . including all obscene enclosures." In general, material placed in the Special File Rooms included what was known as June Mail, ELSUR documents, informant files, and sensitive records on Bureau employees and prominent people, as well as on undercover operations and foreign-source information. The field offices also have special file rooms for informant and ELSUR materials.

FBI June Mail and "Do Not File" memorandums have received widespread public attention. In 1949, Hoover instructed his agents to establish a separate filing procedure for information from or relating to the Bureau's "most sensitive sources" to ensure that such information would not appear in the case files. Such mail was to be sealed in an envelope marked "June," a codeword used because the program began in the month of June. The envelope was then to be placed inside another envelope addressed to the Director, "Personal and Confidential." June Mail was to be used only for the most secretive sources, including unusual investigative techniques (ELSUR materials or surreptitious entry information). In November 1978 the Bureau discontinued the "June" designation but retained the requirements for special handling and the separation of sensitive material. In 1976 extant June Mail was indexed into the General File.

"Do Not File" procedures began with a Hoover memorandum of April 1940. "Do Not File" documents included those concerned with sensitive Bureau matters such as illegal break-ins and political gossip. The designation was also used for documents discussing policymaking decisions. In general, the practice was discontinued in 1950, although Acting Director L. Patrick Gray reinstituted it for a brief period in the 1970s.

ELSUR material refers to wiretaps or microphone surveillance techniques. Both techniques were used by the Bureau beginning in the 1930s, although the legal bases for them changed throughout the years. The Bureau always considered ELSUR records as sensitive materials and until 1978 filed them in the Special File Rooms. At present, ELSUR records are maintained in the regular case files in the Central File and indexed in the ELSUR Index.[4]

The personnel records of the FBI are maintained in Classification 67 Personnel Matters, but they are physically separated from the main file room. They include (1) Official Personnel Files for both out-of-service and in-service personnel, (2) employment applications, and (3) special and general files covering personnel policy matters such as training, overtime, and performance ratings.

FBI budget records are maintained both in the Central File and in separate budget office files. Some are included in Classification 66 Administrative Matters. Since 1979 separate units handle budget formulation and budget execution; each of these maintains its records separately.[5]

The FBI National Academy at Quantico, Virginia, also maintains separate records. They consist of administrative files relating to the training work of the academy and a miscellaneous collection of photograph albums, Bureau publications, and audiovisual materials used in training but maintained in the academy's library.

General, noninvestigative correspondence from the public is handled directly by the FBI's Correspondence Section of the Office of Congressional and Public Affairs. The Bureau replies are increasingly computer formatted and are not indexed or filed in the Central Records System.

Nontextual records are maintained by the Bureau both within the Central Records System as exhibits, or "bulkies," and in "reference collections," such as the Bureau's laboratory, gun, ammunition, typewriter, and photograph collections, or "special collections" held by the Office of Congressional and Public

---

[4] For a more detailed discussion of FBI electronic surveillance methods and techniques, see Special Files, Electronic Surveillance Files, in this volume.

[5] See Special Files, FBI Budget Records, in this volume.

Affairs and containing photographs and audio and video tapes. Public Affairs also has custody of over one hundred boxes of Hoover memorabilia bequeathed to the Bureau by the estate of FBI Associate Director Clyde Tolson.[6]

Automated records in the Bureau, as in the rest of the Federal government, are increasingly replacing older manual systems. Computers have been used by the Bureau for such work as the Uniform Crime Reporting Program, the National Crime Information Center, and for information gathering in missing persons cases. In 1971 the Bureau added a Computerized Criminal History File, and in 1974 the Identification Division initiated automated fingerprint identification capabilities. Plans call for the complete automation of the General Index and the Central Records System in the near future.[7]

Using the *Guide*

The classifications section of *Unlocking the Files of the FBI: A Guide to Its Records and Classification System* contains the following information for researchers interested in making use of the FBI's Central Records System and related records:

(1) The **Number** and **Title** of each classification created by the FBI in its Central Records System.

(2) A **Description** of the classification, containing a general background history detailing when it was established, what legal responsibilities the Bureau has had under the law, how the Bureau has responded, and changes in the nature of the classification and in FBI responsibilities over time. In addition, the description notes basic characteristics of the case files, typical information to be found in the files, and their research potential. Famous or unusual cases are noted, and information released by the Bureau under FOIA in a particular classification is marked with an asterisk (*).

(3) The **Volume** of records in each classification, which pertains to both headquarters and field office records for a particular classification. Where possible, the number of extant cases as of 1980 is provided for both the headquarters and the field office files. Regarding files held at FBI headquarters, the amount is also often given in cubic feet. If the records have been microfilmed, the number of rolls is provided. Since there has been widespread and massive destruction of field office case

---

[6] This section is based on the unpublished study of the FBI Record System, *Appraisal of the Records of the Federal Bureau of Investigation*, pp. 21–29, and the FBI's Research/Drug Demand Reduction Unit, Office of Public Affairs, *Conducting Research in FBI Records* (Federal Bureau of Investigation, 1990), pp. 1–2.

[7] See NARA, "1986 Update to the FBI Records Schedule."

files, the information is more general in nature with regard to these holdings.

(4) The **Date Span** of the classification, derived from the records themselves and not necessarily based on the dates when the classification was officially established or abolished. This section also tells the reader if the classification is still active or has been declared obsolete by the Bureau.

(5) The **Location** of the records as of this writing. Permanent Bureau records are scheduled to be turned over to NARA for storage. None had been transferred at the time this volume was in preparation; however, Appendix XII lists by subject the records that were transferred shortly before this volume went to press.

(6) The **NARA Disposition Recommendation** for each classification, presented for both the headquarters and the field office records in each classification. In 1984 the National Archives proposed and the FBI accepted recommendations for the FBI Records Retention Schedule, which would preserve approximately 20 percent of all Bureau records as permanently valuable and allow for the destruction of the rest. Under this schedule all 00 files for each classification were marked for permanent retention in order to document accurately FBI policies and procedures. Because the field office files have often, but not always, duplicated headquarters files, they are far more likely to be declared nonpermanent and subject to disposal. The schedule also calls for the retention of all records, both at headquarters and in the field offices, in certain classifications. In others it has mandated that all multisectional cases or those with a certain number of serials be preserved. This practice was in line with the "fat file" theory of multisectional cases developed in the Massachusetts Superior Court Records Study conducted by Dr. Michael Hindus, who wrote that "the file size seems to be an important predictor of historical interest." According to this theory, the larger the volume or size of a file or case the more likely it will have substantial research value.[8]

In still other classifications the NARA report called for systematic sampling of the records to be preserved. This selection might take one of two forms: an evidential sample or an informational sample. The former is taken to illustrate the nature of the Bureau's investigations in a particular classification. In an evidential sample a relatively small number of case files are retained that effectively document internal FBI

---

[8] See Michael Hindus, Theodore S. Hammet, and Barbara M. Hobs, *The Files of the Massachusetts Superior Court, 1859–1959: An Analysis and Plan for Action. A Report of the Massachusetts Judicial Records Committee of the Supreme Judicial Court* (Boston, 1979).

operations and procedures, relations with other agencies, investigative policies and techniques, controversial Bureau activities, and the roles of the director and the major policymakers. In the latter, an informational sample, a portion of the records is retained in such a manner as to accurately reflect the characteristics of the larger group. Such a sample relies primarily on the types of statistical research often employed by sociologists, criminologists, and social historians to discern significant patterns in the activities of common people.

In addition, the NARA task force developed, and NARA continues to implement, an Exceptional Case File Index to capture historically significant individuals, events, or organizations investigated by the FBI, precedent-setting programs, unusual investigative techniques, and landmark legal cases involving FBI investigations. All such cases, regardless of classification, are designated as permanent. Over three thousand such exceptional cases already have been identified.[9]

After Judge Greene approved the proposed FBI records retention schedule in 1985, the FBI and NARA reached an agreement on just how to implement the recommendation. The FBI currently marks new and old cases according to the approved schedule. Thus, if a case is determined Permanent, it is marked with a P and labeled "DO NOT DESTROY." If it is part of the sample to be preserved or an Exceptional Case File, it is marked with a P or an X and labeled "DO NOT DESTROY."[10] According to the current schedule, records identified as having permanent value should be transferred to the National Archives fifty years after the date of the last document in a closed case. Under this arrangement all FBI files closed prior to 1941 that have been identified as Permanent should have been transferred to the National Archives in 1991. Evidently, this was not accomplished.

The only FBI records presently in the custody of the National Archives, Record Group 65, Records of the Federal Bureau of Investigation, are the records of such predecessor agencies as the National Bureau of Criminal Identification of the Department of Justice (1896–1924); the National Bureau of Criminal Identification of the International Association of Chiefs of Police (1897–1924); the American Protective League (1917–1919); Papers of Dr. Heinrich F. Albert, the German commercial attaché in New York during World War I; and the records of the BOI (1907–1922). In addition, there are some case files from the FBI Central Records System Classification 61 Treason (1921–1931), Interesting Case Write-Ups (1932–1972), FBI Annual Reports

[9] See the Task Force Report, p. 2, for the criteria used. The Exceptional Case list itself remains classified.
[10] Conversation with NARA archivist and Task Force 1986 leader Dr. Bruce Ambacher, November 1990.

(1921–1951), Uniform Crime Reports (1930–1952), two Exceptional Case Files (1922–1924),[11] and the individual case files listed in Appendix XII.

(7) An **Access** statement, uniform for all FBI records still in the custody of the FBI. A researcher must file an FOIA request with the Bureau in order to gain access to the records.[12] The FBI has released sanitized copies of many records made available to the general public under previous FOIA requests. These records may be viewed at the FBI library reading room or copies may be obtained by writing to the FBI Public Affairs Office.[13]

(8) A list of **Related Records**, suggesting where additional information may be found on a particular subject in other FBI classifications, in the records of other agencies at the National Archives, in state and local records, in court records, or in closely related Department of Justice records.

In addition to the detailed information provided by the *Guide* on each FBI Central Records System classification, this volume offers a brief description of most of the FBI's unclassified indexes and of the FBI special files, such as Hoover's Official and Confidential (O&C) File, the Nichols File, the W. Mark Felt Files, Electronic Surveillance Files, the FBI Interesting Case Program files, FBI Budget Records, and Japanese Activities in the United States. The *Guide* also contains FBI organizational charts tracing the development of the agency and several appendixes detailing FBI record-keeping practices, abbreviations and symbols used, detailed classification information, and FOIA procedures with a sample letter for use in filing an FOIA request. Most importantly, the *Guide* contains a detailed name and subject index to aid the researcher in locating information on a particular subject, organization, or person.

---

[11] See *Conducting Research in FBI Records*, p. 8.

[12] See ibid., pp. 3–4. To assist researchers in filing such requests, the House of Representatives published "A Citizen's Guide to How to Use the Freedom of Information Act and Privacy Act in Requesting Government Documents." For a brief summary of the FOIA requirements and a sample FOIA letter, see Appendix VIII in this volume.

[13] See *Conducting Research in FBI Records*, pp. 29–36, for a listing of the files released. Unfortunately, this listing does not provide the classification number from which the records were obtained. For this information, see the Related Records section within each classification and Appendix V in this volume.

CLASSIFICATIONS

CLASSIFICATION 1

National Academy Matters

Among the many FBI activities are those involved with training and the FBI National Academy at Quantico, Virginia. To establish administrative control over all Bureau training, the FBI created this classification in 1935. Included among the files is documentation relating to the training of FBI personnel as well as local, state, foreign, and other law enforcement personnel. The vast majority of cases opened in this classification relates to applications for FBI training at the academy. Law enforcement agencies nominate individuals through the local FBI field office for such training. The local office then conducts an investigation of the applicant, after which the nomination is sent to headquarters for a final determination. The Bureau maintains a national academy directory of all graduates with pertinent biographical information. The classification also includes a small number of administrative case files documenting such specialized training as the New Special Agents School, Election Laws School, and the Conference of Special Agents in Charge. In addition, there is a file relating to national academy "interesting cases."

Volume HQ: 23,556 cases. FIELD: Unknown. All field offices report extant cases.

Dates 1935 to present

Location FBI

NARA Disposition Recommendation HQ: Systematic evidential sample— Permanent; Administrative/policymaking case files—Permanent; all other files— Destroy. FIELD: Multisectional administrative/policymaking case files —Permanent; all other files—Destroy.

Access To gain access to the records in this classification a researcher must file a Freedom of Information Act request with the FBI.

Related Records See FBI Classifications 230–240 FBI Training Matters.

CLASSIFICATION 2

Neutrality Matters

The Bureau established this classification in June 1940 during the height of concern over possible U.S. involvement in World War II. It covers investigations of violations of a number of statutes relating to neutrality. The Neutrality

Act made illegal such actions as conspiracy to injure the property of a foreign government, enlisting in a foreign military service, organizing a military expedition from the territory of the United States against a country with which it was at peace, and arming vessels of any country to commit hostile actions against a country with which the United States was at peace. Related legislation was the Munitions Control Act, which required the licensing of all persons and businesses engaged in the manufacture, importation, or exportation of articles, ammunition, and implements of war. The FBI had responsibility for violations in both of these areas.

In addition, the FBI shared with the U.S. Customs Service of the Department of the Treasury responsibility for the investigation of other violations covered by this classification. In 1955 the two agencies entered into an agreement dividing primary investigative responsibility. The Bureau took over primary responsibility for the Neutrality Act and the Customs Service investigated violations of the Munitions Control Act. If Customs discovered during the course of its investigation that a conspiracy of major proportions against a foreign government existed, it could request the FBI to take over the investigation. Since violations in this classification have major international implications and, over time, have become increasingly terroristic in nature, other agencies, such as the Department of State, the Department of Justice, the Secret Service, and the National Security Council, have maintained an interest in these investigations. The files also reflect FBI cooperation with the Central Intelligence Agency and international police organizations.

The cases cover private plots to assassinate foreign leaders, military expeditions undertaken from the United States, recruitment of mercenaries and others for foreign service, the illegal import and export of arms, and terrorist activities.

Volume HQ: 2,478 cases. FIELD: 5,541 cases. All field offices have extant cases.

Dates 1940 to present

Location FBI

NARA Disposition Recommendation HQ: 5% evidential sample—Permanent; multisectional cases—Permanent; all others—Destroy. FIELD: Multisectional cases—Permanent; cases with forty or more serials—Permanent; correlates with HQ multisectional cases—Permanent; all others—Destroy.

Access To gain access to the records in this classification a researcher must file a Freedom of Information Act request with the FBI.

Related Records General Records of the Department of State, Record Group 59, and the Records of the United States Secret Service, Record Group 87, both in the National Archives. Related records from the CIA and National Security Agency have not been transferred to the National Archives. See also Department of Justice Classification 9 European War Matters and 71 Neutrality.

CLASSIFICATION 3

Destruction or Overthrow of the Government

The Bureau established this classification in 1941 to cover investigations conducted under the authority of the Hatch Act of 1939 and the Smith Act of 1940. Those acts made it illegal to advocate, abet, advise, or teach the desirability of the destruction or overthrow of the government of the United States or political subdivisions therein by force or violence; to print, publish, issue, or distribute written or printed matter advocating those actions; or to organize a group advocating such actions.

In practice, the Bureau has opened few cases under this classification. Cases that would ordinarily be covered by the classification are handled under Classification 100 Domestic Security, Classification 105 Foreign Counterintelligence, and Classification 176 Antiriot Laws. In addition to files on persons and groups advocating revolution, and on plots and threats to overthrow the government, the files include extensive cases on the 1950 Puerto Rican nationalist assassination attempt on President Harry S. Truman at Blair House and the 1954 Puerto Rican nationalist shooting in the House of Representatives.

Volume HQ: 49 cases. FIELD: 196 cases. Forty-four field offices have extant cases.

Dates This classification opened in 1941. The last headquarters case opened in 1969.

Location FBI

NARA Disposition Recommendation HQ: All cases—Permanent. FIELD: Multisectional cases—Permanent; all others—Destroy.

Access To gain access to the records in this classification a researcher must file a Freedom of Information Act request with the FBI.

Related Records FBI Classifications 100 Domestic Security, 105 Foreign Counterintelligence, and 176 Antiriot Laws.

CLASSIFICATION 4

National Firearms Act

The FBI does not hold primary responsibility for investigating violations of firearms acts. That responsibility rests with the Bureau of Alcohol, Tobacco, and Firearms of the Department of the Treasury. Bureau involvement is and always has been limited to those instances where violations of firearms acts were discovered during the course of an investigation of an offense for which the FBI held primary responsibility. Legislation on firearms covered by this classification includes the National Firearms Act, Unlawful Possession or Receipt of Firearms Statute, and the State Firearms Control Assistance Act (the Gun Control Act of 1968).

This has traditionally been an area of minor investigative activity for the FBI. The Bureau tends to place emphasis in this area only when a strong case against an individual could not be made under other statutory violations, and, as a result, there are relatively few cases in this classification. Most cases included relate to such things as possession of unregistered firearms, possession of stolen firearms, the illegal export of weapons, and other violations of the National Firearms Act.

Volume HQ: 524 cases. Field: 1,938 cases. There has been substantial destruction of files.

Dates 1937 to present

Location FBI

NARA Disposition Recommendation HQ: 5% systematic evidential sample— permanent; multisectional cases—Permanent; microfilm—Permanent; all others—Destroy. FIELD: All cases—Destroy.

Access To gain access to the records in this classification a researcher must file a Freedom of Information Act request with the FBI.

Related Records Records of the Bureau of Alcohol, Tobacco, and Firearms, in General Records of the Department of the Treasury, Record Group 56, National Archives.

CLASSIFICATION 5

Income Tax

The Bureau opened this classification in 1924, although earlier investigations are included. Only violations of Federal income tax laws that are reported to the FBI are documented in this classification. Since the Internal Revenue Service (IRS) holds primary jurisdiction in this area, income tax violations are a minor activity of the Bureau and it has conducted few investigations in this classification. Documentation on cooperation between the IRS and FBI, however, will be found in the records.

Volume HQ: 229 cases. FIELD: 623 cases. Forty-two field offices report opening cases, but nearly all such files have been destroyed.

Dates 1921 to present

Location FBI

NARA Disposition Recommendation HQ: Microfilm—Permanent; multisectional cases—Permanent; all others—Destroy. FIELD: All cases— Destroy.

Access To gain access to the records in this classification a researcher must file a Freedom of Information Act request with the FBI.

Related Records Records of the Internal Revenue Service, Record Group 58, National Archives. The IRS, however, has not transferred the majority of its records to the National Archives.

CLASSIFICATION 6

Interstate Transportation of Strikebreakers

The Interstate Transportation of Strikebreakers Act of 1936 established the Bureau's authority to conduct investigations under this classification. The law prohibited the transportation of people to be employed to interfere with peaceful picketing during labor stoppages. From 1936 to 1949, investigations under this classification required the approval of the attorney general. In 1949 authority to open cases was delegated to the director of the Bureau.

The Bureau has opened relatively few cases in this classification. As would be expected, all relate to the movement of strikebreakers from one state to another. An occasional file includes documentation on vigilante activities tied to strikebreaking.

Volume HQ: 238 cases. FIELD: 238 cases. Forty-two field offices reported opening cases. There has been substantial destruction.

Dates 1936 to present

Location FBI

NARA Disposition Recommendation HQ: Microfilm—Permanent; multisectional cases—Permanent; cases with five or more serials—Permanent; all others—Destroy. FIELD: All cases—Destroy.

Access To gain access to the records in this classification a researcher must file a Freedom of Information Act request with the FBI.

Related Records General Records of the Department of Labor, Record Group 174, National Archives, and Department of Justice Classifications 16 Strikes and 139 Interstate Transportation of Strikebreakers.

CLASSIFICATION 7

Kidnapping

In March 1932 the twenty-month-old son of aviation pioneer Charles A. Lindbergh* was kidnapped from the family's home in New Jersey. The case drew worldwide attention and resulted in the trial and conviction of Bruno Richard Hauptmann* for the kidnapping. As a result of this case, Congress passed the Federal Kidnapping Act or Lindbergh Law, which conferred primary investigative jurisdiction on the FBI whenever three conditions were met in a kidnapping case: (1) the person had been unlawfully seized, (2) the person had been transported across state lines, and (3) the person was held for ransom or reward. Because it was difficult to determine whether or not state lines had been crossed, the Bureau and the Department of Justice determined that after seven days the Bureau would assume that there had been interstate action. A 1957 amendment to the Kidnapping Act reduced the waiting period to one day.

In general, the FBI has taken a strict view of Federal kidnapping law in order to avoid involvement in missing persons cases. The Bureau has had constant problems with cases pertaining to children taken by parents and to runaways in which a domestic dispute was the cause of the complaint or in which a minor willingly accompanied a partner in defiance of parental wishes. The nature of the files, at least at headquarters, seems to have changed over time. During the 1930s the Bureau was especially sensitive to cases with labor or racketeer overtones. In the late 1940s the cases reflect a growing concern over civil rights and child abduction.

Major cases such as the 1972 kidnapping of Virginia Piper, the wife of a wealthy Minneapolis investment banker, of Patricia Hearst,* the daughter of William Randolph Hearst, Jr., who was kidnapped by the radical Symbionese Liberation Army in 1974, and the 1981 Atlanta child kidnapping and murder cases* are heavily documented and reflect a major commitment on the part of the Bureau. There is also a large case file on the activities of the Barker gang,* which was led in a series of bank robberies by Kate (Ma) Barker and her sons until the Barkers were killed in a shoot-out with Bureau agents in January 1936. Most cases, however, were opened and closed quickly, resulting in little actual documentation.

Volume HQ: 18,293 cases. FIELD: Unknown. All field offices reported opening cases. Substantial destruction has occurred.

Dates 1932 to present

Location FBI

NARA Disposition Recommendation HQ: Systematic sample of 1,500 cases—Permanent; cases on microfilm in sample—permanent; multisectional cases—Permanent; all others—Destroy. FIELD: Multisectional cases that correlate with headquarters multisectional cases—Permanent; all others—Destroy.

Access To gain access to the records in this classification a researcher must file a Freedom of Information Act request with the FBI.

Related Records See state and local records and Department of Justice Classification 109 Kidnapping.

CLASSIFICATION 8

Migratory Bird Act

The Bureau established this classification in the early 1920s to cover violations of the Migratory Bird Act. The Bureau does not have primary jurisdiction over the protection of migratory game, fish, and birds, a duty that rests with the Fish and Wildlife Service of the Department of the Interior. Prior to 1939 the Department of Agriculture exercised primary jurisdiction in this area. It is now Bureau policy that it opens an investigation in this classification only upon request of the Department of Justice, which has the option of referring cases to either the FBI or the Department of the Interior.

Even though it is Bureau policy to open a case only in the event of a major violation of the law, most cases reflect minor infractions, including hunting on a wildlife refuge, killing ducks out of season, and threatening game wardens.

Volume HQ: 102 cases. FIELD: Unknown. Thirty-six field offices reported opening cases. There has been substantial destruction.

Dates 1922 to present

Location FBI

NARA Disposition Recommendation HQ: Microfilm—Permanent; all others—Destroy. FIELD: All records—Destroy.

Access To gain access to the records in this classification a researcher must file a Freedom of Information Act request with the FBI.

Related Records See the Records of the Fish and Wildlife Service, Record Group 22, and the Records of the Office of the Secretary of Agriculture, Record

Group 16, both in the National Archives. See also Department of Justice Classification 8 Migratory Bird Act.

CLASSIFICATION 9

Extortion

The Bureau established this classification for investigations of extortion. It
defined extortion as the use of the mail or other means of interstate commerce to
(1) demand ransom for a kidnapped person, (2) threaten to kidnap or injure any
person, or (3) demand money based on threats to injure someone. The Bureau,
however, will not investigate cases in which state or local law enforcement
agencies are already involved. The U.S. Postal Service handles cases involving
the mailing of threats to reveal information in order to harm the recipient's
reputation. The FBI, however, handles cases in which money is demanded under
the threat of informing or as consideration for not informing against persons
who allegedly violate Federal laws.

Throughout the 1960s most extortion cases involved labor disputes and
racial situations. Since 1970, however, there has been an increasing number of
extortion cases involving public officials and businesses, especially banks and
airlines. Extortion attempts directed at banks and airlines are generally prosecuted under the Hobbs Act. The classification includes files on extortion threats
to such famous individuals as Errol Flynn,* Clark Gable,* Congressman Martin
Dies,* and Peter Lawford,* and a file relating to charges that Supreme Court
Justice William O. Douglas,* during his early years as a judge in California, was
paid to stay a sentence. Typical files also include death threat extortions with
racial motives and threats to government officials.

Volume HQ: 65,692 cases. FIELD: 142,592 cases. All field offices reported
opening cases. There has been substantial destruction.

Dates Unknown

Location FBI.

Disposition Recommendation HQ: Systematic sample of 500 cases—Permanent; multisectional cases—Permanent; microfilm cases in sample—Permanent;
all others—Destroy. FIELD: All records—Destroy.

Access To gain access to the records in this classification a researcher must file
a Freedom of Information Act request with the FBI.

Related Records See FBI Classifications 192 Hobbs Act—Financial Institutions and 193 Hobbs Act—Commercial Institutions. See also Department of

Justice Classification 84 Extortion and Records of the U.S. Postal Service, Record Group 28, National Archives.

CLASSIFICATION 10

Red Cross Act

The Bureau established this classification in 1924 for cases involving possible violations of the Red Cross Act, which made it a Federal crime for any person to falsely claim to be a member or agent of the American Red Cross. The act also made it a crime to use the symbol of the Red Cross for trade, advertising, or business without the permission of the Red Cross. This has been a relatively little used classification.

Volume HQ: 893 cases. FIELD: 1,057 cases. Substantial destruction has occurred.

Dates 1924 to present

Location FBI

NARA Disposition Recommendation HQ: Microfilm—Permanent; multisectional cases—Permanent; all others—Destroy. FIELD: All records— Destroy.

Access To gain access to the records in this classification a researcher must file a Freedom of Information Act request with the FBI.

Related Records See Records of the American Red Cross, in the National Archives Gift Collection, Record Group 200, National Archives, and Department of Justice Classification 10 Red Cross.

CLASSIFICATION 11

Tax (Other than Income)

The Bureau opened this classification prior to 1921 to cover cases involving internal revenue laws other than income, alcohol, and social security taxes. In 1951 cases under the Wagering Tax Stamp Act were added to this classification. Very little Bureau activity has taken place under this classification as the Internal Revenue Service (IRS) is the primary investigating agency. Generally the Bureau furnishes the IRS only with information it develops in relation to other investigations. While this classification remains open, the last case was originated in 1951.

Volume HQ: 20 cases. FIELD: None.

Dates 1920 to 1951, but the classification remains open.

Location FBI

NARA Disposition Recommendation HQ: Multisectional cases—Permanent; microfilm—Permanent; all others—Disposition not authorized. FIELD: No extant cases.

Access To gain access to the records in this classification a researcher must file a Freedom of Information Act request with the FBI.

Related Records See the Records of the Internal Revenue Service, Record Group 58, National Archives, and Department of Justice Classification 11 War Tax.

CLASSIFICATION 12

Narcotics

The Bureau uses this classification, which dates from earlier than 1924, for investigations of the illegal sale, possession, or use of narcotics. Since the FBI has never held primary responsibility for drug-law enforcement it has not been a major focus of Bureau activity. The FBI's role has generally been limited to assisting other agencies, particularly the Department of the Treasury's Bureau of Narcotics and its successors, the Department of Justice's Bureau of Narcotics and Dangerous Drugs and the Drug Enforcement Agency. FBI interest in narcotics matters increased in the 1970s because of their connection with organized crime.

FBI activity in this classification has been relatively low. The records include information on the smuggling of drugs into Federal prisons, various violations of narcotics laws, distribution of drugs, and undercover operations. The files also contain documentation on Bureau cooperation with other U.S. government agencies concerned with narcotics.

Volume HQ: 2,075 cases. FIELD: 2,570 cases. All field offices reported opening cases. There has been substantial destruction.

Dates Early 1920s to present

Location FBI

NARA Disposition Recommendation HQ: Multisectional cases—Permanent; microfilm—Permanent; all others—Destroy. FIELD: Multisectional cases—Permanent; all others—Destroy.

Access To gain access to the records in this classification a researcher must file a Freedom of Information Act request with the FBI.

Related Records Records of the Bureau of Narcotics, in the General Records of the Department of the Treasury, Record Group 56, and the Records of the Drug Enforcement Agency, Record Group 170, National Archives. See also Department of Justice Classification 12 Narcotic Act.

CLASSIFICATION 13

National Defense Act, Prostitution, Selling Whiskey within Army Camps (Obsolete)

The Bureau opened this classification in 1920 to cover files generated as a result of investigations into violations of certain provisions of the National Defense Act. Specifically, the Bureau was concerned with prostitution and the sale of liquor within five miles of military bases. This classification was declared obsolete in August 1920. The files include policy documentation on the FBI's responsibilities under the National Defense Act and cases resulting from investigations of prostitution, the sale of liquor, and the improper wearing of a military uniform.

Volume HQ: 44 cases. FIELD: None

Dates 1920

Location FBI

NARA Disposition Recommendation HQ: Microfilm—Permanent (all records are on microfilm). FIELD: No extant cases.

Access To gain access to the records in this classification a researcher must file a Freedom of Information Act request with the FBI.

Related Records See the Records of United States Army Commands, Record Group 338, National Archives, and Department of Justice Classification 23 Liquor.

CLASSIFICATION 14

Sedition

The Bureau established this classification in 1940. It covers investigations into alleged oral and written statements made by nonmilitary persons to members of the armed forces which display the intent to interfere with their loyalty, morale, and discipline and which might tend to cause mutiny, disloyalty, and refusal of duty. The Bureau, however, held no responsibility for investigating seditious activities of members of the armed forces.

While the statutes governing sedition are not limited to wartime, in practice it is virtually impossible to secure a conviction during peacetime and most difficult and rare during wartime. For example, of the approximately two thousand eight hundred cases opened during World War II, only thirty-eight convictions resulted. Activity in this classification was greatest during World War II, although there was activity as well during the war in Korea and the Vietnam conflict. Cases concern the distribution of seditious literature, subversive talk, conscientious objectors, and seditious draft-resistance efforts. There are also files relating to Earl Browder, the head of the American Communist party, who was convicted of using an illegally obtained passport; the poet Ezra Pound,* for collaborating with the enemy during World War II; Tomoya Kawakita, an American citizen sentenced to death in 1948 for mistreating U.S. prisoners of war during World War II; and John W. Powell, an American citizen brought to trial in 1952 for publishing a magazine in Red China during the Korean War.

Volume HQ: 3,113 cases. FIELD: 6,000 cases. Fifty-eight field offices reported opening cases. There has been some destruction.

Dates 1940 to present

Location FBI

NARA Disposition Recommendation HQ: All cases—Permanent. FIELD: Multisectional cases—Permanent; all others—Destroy.

Access To gain access to the records in this classification a researcher must file a Freedom of Information Act request with the FBI.

Related Records See the Records of the Office of the Secretary of the Army, Record Group 335; the General Records of the Department of the Navy, Record Group 80; the Records of the United States Marine Corps, Record Group 127; the Records of the Office of the Secretary of the Air Force, Record Group 340; and the Records of the Office of the Secretary of Defense, Record Group 330, all in the National Archives. See also Department of Justice Classifications 39 Immigration and 146 World War II (internal security).

CLASSIFICATION 15

Theft from Interstate Shipment

The Bureau opened this classification in 1922 to cover investigations of the theft, fraud, or embezzlement of goods that constitute or are a part of an interstate or international shipment. This includes carriers, such as railroad cars, vessels, motor trucks, aircraft, or pipelines, and storage and holding areas, such as stations, platforms, and wharves. Related statutes include theft or misapplication of funds or goods from officers and employees of firms engaged in commerce as a common carrier and breaking the seal or lock on a carrier with the intent to commit larceny.

Because of ambiguities in the law, courts early on interpreted the laws differently, making it difficult for the Bureau to determine its purview in this area. During World War II, thefts from interstate shipments increased as a result of wartime shortages. In 1944 the definition of a "vehicle" was broadened to include pipelines that crossed state lines, and in 1949 theft from aircraft was added to the violations covered. Continued offenses in the postwar period caused the FBI to initiate a strong outreach program to the companies affected by the thefts, local law enforcement officials, civic groups, and the press. The effort continued into the 1970s.

The response that the Bureau received was not always positive. Companies whose losses were covered by insurance expressed dissatisfaction at having to underwrite the cost of sending a representative to testify in court. U.S. Attorneys complained that the Bureau frequently presented them with such minor violations of the law that the cost and effort expended in prosecution were unwarranted. In 1967 the Bureau established a $100 minimum on cases to be presented to the U.S. Attorneys. In 1975 this was increased to $200. By the late 1970s the Bureau's interest in such criminal activities decreased as it concentrated on white-collar crime.

Volume   HQ: 84,442 cases. FIELD: 657,062 cases. All field offices reported opening cases. There has been substantial destruction.

Dates   1922 to present

Location   FBI

NARA Disposition Recommendation   HQ: Systematic informational sample of 1,500 cases—Permanent; microfilm cases in sample—permanent; all others—Destroy. FIELD: All records—Destroy.

Access   To gain access to the records in this classification a researcher must file a Freedom of Information Act request with the FBI.

Related Records   Department of Justice Classification 15 Theft from Interstate Commerce.

CLASSIFICATION 16

Violation of Federal Injunction

The FBI merged this classification with Classification 69, Contempt of Court. There are no extant cases.

Volume HQ: None. FIELD: None

Dates NA

Location NA

NARA Disposition Recommendation NA

Access NA

Related Records See FBI Classification 69 Contempt of Court.

CLASSIFICATION 17

Fraud against the Government—Veterans Administration

The Bureau opened this classification in 1921. It includes files opened for investigations of possible fraudulent activity by or against veterans, primarily in the areas of benefits, educational and training allowances, hospitalization benefits, and pension and insurance benefits. Even though the FBI maintains primary investigative jurisdiction in this area, the Veterans Administration (now the Department of Veterans Affairs), the Secret Service, and the Department of Labor have also been responsible for investigating some aspects of criminal fraud against veterans. This shared responsibility has on occasion caused problems; in 1945, for example, a jurisdictional dispute arose between the Bureau and the Veterans Administration that was not resolved until 1954.

For the most part the FBI has not been aggressive in seeking prosecution of fraud by veterans. The attorney general has advised U.S. Attorneys that veterans are to be prosecuted only in aggravated instances; violations typically include applying for unemployment compensation while employed, making false statements on home loan applications, falsely claiming to attend class in order to qualify for educational benefits, and otherwise making false claims for benefits. Some cases also relate to institutions attempting to defraud veterans, such as training schools charging veterans higher tuition than nonveterans.

Volume HQ: 32,752 cases. FIELD: 53,894 cases. All field offices reported opening cases. Some destruction has occurred.

Dates 1921 to present

Location FBI

NARA Disposition Recommendation HQ: Systematic evidential sample of 500 cases—Permanent; multisectional cases—Permanent; microfilm cases in sample—permanent; all others—Destroy. FIELD: All records—Destroy.

Access To gain access to the records in this classification a researcher must file a Freedom of Information Act request with the FBI.

Related Records Records of the Veterans Administration, Record Group 15, the General Records of the Department of Labor, Record Group 174, and the Records of the United States Secret Service, Record Group 87, all in the National Archives. See also Department of Justice Classification 46 Fraud against the Government.

CLASSIFICATION 18

May Act

The Bureau opened this classification in 1941 to cover violations of the May Act, which was intended to prevent prostitution in restricted zones surrounding military bases. The act was invoked primarily during wartime and then only in a limited area, primarily in North and South Carolina and Tennessee.

Volume HQ: 2,062 cases. FIELD: 2,761 cases. Thirty-one field offices reported opening cases. There has been substantial destruction.

Dates 1942 to present

Location FBI

NARA Disposition Recommendation HQ: All records—Permanent. FIELD: All records—Destroy.

Access To gain access to the records in this classification a researcher must file a Freedom of Information Act request with the FBI.

Related Records See the Records of the United States Army Continental Commands 1920–42, Record Group 394, National Archives.

CLASSIFICATION 19

Censorship Matters
(Obsolete)

During World War II the U.S. government established regulations relating to the censorship of communications. The Office of Censorship held primary responsibility for investigations of censorship matters, but it could request that the FBI undertake an investigation in this area, to be conducted under the authority of the First War Powers Act and the Trading with the Enemy Act. The Bureau established this classification in September 1942 by teletype message to all Special Agents in Charge. Included are investigations of attempts to avoid submitting communications to wartime censorship or using codes or other devices to conceal the true content of communications from censorship review. Since the Bureau did not hold primary responsibility for investigations of censorship matters, it opened relatively few cases. All censorship investigations ceased on September 5, 1945.

Volume HQ: 1,248 cases. FIELD: Unknown. Nine field offices reported opening cases.

Dates 1942 to 1945

Location FBI

NARA Disposition Recommendation HQ: Systematic evidential sample—Permanent; multisectional cases—Permanent; all others—Destroy. FIELD: Multisectional cases that correlate with headquarters multisectional cases—Permanent; all others—Destroy.

Access To gain access to the records in this classification a researcher must file a Freedom of Information Act request with the FBI.

Related Records Records of the Office of Censorship, Record Group 216, National Archives.

CLASSIFICATION 20

Federal Grain Standards Act
(Obsolete)

The Federal Grain Standards Act of 1920 required that companies report the quality of the grain they sold. The Bureau established this classification in September 1920 for investigations of possible violations of the act. The two extant cases relate to a citizen complaint pertaining to the improper grading of corn and a grain inspector alleging fraud in loading wheat. The Bureau declared this classification obsolete in 1921.

Volume HQ: 2 cases (1 roll of film). FIELD: None

Dates 1920 to 1921

Location FBI

NARA Disposition Recommendation HQ: Microfilm—Permanent. FIELD: No extant cases.

Access To gain access to the records in this classification a researcher must file a Freedom of Information Act request with the FBI.

Related Records Records of the Office of the Secretary of Agriculture, Record Group 16, National Archives. See also Department of Justice Classifications 20 Standard Grain Act and 86 Federal Seed Act (misbranding).

CLASSIFICATION 21

Food and Drugs

The Bureau established this classification in 1924 for investigations of complaints received under the criminal provisions of the Food and Drug Act, although complaints under the Meat Inspection Act are also included. Most complaints were referred to and handled by the Food and Drug Administration, which holds primary investigatory jurisdiction in this area. The FBI does assist in apprehending fugitives who have violated the act, but it does little investigative work in this area.

Volume HQ: 51 cases (1 roll of film). FIELD: 58 cases. Twenty-four field offices opened cases.

Dates 1924 to present

Location FBI

NARA Disposition Recommendation HQ: Microfilm—Permanent; multisectional cases—Permanent, all others—Destroy. FIELD: All records—Destroy.

Access To gain access to the records in this classification a researcher must file a Freedom of Information Act request with the FBI.

Related Records Records of the Food and Drug Administration, Record Group 88, National Archives. See also Department of Justice Classifications 21 Food and Drug (Prosecution) and 22 Food and Drug (Seizure).

CLASSIFICATION 22

National Motor Vehicle Traffic Act
(Obsolete)

Although the Bureau opened some cases as early as August 1922, this classification was formally established on March 23, 1923. It served to document the Bureau's role in determining whether vehicles seized by Federal prohibition agents were stolen. When notified by the Prohibition Bureau that it had seized a vehicle, the FBI contacted the Automobile Protection and Information Bureau (APIB) and requested a trace of that vehicle's ownership. The APIB in turn referred such requests to local detective agencies maintained by a consortium of insurance companies. If the detective agency proved unable to trace the ownership of a vehicle, the Bureau referred the matter to the local field office for investigation.

Of all cases opened in this classification, 90 percent were opened between 1922 and 1924. Typical cases included requests for a trace of ownership and investigations of the use of stolen cars in committing other crimes. The Bureau declared this classification obsolete in 1927.

Volume HQ: 495 cases (9 rolls of microfilm). FIELD: None extant.

Dates 1922 to 1927

Location FBI

NARA Disposition Recommendation HQ: Microfilm—Permanent; multisectional cases—Permanent; no other extant cases. FIELD: No extant cases.

Access To gain access to the records in this classification a researcher must file a Freedom of Information Act request with the FBI.

Related Records Records of the Prohibition Bureau, in Records of the Bureau of Narcotics and Dangerous Drugs, Record Group 170, National Archives. See also the records of the Automobile Protection and Information Bureau and Department of Justice Classifications 26 Dyer Act (Automobile Theft) and 23 Liquor.

CLASSIFICATION 23

Prohibition
(Obsolete)

The Bureau established this classification in 1924 for investigations of violations of the Eighteenth Amendment and its implementing legislation. When the classification was first opened, the Bureau was not the agency with primary jurisdiction in this area, and it conducted investigations only at the request of the Department of Justice. In 1928, however, it gained authority to initiate investigations on its own. The records include information on the operation of illegal stills, smuggling and bootlegging across borders, and attempts at intimidating juries and otherwise obstructing judicial proceedings in prohibition cases. The records are a good source of information on social conditions in the United States during the Prohibition era.

After the repeal of Prohibition in 1933, virtually all further investigatory responsibility was transferred to the Department of the Treasury. The FBI continued to investigate the shipment of liquor from wet to dry states until 1936, when that function also shifted to the Department of the Treasury.

Volume HQ: 4,740 cases (24 rolls of film). FIELD: Unknown. All records are believed to have been destroyed.

Dates 1924 to 1936

Location FBI

NARA Disposition Recommendation HQ: Systematic evidential sample of 500 cases—Permanent; multisectional cases—Permanent; all others—Destroy. FIELD: Multisectional cases—Permanent; all others—Destroy.

Access To gain access to the records in this classification a researcher must file a Freedom of Information Act request with the FBI.

Related Records General Records of the Department of the Treasury, Record Group 56, National Archives. See also Department of Justice Classification 23 Liquor.

CLASSIFICATION 24

Profiteering
(Obsolete)

The Bureau opened this classification in 1920 to cover investigations of reported violations of the Lever Act, which prohibited the making of excess profits on food and clothing. The Bureau opened most of the cases in 1920 with virtually no activity between 1921 and 1938. In 1939 the Bureau once again undertook investigations for a brief period. In the early 1940s the classification was declared obsolete.

The Bureau's standard procedure after receiving a citizen complaint about a merchant's prices was to review comparative price lists. There are files on profiteering concerning coal, sugar, shoes, women's clothing, milk, and other consumer goods.

Volume HQ: 1,298 cases (6 rolls of film). FIELD: Unknown. Only one field office reported opening a case.

Dates 1920 to 1943

Location FBI

NARA Disposition Recommendation HQ: Microfilm—Permanent (all extant cases). FIELD: All records—Destroy.

Access To gain access to the records in this classification a researcher must file a Freedom of Information Act request with the FBI.

Related Records Department of Justice Classifications 14 Cotton Futures Act, 20 Standard Grain Act, 24 High Cost of Living, and 53 Excess Wool Profits.

CLASSIFICATION 25

Selective Service Act

The FBI formally established this classification on July 28, 1924; however, some cases were opened as early as June 1922. This classification covers investigations of all aspects of the Selective Service Act, including failure to register for the draft; furnishing false information to a local draft board; refusal to serve; interference with the draft, such as encouraging draft evasion or resistance; and offenses committed by local boards, such as accepting bribes.

For the World War II period there is a file relating to Errol Flynn* and his deferment case. Post-World War II cases also cover reemployment rights of returning servicemen. From 1924 to 1967 the Bureau investigated applications for conscientious-objector status for persons whose claims were disallowed by the local draft board and who appealed their cases to the Department of Justice. In 1967 the Selective Service System assumed responsibility for that function.

Using authority granted to it in the early 1950s, the FBI has destroyed all files covering investigations during which it was revealed "that the delinquency was not wilful or no aggravated circumstances involved and no prosecutive action taken." As a result, more than 75 percent of all cases have been destroyed, particularly files created at the beginning of World War II and in the early 1960s. Files that remain document investigations involving background checks of conscientious objectors, failure to register for the draft, refusals to report for induction, attempts to bribe draft board officials, failure to notify local draft boards of changes in residence, counseling of individuals to avoid the draft, failure of conscientious objectors to report for alternative service, failure to possess a draft card (usually in conjunction with another offense), use of fake draft cards, and antidraft activities. The records also document the complexities of the U.S. draft laws, especially as they relate to aliens residing in the United States.

Volume HQ: 650,938 cases (22 rolls of film). FIELD: 1,415,763 cases. All field offices reported opening cases. There has been massive destruction, however, and few cases predating the early 1970s remain.

Dates 1922 to present

Location FBI

NARA Disposition Recommendation HQ: Multisectional cases—Permanent; microfilm—Permanent; all cases involving organized efforts to obstruct or interfere with the draft (including counseling of draft evasion or resistance)— Permanent; cases involving offenses committed by members of local draft boards or other government officials—Permanent; all others—Destroy. FIELD: All records—Destroy.

Access To gain access to the records in this classification a researcher must file a Freedom of Information Act request with the FBI.

Related Records Records of the Selective Service System (World War II), Record Group 163, and the Records of the Selective Service System, Record Group 147, both in the National Archives. See also Department of Justice Classification 25 Military Draft.

CLASSIFICATION 26

Interstate Transportation of Stolen Motor
Vehicles and Stolen Aircraft

The Bureau established this classification on July 28, 1924, and its case load in these matters continued to grow from the 1920s until 1971. Cases opened in this classification reflect the growing involvement of the Bureau with statutes making the transportation, sale, or receipt of stolen motor vehicles in interstate or foreign commerce a Federal offense. The extant cases reflect America's infatuation with the automobile and its influence on American life, including the perpetration of crimes. There is a wealth of biographical data on individuals and suspects including sex, education, race, age, arrest records, military service, and residential information. The files also reflect changing American tastes. In the 1940s, for example, Chrysler roadsters seem the most popular car stolen, in the 1950s the Chevrolet, in the 1960s the Ford Mustang; in the 1970s the emphasis shifted to imports and luxury automobiles, such as the Mercedes-Benz and the Cadillac. There is also information on organized crime and its involvement in stolen car rings, including international gangs that dealt in European cars and the selling of parts from U.S. automobiles. Many cases involved juveniles and local family and domestic disputes. In the 1960s and 1970s the files reflect an increase in the use of stolen automobiles in the transportation of marijuana and narcotics.

Although most of the cases deal with stolen automobiles, some involve motorcycles (primarily Harley-Davidsons), airplanes, trucks (primarily pickups), helicopters, and even tractor-trailers. There are also large files relating to John Dillinger and his gang, including his sweetheart Marian Evelyn Freschette. Dillinger, after escaping from prison in 1933, began a crime spree that earned him the title "Public Enemy Number One." Bureau agents led by Melvin Purvis killed him outside a movie theater in Chicago in July 1933. Other files concern the Barker gang and its famous gunfight with local law enforcement officials in 1927. The files contain extensive newspaper clippings on the gangs and on Anna Sage, the "Woman in Red" who set up Dillinger and who was herself later deported to Romania. There is also a case file on Bonnie Parker and Clyde Barrow* who were brought renewed fame by the 1967 motion picture *Bonnie and Clyde*.

In 1970 the Department of Justice issued new guidelines for the prosecution of cases in this area. The FBI and U.S. Attorneys were to refer most of the cases to state and local authorities, prosecution of "joy riding" thefts was eliminated, and juvenile cases greatly restricted. The Bureau, however, continued the investigation and prosecution of more complex cases, such as international incidents and major car theft rings. Accordingly, there is a steep decline in cases opened after 1970. Statistics on motor vehicle theft are now available through the FBI's

Uniform Crime Reports, which cover all auto thefts and not simply interstate stolen vehicles.

Volume HQ: As of 1978, 449,120 cases (308,480 of these cases are on microfilm that is of very poor quality). FIELD: As of 1978, 2,019,393 cases. There has been substantial destruction of case files in this classification both at headquarters and in the field.

Dates Classification opened in 1924, but some extant cases date from as early as 1921. The classification remains open today.

Location of Records FBI

NARA Disposition Recommendation HQ: Four- or more section cases—Permanent; all others—Destroy. FIELD: Four- or more section cases—Permanent; all others—Destroy.

Access To gain access to the records in this classification a researcher must file a Freedom of Information Act request with the FBI.

Related Records See state and local files and Department of Justice Classification 26 Dyer Act (Automobile Theft).

CLASSIFICATION 27

Patent Matters

The Bureau formally opened this classification in 1924. As the extant cases from this classification reflect, patent matters are only a minor activity for the FBI. The Bureau does not investigate civil disputes—such as patent infringements and claims of stolen patent ideas. It does, however, investigate patent law violations that have a possibility of becoming criminal prosecutions, including such cases, for example, as debarred patent attorneys continuing to practice and fraud relating to misrepresentation. The classification does contain some interesting cases: one involves a violation of U.S. copyright laws by the producers of the Harry Houdini film *The Master Mystery*, another a patent dispute regarding "Sesame Street" characters, and a third the *Lord Manufacturing v. U.S. Government* case that revolved around designs for shock motor mountings. Although Lord won its case, the file itself is of more value for the light it sheds on the attitudes and workings of the automobile industry. In the cases with which the Bureau does get involved, the records show clearly the close cooperation of the Bureau with the U.S. Patent Office and U.S. Attorneys.

Volume HQ: 402 cases as of 1978 (216 cases microfilmed). FIELD: 58,252 cases, most of which have been destroyed.

Dates 1921 to present

Location FBI

NARA Disposition Recommendation HQ: All records—Permanent. FIELD: All records—Destroy.

Access To gain access to the records in this classification a researcher must file a Freedom of Information Act request with the FBI.

Related Records See the Records of the Patent Office, Record Group 241, National Archives, and Department of Justice Classification 27 Patents.

CLASSIFICATION 28

Copyright Matters

In 1924 the Bureau established this classification to parallel a similar classification in the Department of Justice files. It covers Bureau investigations of criminal violations of the copyright laws; under this classification the Bureau investigated infringements of copyrights, fraudulent notices of copyrights, and false representations in applications for copyrights. With the inclusion of sound recordings and motion pictures within the copyright law in the 1960s the number of cases opened annually dramatically increased. Early files included cases involving sheet music and silent films.

The files document the difficulty in proving the infringement of copyright, as well as early Bureau techniques for distinguishing authentic from illegal materials. The focus of the files is on the illegal manufacturing, distribution, and sale of bootleg song sheets, recordings, tapes, cassettes, and commercial films. As might be expected, the Los Angeles field office files are particularly rich in this area. The entertainment industry, especially major film producers such as Twentieth-Century Fox, Metro-Goldwyn-Mayer, Warner Brothers, and Paramount, and the major recording companies, including RCA, have been and continue to be concerned with this issue. For example, in the 1970s and 1980s the Motion Picture Association of America complained to the FBI about a number of movie theaters showing pirated or unauthorized copies of major films, such as *The Hustler* and *Star Wars*.

Complaints in the recording industry ranged from unauthorized copying of rock-and-roll records to the distribution of illegal W. C. Fields tapes. The Bureau developed a case against an international Arab distributor who planned to distribute tapes in the Middle East. The Bureau even investigated a complaint that classic American works of art by artists such as Frederic Remington and Charles Marion Russell were being reproduced and sold as originals. Today, of course, the focus is on pirated compact discs and digital tapes—a multimillion-dollar industry.

Volume HQ: 4,802 case files as of 1978 (597 of these, all prior to 1945, are on microfilm). FIELD: 8,156 cases (Los Angeles). Extensive destruction has occurred, however, and as of 1978 only 1,000 cases were extant.

Dates 1924 to present

Location FBI

NARA Disposition Recommendation HQ: All records—Permanent. FIELD: Multisectional cases—Permanent; all others—Destroy.

Access To gain access to the records in this classification a researcher must file a Freedom of Information Act request with the FBI.

Related Records Justice Department Classification 28 Copyrights.

CLASSIFICATION 29

Bank Fraud and Embezzlement

The Bureau established this classification in 1924 to cover investigations of fraud against financial institutions protected by Federal law. The types of cases investigated under this classification include embezzlement, bribery of bank officials, kickback schemes, willful misapplication of funds, false bank entries, giving false information on loan applications, and false certification of checks. Although the basic definition of fraud and the types of cases investigated under this classification have changed little over time, the Bureau's jurisdiction in this field has expanded considerably. It now includes investigations concerning the Federal reserve banks, state banks that are members of the Federal Deposit Insurance Corporation (FDIC), all banks in the District of Columbia, Federal credit unions, and savings and loan institutions insured by the FDIC.

Most investigations in this classification are initiated when a cashier or teller is unable to balance. Few such cases are ever prosecuted because of the low dollar amounts involved. The records do reflect some fraudulent banking practices, early social attitudes in the United States, and FBI investigation techniques including the use of the polygraph. Generally, the Bureau attitude has been "no loss, no fraud, no investigation." One unusual case involved the disappearance from the U.S. Treasury of eighteen cases of old currency. No suspect was ever prosecuted in the case, although the Bureau polygraphed more than twenty treasury employees.

Volume HQ: 91,804 cases (978 cu. ft. of records); 33,385 of those cases are on 42 rolls of microfilm. FIELD: 196,047 cases.

Dates 1924 to present

Location FBI

NARA Disposition Recommendation HQ: Microfilmed cases—Permanent; multisection cases—Permanent; systematic informational sample of 1,500 of the pre-1978 extant cases—Permanent; post-1978 cases, evidential sample— Permanent; all others—Destroy. FIELD: All files—Destroy.

Access To gain access to the records in this classification a researcher must file a Freedom of Information Act request with the FBI.

Related Records Department of Justice Classification 29 National Banking Act.

CLASSIFICATION 30

Interstate Quarantine Law
(Obsolete)

The Bureau established this classification in 1924 to investigate violations of the Interstate Quarantine Act of 1893. The law prohibited the interstate travel of persons or animals carrying infectious diseases. There are only eight extant cases in this classification; most of these relate to persons infected with venereal disease, and the cases were referred to the Public Health Service. Investigations relating to diseased animals being transported across state lines were referred to the Department of Agriculture. One particular case presents a vivid picture of small-town life in Minnesota in 1924. In 1925 the Bureau abandoned this classification.

Volume HQ: 8 cases, all on microfilm. FIELD: None

Dates 1924 to 1925

Location FBI

NARA Disposition Recommendation HQ: All records—Permanent. FIELD: NA

Access To gain access to the records in this classification a researcher must file a Freedom of Information Act request with the FBI.

Related Records See Justice Department Classifications 2 Plant Quarantine Act and 30 Animal Quarantine. See also Records of the Office of the Secretary of Agriculture, Record Group 16, National Archives.

CLASSIFICATION 31

White Slave Traffic Act

Investigations in this classification are one of the oldest functions of the Bureau. In 1910, Congress passed the White Slave Traffic Act (the Mann Act), which prohibited the transportation of women or girls in interstate or foreign commerce for the purposes of prostitution, debauchery, or other immoral acts, the coercion or enticement of women or girls for these purposes, and the coercion or enticement of female minors for these purposes. Prostitution has been a major social issue in the United States and the Bureau files reflect changing American social mores and attitudes. Enforcement of the act has also changed over the years. Although the files are full of noncommercial cases, domestic disputes, and family quarrels (runaway children and wives), by the 1960s the FBI concentrated its activities on commercial prostitution, houses of prostitution, and organized crime involvement. Most cases are currently handled by local authorities and the act is given low priority in FBI field offices. Nevertheless, the extant cases provide a great deal of biographical detail on individuals and insight into the prostitution profession in the early twentieth century, including prostitution rings involving truck stops, motels, clubs, and massage parlors; the corruption of public officials and police departments; racial stereotypes; pimps; and high-society call-girl services. There is also some information on Errol Flynn,* who was investigated on moral charges in connection with underage girls, and some information relating to Marilyn Monroe* (Norma Jean Baker) and her death.

Volume HQ: 94,018 cases (88,007 on 508 rolls of microfilm). FIELD: 315,973 cases opened.

Dates 1910 to present. Classification opened in 1910. The early cases are incorporated in the FBI filing system set up in 1921.

Location FBI

NARA Disposition Recommendation HQ: All cases opened between 1910–1921—Permanent; systematic sampling of 1,500 cases per decade beginning in 1922—Permanent; all others including microfilm—Destroy. FIELD: Multisection cases—Permanent; all others—Destroy.

Access To gain access to the records in this classification a researcher must file a Freedom of Information Act request with the FBI.

Related Records Justice Department Classification 31 White Slave Act and 50 Peonage.

CLASSIFICATION 32

Fingerprint Matters

Created in 1924, this classification contains primarily administrative information on the subject of fingerprints. Most of the headquarters files contain correspondence with state, city, or county law enforcement officials concerning the establishment of a fingerprint program and requests for FBI fingerprint cards and identification of criminals or accident victims. FBI official fingerprint information is maintained in the FBI's Identification Division and includes prints both of applicants and criminal suspects. During World War II the FBI encouraged local law enforcement agencies to contribute fingerprints of all local criminals. The FBI, beginning in the 1950s, also encouraged the general public to contribute fingerprints under its Voluntary Civilian Fingerprint Program. Such fingerprints may be destroyed when the individual reaches seventy-five years of age or after notice of the person's death, according to expungement procedures established by the archivist of the United States. Criminal fingerprints may not be destroyed until an individual is eighty years old or seven years after notification of the person's death. Federal legislation passed in 1972 limited fingerprint dissemination by the FBI and permitted expungement of the records of nonserious offenders under the age of twenty-one.

Most files simply contain requests for statistics and help in identifying individuals. Some contain information relating to major disasters, such as aviation and railroad accidents, and the Jonestown massacre in 1978, where the FBI was asked to provide fingerprint cards to help identify victims. There is also a file relating to Alphonse (Al) Capone* and gang warfare in Chicago in the 1930s.

Volume HQ: 32,573 cases (630 cu. ft.). FIELD: Two-thirds of the field offices opened more than 100 cases in this classification.

Dates 1924 to present

Location FBI

NARA Disposition Recommendation HQ: Evidential sample—Permanent; all others—Destroy. FIELD: All records—Destroy.

Access To gain access to the records in this classification a researcher must file a Freedom of Information Act request with the FBI.

Related Records NA

CLASSIFICATION 33

Uniform Crime Reporting

The Bureau established this classification in 1938 to collect and compile statistics on crime in the United States. Congress granted the FBI this authority in 1930, and during the following decade state and local authorities submitted data directly to it. In the 1940s this procedure changed as state data collection centers were established. These state centers sent the data on to the FBI's Uniform Crime Reporting Section. The records of this section are not part of Classification 33 but relate closely to the records contained within it. No cases have been opened in this classification since 1948 and none of the cases is investigatory in nature. For the 1930s, however, there is a subsection for each state and geographic area. There is also in the files a *Crime Statistics Reporting Handbook*, material on FBI coordination with state and local officials on the gathering of criminal and judicial statistics, and a variety of Bureau and other agency publications on crime and crime statistics.

Volume HQ: 11 cases (18 cu. ft.). FIELD: None

Dates 1938 to 1948

Location FBI

NARA Disposition Recommendation HQ: Cases 1,2,6,7—Permanent; all others—Destroy. FIELD: NA

Access To gain access to the records in this classification a researcher must file a Freedom of Information Act request with the FBI.

Related Records Statistics from state and local law enforcement authorities.

CLASSIFICATION 34

Violation of Lacy Act
(Obsolete)

In 1922 the U.S. Congress passed a law that prohibited the interstate transportation of black bass and fur-seal skins. The FBI therefore established this classification to investigate violations of this act. During the 1920s only two investigative cases files were opened, and in the 1930s the FBI declared the classification obsolete.

Volume HQ: 2 files (microfilmed on one roll). FIELD: None

Dates 1922 to 1928

Location FBI

NARA Disposition Recommendation HQ: All records—Permanent. FIELD: NA

Access To gain access to the records in this classification a researcher must file a Freedom of Information Act request with the FBI.

Related Records Department of Justice Classification 138 Black Bass Act and 34 Lacy Act.

CLASSIFICATION 35

Civil Service

Although this classification remains open, no new cases have been filed since 1943. Altogether, there are only twenty-five extant cases at FBI headquarters. The Bureau established the classification in 1921 to cover investigations involving the character and suitability of applicants for civil service positions and complaints relating to civil service laws. Most cases resulted from a request by the Civil Service Commission (CSC) to have the FBI investigate and date from the 1920s. Generally these cases appear to question an individual's loyalty to the United States, especially focusing on suspected pro-German sentiments during World War I. Information gathered by the Bureau in these investigations was turned over to the CSC for action.

Volume HQ: 25 cases (1 roll of microfilm). FIELD: 20 cases opened; most have been destroyed.

Dates 1921 to 1948

Location FBI

NARA Disposition Recommendation HQ: All records—Permanent. FIELD: All records—Destroy.

Access To gain access to the records in this classification a researcher must file a Freedom of Information Act request with the FBI.

Related Records Records of the United States Civil Service Commission, Record Group 146, National Archives, and Department of Justice Classification 35 Civil Service Act.

CLASSIFICATION 36

Mail Fraud

The Bureau opened this classification in 1924. Although the U.S. Postal Service has the primary responsibility for cases involving fraud through the mails, the FBI also investigates such cases, especially when the mail fraud relates to other matters within the Bureau's jurisdiction. The records themselves reflect the close coordination between the FBI and postal authorities in these matters and the linkage with such criminal activities as stock fraud and real estate scams, insurance swindles, and nonexistent bank and mining companies. The early cases also document Bureau administrative procedures and American social mores. For example, in the 1950s the Bureau investigated a mail fraud case in which books listed as pornography included John Cleland's *Fanny Hill* and John Steinbeck's *The Grapes of Wrath*. There are also excellent materials on U.S. businesses and their practices. In one such case the Warren Feed Company claimed that the Kellogg Company stole its formula for "pop" cereals.

Volume HQ: 2,776 cases (6.35 cu. ft.). 2,492 of the cases are on 38 rolls of microfilm. FIELD: None.

Dates 1924 to present, although there are some cases extant as early as 1921.

Location FBI

NARA Disposition Recommendation HQ: All records—Permanent. FIELD: NA

Access To gain access to the records in this classification a researcher must file a Freedom of Information Act request with the FBI.

Related Records Records of the Post Office Department, Record Group 28, National Archives, and Department of Justice Classification 36 Mails to Defraud.

CLASSIFICATION 37

False Claim against the Government
(Obsolete)

The Bureau established this classification in 1921 to handle its investigations of false claims for compensation by veterans under the Sweet Act and the War Risk Insurance Act. The programs established under these acts provided for the vocational rehabilitation of disabled veterans of World War I and were administered by the U.S. Veterans Bureau from 1921 to 1928. During this period the FBI investigated fraudulent claims for monthly compensation by veterans receiving vocational training. The Bureau declared the classification obsolete in 1928 when the programs expired.

Volume HQ: 3ʑ cases on 1 roll of microfilm (the microfilm is of very poor quality). FIELD: None

Dates 1921 to 1928

Location FBI

NARA Disposition Recommendation HQ: All records—Permanent. FIELD: All records—Destroy.

Access To gain access to the records in this classification a researcher must file a Freedom of Information Act request with the FBI.

Related Records The principal source for information on vocational rehabilitation for veterans is the Records of the Veterans Administration, Record Group 15, National Archives. There are 2,265 linear feet of records on vocational rehabilitation from 1918 to 1928 already at the National Archives. In addition, the Records of the Bureau of War Risk Litigation, Record Group 190, contain an index of claims from 1919 to 1929. See also Department of Justice Classification 37 Bonus Overpayment.

CLASSIFICATION 38

Application for Pardon to Restore Civil Rights
(Obsolete)

The Bureau established this classification for its investigations of naturalized citizens who obtained citizenship by fraudulent means or persons who pretended to be citizens of the United States. Most of the cases were opened when the Department of Justice asked the Bureau to investigate. Most involved false claims of citizenship in order to obtain employment in the 1920s and 1930s, false claims of military service during World War I, and attempts to bribe Immigration and Naturalization Service personnel for approval of citizenship applications. The records are of value to those studying immigration history and the impact of the Great Depression, especially upon recent immigrants. The Bureau declared the classification obsolete in 1938.

Volume HQ: 454 cases (1.5 cu. ft.). FIELD: None. All were destroyed.

Dates 1924 to 1938

Location FBI

NARA Disposition Recommendation HQ: All records—Permanent. FIELD: NA

Access To gain access to the records in this classification a researcher must file a Freedom of Information Act request with the FBI.

Related Records Records of the Immigration and Naturalization Service, Record Group 85, National Archives, and Department of Justice Classifications 38 Naturalization and 39 Immigration. See also FBI Classification 39 Falsely Claiming Citizenship.

CLASSIFICATION 39

Falsely Claiming Citizenship

The Bureau established this classification in 1924 as Immigration and Naturalization Matters but changed the title in 1938 to Falsely Claiming Citizenship. The Bureau focused its investigations primarily on alien radicals and Communists, especially during the 1950s. There is, for example, a file relating to Harry Bridges, president of the International Longshoremen's and Warehousemen's Union, who was convicted of falsely swearing in a naturalization proceeding that he had never belonged to the Communist party. Earlier records relate to German and Japanese aliens, German prisoner-of-war escapees, and undesirable aliens such as Italian mafia subjects. The early records provide information on immigrants and the various procedures for entering the United States. By the 1950s the focus is almost entirely on Soviet-bloc countries and their efforts to infiltrate the United States. Included, for example, is a file devoted to Communist programs designed to entice Americans abroad to marry foreigners and bring them back home. The FBI believed that this was a technique used by the Soviet bloc to infiltrate agents into the United States. In the 1960s the focus changed to black radicals and New Left groups.

The jurisdictional responsibility in this classification has been divided between the Bureau and the Immigration and Naturalization Service (INS). In 1980 the Justice Department recommended that the Bureau transfer its authority in this area to the INS, but as of 1990 this had not been implemented by the Bureau. The files also contain a large amount of biographical data on individuals and groups and highlight the working relationship between the Bureau and the INS.

Volume HQ: 2754 cases (46.5 cu. ft.). FIELD: 3,630 cases in fifty-five field offices. Substantial destruction has occurred.

Dates 1924 to present

Location FBI

NARA Disposition Recommendation HQ: Systematic informational sample of 1,500 cases—Permanent; multisectional cases—Permanent; all others—Destroy. FIELD: Multisection cases—Permanent; all others—Destroy.

Access To gain access to the records in this classification a researcher must file a Freedom of Information Act request with the FBI.

Related Records Records of the Immigration and Naturalization Service, Record Group 85, National Archives; FBI Classification 38, Application for Pardon to Restore Civil Rights; and Department of Justice Classifications 38 Naturalization and 39 Immigration.

CLASSIFICATION 40

Passport and Visa Matters

The Bureau opened this classification in 1924 for investigations of false passport and visa applications, counterfeit passports, and the use of one person's passport by another person. The focus in the 1920s and early 1930s was on the use of false passports by aliens and refugees as the Bureau looked for Communists and Socialist radicals. During World War II the Bureau was primarily concerned with German and Italian agents, but the focus shifted back to Communists during the Cold War years after the passage of the Internal Security Act of 1950. In the early 1960s primary concern in this classification appeared to be Cuba and Cuban travel, particularly after the 1962 U.S. ban on travel to Cuba. After the Vietnam War the focus shifted once again to radicals and immigrants. In 1973, for example, the Bureau uncovered a counterfeit ring that collected the names of deceased infants for use in the creation of false passports for people in Latin America. The Bureau cooperated fully with the Department of State Passport Office on these issues. The records themselves are full of biographical data that document refugee and immigrant problems in the United States and the Bureau's obsession with rooting out Communists and radicals. Included, for example, are case files relating to Communist party head Earl Browder, leader of the American Communist party, and his use of an illegally obtained passport, and William Schneiderman, a Communist at the time he took the citizenship oath, who was pursued by the Bureau, eventually denaturalized, and deported in 1942.

Volume HQ: 85,330 case (79.5 cu. ft.). FIELD: Varies widely from office to office.

Dates 1924 to present. There are some cases dated as early as 1917, however.

Location FBI

NARA Disposition Recommendation HQ: All cases through 1950—Permanent; evidential statistical sample of cases created after 1959—Permanent; all others—Destroy. FIELD: All records—Destroy.

Access To gain access to the records in this classification a researcher must file a Freedom of Information Act request with the FBI.

Related Records Records of the Immigration and Naturalization Service, Record Group 85, and Passport Office Files, in the General Records of the Department of State, Record Group 59, both in the National Archives; and Department of Justice Classification 40 Passport and Visa.

CLASSIFICATION 41

Explosives
(Obsolete)

The Bureau established this classification in 1924 for investigations involving violations of the Federal Explosives Act, which regulated the manufacture, sale, possession, and interstate transportation of explosives. During World War II, Congress amended the act in order to establish a licensing system for explosives. Accordingly, the FBI suspended its investigations relating to the act and in 1958 declared the classification obsolete. The extant cases are, in general, small, with fewer than ten serials, and document rather routine requests for the Bureau to investigate the theft of explosives from government installations and construction sites. In general, the Bureau took little interest in cases of this type. In one case the Du Pont Company notified the Bureau that a substantial quantity of explosives was missing from its Jackson, Mississippi, plant, but the Bureau declined to become involved since, according to a Bureau memo, it could find no evidence of a violation of the actual law. Interestingly, one multisectional case file at headquarters details a number of state and local police brutality cases throughout the 1950s and 1960s as they investigated stolen explosive complaints.

Volume HQ: 757 cases on 3 rolls of microfilm. FIELD: Nine field offices reported extant cases, but there has been extensive destruction in this classification.

Dates 1924 to 1958

Location FBI

NARA Disposition Recommendation HQ: Multisection cases—Permanent. All others—Destroy. FIELD: All records—Destroy.

Access To gain access to the records in this classification a researcher must file a Freedom of Information Act request with the FBI.

Related Records Records of the Office of the Secretary of the Interior, Record Group 48, National Archives, and Department of Justice Classification 41 Explosives.

CLASSIFICATION 42

Deserter

The Bureau established this classification in 1920 when it first began investigating and arresting military deserters. Only a few such cases, however, were opened by the Bureau until near the end of World War II, at which time the War Department and the FBI reached an agreement on who would investigate what cases, and the number investigated by the Bureau exploded. The number grew still more during the Korean conflict and again during the Vietnam War. In 1978 the Bureau, in an agreement with the Department of Defense, sharply restricted its activities in this area, agreeing to limit its investigations to those cases involving more than simple desertion. The number of cases opened at headquarters subsequently dropped from more than 8,000 in 1978 to 11 in 1979.

Because the Bureau's role was to provide assistance to the military services in deserter investigations, most of the cases opened simply consist of a notification from the army, navy, air force, or marine corps of a deserter, a memorandum assigning the case, and a form completed by the field office reporting the circumstances under which the deserter was apprehended. Taken as a whole, however, the files document extensive and continuing investigations initiated by the Bureau in trying to apprehend deserters. In one case, the Bureau pursued an individual for more than fifteen years. There is also a large amount of social history in the files. For example, there are interviews with the deserters, both men and women and even including on occasion an officer. The files document living conditions in America: one dating from 1945 follows a black deserter who became a musician in Harlem and evaded capture for more than ten years; another concerns a youth from Colorado who at first evaded the draft, was caught and inducted into the army, deserted, was apprehended and returned to military service, deserted again, stole a car, and finally led the FBI and local and military authorities on a chase throughout the Western states. He was caught, tried, convicted, and sentenced to prison. The FBI interviews in the case provide a detailed look at living conditions in the West during the 1950s. In a similar manner, cases from the 1960s and early 1970s document the general political atmosphere of the Vietnam War era.

Volume HQ: 503,251 cases (2,702 cu. ft.). 165,533 of the cases are on 823 rolls of microfilm. FIELD: All field offices opened cases in this classification. There has been extensive destruction of these files.

Dates 1921 to present

Location FBI

NARA Disposition Recommendation HQ: Pre-1978, Systematic eviden- tial sample of 500 cases—Permanent; multisectional cases—Permanent; microfilm—Permanent; all others—Destroy. Post-1978, all records— Permanent. FIELD: Pre-1978 records—Destroy; post-1978 records—Destroy.

Access To gain access to the records in this classification a researcher must file a Freedom of Information Act request with the FBI.

Related Records See the individual service records in the various record groups in the National Archives: Records of the Office of the Secretary of the Army, Record Group 335; General Records of the Department of the Navy, Record Group 80; Records of the Office of the Secretary of the Air Force, Record Group 340; and Records of the United States Marine Corps, Record Group 127. See also the Records of the Selective Service System (World War II), Record Group 163, and the Records of the Selective Service System, Record Group 147, both in the National Archives; and Department of Justice Classification 42 Desertion.

CLASSIFICATION 43

Illegal Wearing of Uniform

The Bureau established this classification in 1924. Originally titled National Defense, it pertained almost exclusively to investigations regarding the illegal wearing of U.S. military uniforms. The classification presently covers a variety of statutes relating not only to the illegal wearing of uniforms of the armed forces and other Federal agencies but also to the manufacturing or selling of congressionally authorized decorations, medals, and badges, forgery or alter- ation of military discharge papers and government identification cards and documents, and the unauthorized use of agency seals or symbols, such as Smokey the Bear.

Cases opened in this classification primarily deal with the illegal wearing of a uniform and, on the whole, reflect minor infractions. For example, in cases investigated by FBI agents, violators often wore a uniform illegally to impress a member of the opposite sex, to gain more status, or simply to aid themselves in hitchhiking. At times the uniform was employed to help individuals pass bad checks. The classification is closely related to Classification 47 Impersonation. The Bureau, however, encouraged its field offices to seek convictions in Classification 43, since it was generally easier to establish proof of a violation and therefore easier to obtain a conviction in this classification. In addition to cases concerning the illegal wearing of uniforms, there are those involving forgery and the altering of military identification, primarily for obtaining alcoholic beverages, and the forging of discharge papers for obtaining employment. More recently, the counterfeiting of immigration green cards has become a major problem. The Bureau has also investigated cases involving the illegal use of Federal agency seals. A toy manufacturer in New York, for example, placed the FBI seal on a toy water pistol. The Bureau asked the manufacturer to remove the seal or face prosecution.

Volume   HQ: 17,583 cases (15,190 of them on 64 rolls of microfilm). FIELD: 54,469 cases opened. There has been substantial destruction in this classification.

Dates 1921 to present

Location FBI

NARA Disposition Recommendation HQ: Multisectional cases—Permanent; systematic evidential sample of 500 cases—Permanent; all others, including microfilm—Destroy. FIELD: All records—Destroy.

Access To gain access to the records in this classification a researcher must file a Freedom of Information Act request with the FBI.

Related Records See FBI Classification 47 Impersonation; Records of the Immigration and Nationalization Service, Record Group 85; Records of the Office of the Secretary of the Army, Record Group 335; General Records of the Department of the Navy, Record Group 80; and Records of the Office of the Secretary of the Air Force, Record Group 340, all in the National Archives; and Department of Justice Classification 43 Illegal Wearing of Uniform.

CLASSIFICATION 44

Civil Rights

By a J. Edgar Hoover memorandum of January 1924 the Bureau established this classification primarily for investigations of Ku Klux Klan activities. Hoover based his authority on the civil rights acts of the Reconstruction period that prohibited actions or conspiracies to stop U.S. citizens from exercising the rights secured by the Constitution. In the mid-1930s the Bureau expanded its investigations to include violence against labor union organizers. During World War II and the early Cold War period the Bureau focused on racial disturbances and police brutality claims.

After *Brown v. Topeka Board of Education* in 1954 the Department of Justice pressed the Bureau to initiate investigations of school discrimination cases. Meeting with President Dwight D. Eisenhower and Attorney General Herbert Brownell, Hoover refused to expand FBI responsibilities in this area. He deprecated the nascent civil rights movement, stating that the Ku Klux Klan was moribund and that the National Association for the Advancement of Colored People (NAACP) was infiltrated by Communists. Hoover's attitudes set the tone for all FBI investigations in this classification until his death in 1973. During the 1960s, for example, although Presidents Kennedy and Johnson urged Hoover and the Bureau not only to investigate civil rights abuses but to actively protect civil rights advocates during demonstrations, voter registration drives, and mass marches, Hoover adamantly refused, taking the position that the FBI could only investigate crimes, not protect individuals. This led Kennedy and Johnson to rely on Federal troops and U.S. Marshals in protecting citizens engaged in civil rights activities. The passage of the Voting Rights Act of 1965, the Civil Rights Act of 1968, and the Voting Rights Act of 1975 nevertheless increased pressure on the Bureau to take action. By the mid-1970s most of the investigations opened by the Bureau in this classification were once again related to police and prison brutality complaints. There is an early case, however, that relates to Arthur Mitchell, who later established the Dance Theater of Harlem, and his efforts in the 1940s to contest the railroads' policy of not providing first-class passenger accommodations to blacks.

Taken as a whole, the records in this classification document the great domestic and social changes in American life in the twentieth century. The early records from 1921 to 1950, when interest in civil rights matters by the Bureau and by the general public was minimal, nevertheless document FBI involvement in stopping the Ku Klux Klan, lynching, and institutional segregation, and in ensuring voting and other constitutional rights for all American citizens. The records of the 1960s and early 1970s capture the dramatic changes in election laws and the civil unrest that rocked the United States. The later records illustrate the Bureau's return to investigating more routine police brutality matters.

In addition to clearly defined civil rights matters, this classification contains some rather eclectic cases. Although most of the files simply document police brutality charges and prison condition complaints that were only rarely prosecuted, some illustrate Bureau indifference and perfunctory investigative habits. There are also files richly documenting the Detroit riots of 1967; attacks on Jehovah's Witnesses; threats against President Jimmy Carter; evidence pertaining to Jack Ruby* and his killing of Lee Harvey Oswald*; the unsolved 1964 murder in Georgia of black Lieutenant Colonel Lemuel A. Penn*; the burning in June 1964 of the black Mt. Zion Methodist Church, in Meridian, Mississippi, which led to the deaths of three civil rights workers killed on their way to the site; and on Martin Luther King, Jr.,* and his killer James Earl Ray in 1968. Other files in this classification relate to the Little Rock, Arkansas, school desegregation issue; the murder of civil rights workers Viola Gregg Liuzzo* and Leroy Gerome Moton near Selma, Alabama, in March 1965; the 1968 Democratic Party Convention in Chicago; the attempted assassination of George Wallace* in 1972; and Nixon presidential advisor John Ehrlichman. There is even a file on motorcycle gangs and their civil rights.

Volume HQ: 86,379 cases (1,662 cu. ft.). FIELD: 148,000 cases opened. There has been substantial destruction in all field office files.

Dates 1924 to present. Most cases date from the 1950s.

Location FBI

NARA Disposition Recommendation HQ: All records, pre-1977—Permanent; for post-1977 records, a statistical sample of 1,500 cases per decade beginning in 1975—Permanent; all multisectional cases—Permanent; all other records—Destroy. FIELD: All records, pre-1977—Permanent; all post-1977, multisectional cases—Permanent; all other records—Destroy.

Access To gain access to the records in this classification a researcher must file a Freedom of Information Act request with the FBI.

Related Records See the following FBI classifications: 56 Election Laws, 157 Civil Unrest, 170 Extremist Informants, 176 Antiriot Laws, 7 Kidnapping, 100 Domestic Security, 137 Informants, 173 Civil Rights Act of 1964. See also Justice Department Classifications: 175 Discrimination in Housing, 144 Civil Rights, 168 Desegregation of Public Facilities, 169 Desegregation of Public Education, 170 Desegregation of Equal Employment Opportunity, 171 Miscellaneous Discrimination Matters, 173 Jury Discrimination, and 167 Desegregation of Public Accommodations.

CLASSIFICATION 45

Crime on the High Seas

The Bureau opened this classification in 1924 to cover a variety of crimes committed at sea. Since J. Edgar Hoover was interested in expanding Bureau activity involving the high seas, the FBI constantly pressed the Justice Department for increased authority to investigate cases in this area. The Bureau's campaign resulted in laws against gambling on ships (1939), stowaways (1940), and gambling ships (1948). After World War II the Bureau expanded its operations to cover aircraft as well. This expansion brought the Bureau into jurisdictional conflicts with such agencies as the Coast Guard and the Immigration and Naturalization Service. Most of the cases opened involved stowaways from Africa, Latin America, Eastern Europe, the Philippines, and later Cuba and Vietnam. Other cases varied from the investigation of the theft of a tuna catch to murder and rape on the high seas, to smuggling and organized crime. One of the most interesting cases involved the Cuban exile group led by Dr. Orlando Bosch Avila during the 1960s, and its bombing of freighters bound for Fidel Castro's Cuba. The records, taken as a whole, contain an immense amount of biographical data and in-depth interviews by agents and could be used successfully by those interested in immigration and social history.

Volume HQ: 11,603 cases (52.76 cu. ft.). 7,485 cases are on 28 rolls of microfilm, covering the classification through 1952. FIELD: Fifty-six field offices reported opening cases in this classification. Substantial destruction has occurred.

Dates 1921 to present

Location FBI

NARA Disposition Recommendation HQ: Microfilm—Permanent; multisectional cases—Permanent; systematic sample—Permanent; all others— Destroy. FIELD: All records—Destroy.

Access To gain access to the records in this classification a researcher must file a Freedom of Information Act request with the FBI.

Related Records Records of the United States Coast Guard, Record Group 26, and Records of the Immigration and Naturalization Service, Record Group 85, both in the National Archives, and Justice Department Classification 45 Crime on the High Seas.

CLASSIFICATION 46

Fraud against the Government

The Bureau established this classification in 1921 for its investigations into individuals and corporations that might be defrauding the U.S. government. The Bureau investigated allegations such as overcharges in procurement and construction contracts, the use or provision of substandard parts and merchandise, claims for work not performed, the falsification of time and attendance data by government employees, false statements on applications for government loans or employment, and the offering or accepting of bribes in connection with government contracts. Prior to 1978 the Bureau filed all such investigations in this classification regardless of the Federal agency involved. Beginning in 1978, however, the Bureau established separate classifications for the Department of Defense (Classification 206); the Environmental Protection Agency, Department of Energy, National Aeronautics and Space Administration, and the Department of Transportation (Classification 207); the General Services Administration (GSA) (Classification 208); the Department of Health and Human Services (Classification 209); the Department of Labor (Classification 210); and the Department of Education (Classification 213).

The cases in this classification range from Bureau investigations of U.S. Navy ship-building contracts involving rigged bidding, kickbacks, excessive profits, and the misuse of funds, to GSA scandals involving strategic materials and stockpiling, Vietnam War commodity contracts that relied on the pay-off of inspectors, and investigations of the Federal school-lunch program, to the filing of false travel vouchers, and embezzlement by government employees. One case at the Department of Transportation involving embezzlement resulted in the U.S. government owning the Lone Star Café, a striptease bar in Washington, DC. Surprisingly, there are also files relating to Adam Clayton Powell, Jr., the black former congressman from New York, and James R. Hoffa, the former president of the Teamsters Union. The Hoffa file involves an investigation into his misuse of union pension funds. There is also some information relating to Howard Hughes.*

Volume HQ: 74,162 cases. 46,929 cases are on 558 rolls of microfilm. They primarily predate 1964. FIELD: Fifty field offices reported opening cases in this classification. Of the 203,000 cases, the largest numbers are in Los Angeles, Washington, DC, San Francisco, New York, and Indianapolis. There has been substantial destruction.

Dates 1921 to present

Location FBI

NARA Disposition Recommendation HQ: Systematic informational sample of 1,500 cases—Permanent; multisectional cases—Permanent; all others including the microfilm—Destroy. FIELD: Multisectional cases at Washington field office—Permanent; all other records—Destroy.

Access To gain access to the records in this classification a researcher must file a Freedom of Information Act request with the FBI.

Related Records FBI Classifications 206–210 and 213 Fraud against the Government, and Department of Justice Classification 46 Fraud against the Government.

CLASSIFICATION 47

Impersonation

The Bureau established this classification in 1924 for investigations involving the impersonation of U.S. government officials or foreign diplomats. The courts have increasingly restricted application of the law. To be in violation today the impersonator must obtain or attempt to obtain money, documents, or other items of value. In addition, the government must prove the subject's intent to act under the "color of authority" and prove intent to defraud. In general, the FBI and the Department of Justice have given low priority to such cases, considering them "petty violations." Since 1961 cases in this classification have been handled by U.S. Commissioners as "petty offenses." Most of the cases opened involved individuals impersonating military officers or FBI agents for the purpose of passing bad checks. One case involved the elaborate development of a scam where the subject passed as a Federal bank examiner in order to bilk money from widows and widowers. Another involved the impersonation of former Speaker of the House Sam Rayburn in order to gain admittance to the White House.

Volume HQ: 57,263 cases (171 cu. ft.); 50,247 of the cases have been microfilmed on 175 rolls. FIELD: All fifty-nine field offices reported opening cases in this classification, totaling 218,743 cases. There has been substantial destruction.

Dates 1924 to present

Location FBI

NARA Disposition Recommendation HQ: Systematic evidential sample—Permanent; multisectional cases—Permanent; all others—Destroy. FIELD: All records—Destroy.

Access To gain access to the records in this classification a researcher must file a Freedom of Information Act request with the FBI.

Related Records FBI Classification 43 Illegal Wearing of Uniform and Department of Justice Classifications 43 Illegal Wearing of Uniform and 47 Impersonation of a Federal Officer.

CLASSIFICATION 48

Postal Violations (Except Mail Fraud)

The Bureau established this classification in 1924 for its investigations into postal violations including the reproduction of postal stamps, theft of postal money orders, the counterfeiting of postal meters, and theft from mail boxes. Mail fraud cases are not covered by this classification. The Bureau has opened only fifty cases at headquarters in the last thirty years in this classification. In general, the cases consist of requests by postal inspectors for FBI fingerprint checks and FBI referral letters to the Postal Service for handling. Other extant cases deal with such matters as obscene letters, pornographic literature, threats being sent through the mail, and the forging of postal money orders.

Volume HQ: 12,110 cases. 1,169 cases on 3 rolls of microfilm. FIELD: Unable to determine as a result of substantial destruction.

Dates 1924 to present

Location FBI

NARA Disposition Recommendation HQ: Microfilm—Permanent; multisectional cases—Permanent; informational sample—Permanent; all others—Destroy. FIELD: All records—Destroy.

Access To gain access to the records in this classification a researcher must file a Freedom of Information Act request with the FBI.

Related Records Records of the U.S. Postal Service, Record Group 28, National Archives, and Department of Justice Classification 48 Postal Violations.

CLASSIFICATION 49

National Bankruptcy Act

The Bureau established this classification in 1921 when it adopted the Department of Justice filing system. Cases found in this classification document FBI investigations under the criminal provision of the National Bankruptcy Act, including cases that concern the concealment or transfer of assets in contemplation of filing for bankruptcy, the destruction of records relating to the property or financial affairs of a debtor, and investigations of trustees or bank officers acting improperly in bankruptcy proceedings. Prior to 1944 the Bureau initiated investigations only at the request of the U.S. Attorneys. After World War II, however, Bureau agents periodically checked bankruptcy court dockets in an effort to identify violators. Peak case loads appeared in 1950, 1965, and 1976. The records document attempts by individuals to conceal assets, the filing of false statements on bankruptcy petitions, and bribery attempts of bankruptcy referees. Although bankruptcy cases in court records are heavily used by genealogists, the records in this classification relate only to criminal activities and therefore offer the genealogist less useful information.

Volume HQ: 22,642 cases. FIELD: 53,827 cases. All field offices report extant cases.

Dates 1921 to present

Location FBI

NARA Disposition Recommendation HQ: Systematic evidential sample of 500 cases—Permanent; all others—Destroy. FIELD: All records—Destroy.

Access To gain access to the records in this classification a researcher must file a Freedom of Information Act request with the FBI.

Related Records Records of District Courts of the United States, Record Group 21, National Archives, and Department of Justice Classification 49 Bankruptcy.

CLASSIFICATION 50

Involuntary Servitude and Slavery

The Bureau adopted this classification in 1921 as one of the original classifications from the Department of Justice filing system. Under this classification, the Bureau has investigated cases involving the holding or returning of a person to peonage, enticement into slavery, sale into servitude, deprivation of rights under the Thirteenth Amendment, and conspiracy to violate the rights of citizens. Prior to 1942 the classification was titled Peonage and violations had to include involuntary servitude plus debt. On December 12, 1941, the Department of Justice instructed the Bureau and U.S. Attorneys to disregard entirely the element of debt and concentrate on the issue of involuntary servitude and slavery. The cases clearly reflect the change in focus of investigations, as well as providing a clear illustration of changing American social and labor conditions. Early cases, for example, concentrate on state and local prison conditions and forced labor issues, especially chain gangs in the South and Jim Crow laws. In the 1940s and 1950s the focus was on the exploitation of black tenant farmers and sharecroppers in the South. By the 1960s and 1970s migrant labor conditions, especially concerning Mexican and Central and South American workers, are the focus.

In addition, there is a wealth of information on prostitution rings and some information on nursing homes and the growing problems of the elderly. Many cases present research potential for labor, social, criminal, women, race, and ethnic scholars with many in-depth interviews of plaintiffs and subjects. The records document living conditions in the South and in California especially. There is also some information relating to the National Association for the Advancement of Colored People and its leader, Roy Wilkins.*

Volume HQ: 3,598 cases, of which 2,224 are on 7 rolls of microfilm. FIELD: 5,201 cases. All field offices reported extant cases. There has been substantial destruction in this classification.

Dates 1921 to present

Location FBI

NARA Disposition Recommendation HQ: All records—Permanent. FIELD: All records—Permanent.

Access To gain access to the records in this classification a researcher must file a Freedom of Information Act request with the FBI.

Related Records Records of the Office of the Secretary of Agriculture, Record Group 16, National Archives, and Department of Justice Classifications 31 White Slave Act, 50 Peonage, and 144 Civil Rights.

CLASSIFICATION 51

Jury Panel Investigations

This classification, established in 1924, contains the Bureau's files relating to its assistance to the Department of Justice in the selection of possible jury members. Before the FBI undertakes an investigation, the approval of the attorney general or the appropriate assistant attorney general is required. Typically, the Bureau's response has involved a check of the prospective jury panel member's criminal record, a credit check, and a search of appropriate field office files. The passage of the Fair Credit Reporting Act of 1971 forced the Bureau to eliminate the credit check.

Volume HQ: 520 cases (1 roll of film). FIELD: 555 cases. Forty-two field offices reported opening cases. There has been substantial destruction.

Dates 1924 to present

Location FBI

NARA Disposition Recommendation HQ: Microfilm (all extant cases)— Permanent. FIELD: All records—Destroy.

Access To gain access to the records in this classification a researcher must file a Freedom of Information Act request with the FBI.

Related Records Department of Justice Classification 51 Bribery and Perjury.

CLASSIFICATION 52

Theft or Destruction of Government Property

The Bureau opened the first case in this classification in 1921. There are two types of investigations included in this classification: the first covers theft, robbery, embezzlement, illegal possession, and receipt or destruction of government property; the second, interference with government communications. This classification is closely related to several others: Classification 17 Fraud against the Government—Veterans Administration; Classification 46 Fraud against the Government; Classification 86 Fraud against the Government—Small Business Administration; Classification 206 Fraud against the Government—Department of Defense; Classification 207 Fraud against the Government—Environmental Protection Agency, Department of Energy, National Aeronautics and Space Administration, and the Department of Transportation; Classification 208 Fraud against the Government—General Services Administration; Classification 209

Fraud against the Government—Department of Health and Human Services; Classification 210 Fraud against the Government—Department of Labor; Classification 213 Fraud against the Government—Department of Education; Classification 70 Crime on Government Reservation (including crimes on Indian reservations, inducing conveyance of Indian Trust Land, and embezzlement or theft of Indian property); and Classification 198 Crime on Indian Reservation. Investigations of interference with government communications became part of this classification in 1977. Before this time, they had been included in Classification 92 Racketeering Enterprise Investigations.

The FBI has been aggressive in its assertion of authority to investigate the theft of government property. Suggestions that the military should investigate theft by military personnel and that other agencies should investigate thefts by their own employees have almost always been rejected by the Bureau. While the value of the goods stolen or destroyed played no part in determining jurisdiction, value was used to establish investigative priorities. By the late 1960s, after U.S. Attorneys refused to prosecute the large number of minor offenses, the Bureau allowed other agencies to investigate them. By the late 1970s, the FBI began placing its emphasis on investigations involving more than $5,000. The Bureau has always acknowledged the generally routine nature of these investigations. A 1947 Bureau Bulletin, for example, stated that no investigative reports other than a summary of the closing report need be forwarded to FBI headquarters except for major cases and cases involving electronic surveillance, peculiar crimes, and important perpetrators.

Typical violations include minor offenses such as theft of typewriters, tools, items from post exchanges, vehicles, and machinery. Beginning in the 1960s, the Bureau urged its agents to watch for the theft of weapons and explosives by extremists and hate groups. This classification also contains files on the destruction of government property and the use of government property for personal benefit. One of the most interesting cases involves the break-in and burglary of the FBI-in-residence agency in Media, Pennsylvania, in 1971. The Bureau concluded it was part of the anti-Vietnam War, antidraft activities of the Citizens' Commission to Investigate the FBI.* There is also some information relating to Bonnie Parker and Clyde Barrow* and their accomplices.

Volume HQ: 105,015 cases (329 rolls of microfilm). FIELD: 375,639 cases. All field offices reported opening cases. There has been substantial destruction.

Dates 1921 to present.

Location FBI

NARA Disposition Recommendation HQ: Microfilm (all extant cases)—Permanent. FIELD: All records—Destroy.

Access To gain access to the records in this classification a researcher must file a Freedom of Information Act request with the FBI.

Related Records See FBI Classifications 17, 46, 86, 206, 207, 208, 209, 210, and 213 Fraud against the Government (various agencies and departments), 70 Crime on Government Reservation, 92 Racketeering Enterprise Investigations, and 198 Crime on Indian Reservation. See also Department of Justice Classification 46 Fraud against the Government and 52 Theft of Government Property.

CLASSIFICATION 53

Excess Profits on Wool
(Obsolete)

The Bureau established this classification to cover its investigations of violations of World War I-era regulations on the price of wool as set by the War Industries Board. The Bureau, however, opened only three cases in this classification.

Volume HQ: 3 cases. FIELD: NA

Dates 1918 to 1925

Location FBI

NARA Disposition Recommendation HQ: Microfilm (all extant cases)— Permanent. FIELD: No extant cases.

Access To gain access to the records in this classification a researcher must file a Freedom of Information Act request with the FBI.

Related Records Records of the War Industries Board, Record Group 61, National Archives.

CLASSIFICATION 54

Customs Laws and Smuggling

The Bureau established this classification on July 28, 1924. It includes cases involving smuggling that did not fall under the jurisdiction of the Bureau of Customs. Most files in this classification date from between 1924 and 1950, when the Bureau of Customs assumed responsibility for investigating most Federal smuggling violations. In 1939 the Bureau placed investigations of most arms smuggling cases in Classification 2 Neutrality Matters.

The cases break down into broad categories. During the 1920s, most investigations related to the smuggling of alcohol, drugs, and Chinese nationals.

During the 1930s, cases relating to the smuggling of arms to Spain, Latin America, and Asia and other violations of the Neutrality Act of 1935 predominate. The 1940s find most investigations covering the smuggling of a wide variety of items including jewelry, wool, watches, radio tubes, and precious metals and gems.

Volume HQ: 1,483 cases. FIELD: 903 cases. Forty-six field offices reported opening cases. There has been substantial destruction.

Dates 1924 to 1973. The classification remains open, however.

Location FBI

NARA Disposition Recommendation HQ: Multisectional cases—Permanent; all cases opened prior to 1939—Permanent; systematic evidential sample— Permanent; all others—Destroy. FIELD: Multisectional cases—Permanent; all others—Destroy.

Access To gain access to the records in this classification a researcher must file a Freedom of Information Act request with the FBI.

Related Records Records of the Bureau of Customs, Record Group 36, National Archives, FBI Classification 2 Neutrality Matters, and Department of Justice Classification 54 Customs Violations.

CLASSIFICATION 55

Counterfeiting

This classification predates 1924 and includes FBI files relating to the counterfeiting of U.S. coins, stamps, paper money, and securities. Primary jurisdiction for the investigation of counterfeiting rests with the Secret Service; the FBI merely refers such matters to the other agency. As a result, this is a relatively unimportant classification insofar as the Bureau is concerned. Virtually all cases predate 1945.

Volume HQ: 689 cases (1 roll of microfilm). FIELD: 691 cases. Forty-six field offices report opening cases. There has been substantial destruction.

Dates 1924 to present

Location FBI

NARA Disposition Recommendation HQ: Multisectional cases—Permanent; microfilm—Permanent; all others—Destroy. FIELD: All records—Destroy.

Access To gain access to the records in this classification a researcher must file a Freedom of Information Act request with the FBI.

Related Records Records of the United States Secret Service, Record Group 87, National Archives, and Department of Justice Classification 55 Counterfeit and Forgery.

CLASSIFICATION 56

Election Laws

Records in this classification cover Bureau investigations into violations of Federal election laws. These laws include the Federal Corrupt Practices Act of 1925, the Hatch Act of 1939, and the Federal Election Campaign Act of 1972, with its 1974 and 1976 amendments. The Bureau established this classification in 1924. Violations of election laws generally involve conspiracies to injure, oppress, threaten or intimidate citizens in their right to vote; conspiracies by election officials to stuff ballot boxes with fraudulent votes; conspiracies to prevent the official count of ballots; conspiracies to illegally register voters and to count absentee ballots in their names; illegal expenditures to influence voting; and illegal campaign contributions and illegal solicitation of campaign contributions.

As might be expected, the Bureau opened most of these cases during election years. They include investigations of the unauthorized use of candidates' names, misuse of absentee ballots, false registration, voting by noncitizens, vote buying, and unfair campaign literature. Generally, twice as many cases are opened in years with a presidential election than in years with only congressional elections, with the Bureau opening more cases in 1960 (748) than in any other year. Since 1975 the number of cases opened each year has dropped to less than 100. While a number of cases in this classification relate to possible violations of the civil rights of blacks living in the South, especially with regard to the white primary, most such cases are incorporated into Classification 44 Civil Rights. During the 1970s, several investigations of Federal campaign-finance laws connected with the Watergate affair fell into this classification. There is also an election fraud case in Kansas City, Missouri, involving the Pendergast machine in which President Truman showed great interest.

Volume HQ: 8,897 cases. FIELD: 11,608 cases. All fifty-nine field offices reported opening cases. There has been substantial destruction.

Dates 1924 to present

Location FBI

NARA Disposition Recommendation HQ: All records—Permanent. FIELD: All records—Destroy.

Access To gain access to the records in this classification a researcher must file a Freedom of Information Act request with the FBI.

Related Records FBI Classification 44 Civil Rights and Department of Justice Classifications 72 Election Frauds—Hatch Act and 166 Voting Rights—Discrimination and Intimidation.

CLASSIFICATION 57

War Labor Dispute Act
(Obsolete)

The Bureau established this classification in the early 1920s to cover investigations of labor strikes. In November 1943 the Bureau's Executive Conference determined that this classification should cover investigations of violations of the War Labor Dispute Act, also known as the Smith-Connolly Anti-Strike Law. Between June and November 1943 violations of the War Labor Disputes Act were filed in Classification 98 Sabotage.

Before the passage of that law, the FBI had disseminated to other appropriate agencies information about potential strikes, lockouts, and other aspects of labor unrest. After the bill became law over President Franklin Roosevelt's veto, the Bureau and the Department of Justice reached an understanding. The existing policy of dissemination would remain essentially intact and the Bureau would conduct no investigations without express authority from the Criminal Division of the Department of Justice. Hoover was content with that arrangement only as it related to the conduct of investigations. He complained to the attorney general in July 1943, however, that the agreement also prohibited his agents from developing informants and contacts, a situation he believed would leave the FBI unprepared to respond if and when an overt act of sabotage was committed.

In August 1943, in the course of World War II, the Bureau authorized agents to develop "discreet informant coverage" and asked all field offices to keep headquarters up to date with information on lockouts, strikes, slowdowns, and other work stoppages. The FBI attached primary importance to government-controlled plants and to evidence of subversive activities and strikes affecting vital defense-related activities. With the end of the war and the return of industry to private ownership, the Bureau informed its field offices that investigations in this classification should emphasize labor unrest with possible Communist origins. The FBI declared this classification obsolete in 1951.

The records in this classification detail the Bureau's considerable involvement in the coal miners' strike of 1944, the New England railroad strike of 1922, World War II strikes in government-operated mines and plants, and the influence of the Communist party on American labor.

Volume HQ: 946 cases. FIELD: NA. All field office files have been destroyed.

Dates 1922 to 1951

Location FBI

NARA Disposition Recommendation HQ: All records—Permanent. FIELD: NA

Access To gain access to the records in this classification a researcher must file a Freedom of Information Act request with the FBI.

Related Records General Records of the Department of Labor, Record Group 174, National Archives, and Department of Justice Classification 16 Strikes.

CLASSIFICATION 58

Bribery, Conflict of Interest

Hoover established the Bureau's authority to conduct investigations in this classification in 1924. Bribery investigations initially required the approval of the attorney general; however, in 1938 authority to open such cases was delegated to the director of the FBI.

The files in this classification cover investigations of charges of conflict of interest against and bribery of Federal officials, members of Congress, and Federal judges. Many cases also cover the impersonation of government officials. Cases relate to attempts to influence officials, such as meat inspectors and Internal Revenue Service agents, in their decision-making capacity; government employees selling favors such as immigration green cards; and contract and procurement fraud involving former government officials working in private industry. One such case involved William Woolridge, a sergeant major in the U.S. Army, and charges of corruption in the procurement area during the 1950s. There is also some information relating to Alger Hiss,* some on the investigation of then Vice President Spiro Agnew, and a file relating to the Abscam investigation of Congress and the consequent conviction of Congressman John Jenrette (D., South Carolina) for bribery.

Volume HQ: 10,627 cases (76 rolls of microfilm). FIELD: 23,598 cases. All fifty-nine field offices reported opening cases. There has been substantial destruction.

Dates 1921 to present

Location FBI

NARA Disposition Recommendation HQ: Systematic informational sample of 2,500 cases—Permanent; multisectional cases—Permanent; microfilm cases in sample—Permanent; all others—Destroy. FIELD: Multisectional cases—Permanent; all others—Destroy.

Access To gain access to the records in this classification a researcher must file a Freedom of Information Act request with the FBI.

Related Records Records of the Immigration and Naturalization Service, Record Group 85, National Archives, and Department of Justice Classification 51 Bribery and Perjury.

CLASSIFICATION 59

World War Adjusted Compensation Act
(Obsolete)

The Bureau established this classification in 1924 to include files generated by investigations of violations of legislation providing special compensation for veterans of World War I. Violations included the filing of false claims and charging of excessive fees for assisting veterans in applying for benefits. Cases cover investigations of illegal loans made under the act, theft of compensation certificates, and fraudulent claims. The FBI declared this classification obsolete in 1928 but continued to add documents to existing cases as late as 1944.

Volume HQ: 190 cases (1 roll of microfilm). FIELD: Unknown. Only two field offices reported opening any cases in this classification.

Dates 1924 to 1944

Location FBI

NARA Disposition Recommendation HQ: Microfilm (all extant cases)—Permanent. FIELD: All records—Destroy.

Access To gain access to the records in this classification a researcher must file a Freedom of Information Act request with the FBI.

Related Records   Records of the Veterans Administration, Record Group 15, National Archives, and Department of Justice Classification 37 Bonus Overpayment.

CLASSIFICATION 60

Anti-Trust

The Bureau opened this classification in 1921 for files relating to investigations of Federal antitrust laws. Beginning in 1890, Congress passed three major laws on antitrust matters. The first, the Sherman Antitrust Act of 1890, prohibited the restraint of trade. The second, the Clayton Antitrust Act of 1914, supplemented the Sherman Act by prohibiting price discrimination between purchasers of commodities in interstate commerce if such discrimination resulted in decreased competition or the creation of a monopoly. The third, the Robinson-Patman Act of 1936, expanded the Clayton Act by prohibiting any discrimination that lessened competition, not just discrimination based on price. The type of cases investigated by the FBI under this classification has varied over time. During the early 1940s the Bureau concentrated on industries connected with defense and international cartels. In the late 1940s the emphasis switched to concern with conspiracies to raise prices. The 1950s saw a concern with larger corporations. In addition to material relating to the FBI's investigations, the files include substantial data on business practices and economic conditions in the United States.

There are also files on local and nationwide investigations of such diverse establishments as the newsprint industry, General Motors, the concrete industry, International Business Machines (IBM), the fur-dressing industry, Volkswagen of America, and the housing industry. Many of the cases, for example the IBM case, document FBI support and assistance to U.S. Attorneys and to the Antitrust Division of the Department of Justice. There is information, for example, relating to the early Du Pont Company divestiture of its ownership of General Motors; the separation of Aluminum Company of America from other aluminum-production firms; the separation of taxi-cab manufacturing (by Checker) from taxi-operating companies (particularly Yellow Cab); investigations of General Motors and its control of 85 percent of all bus sales in the United States; the breakup of American Telephone and Telegraph; the investigation of the American Bar Association and the restriction of advertising by lawyers; and monopoly practices in the meatpacking industry.

Volume HQ: 7,720 cases (102 rolls of microfilm). FIELD: Unknown. All fifty-nine field offices reported opening cases. There has been substantial destruction.

Dates 1921 to present

Location FBI

NARA Disposition Recommendation HQ: Multisectional cases—Permanent; microfilm—Permanent; all others—Destroy. FIELD: Multisectional cases— Permanent; all others—Destroy.

Access To gain access to the records in this classification a researcher must file a Freedom of Information Act request with the FBI.

Related Records Department of Justice Classification 60 Antitrust Violations.

CLASSIFICATION 61

Treason

The earliest case in this classification dates from 1921. The Bureau included under this heading investigations of persons or organizations engaged in treasonous activities or in concealing such activities. Also included in the definition is service in or recruitment of others to serve in armed hostility against the United States and aiding or procuring the escape of interned enemy aliens. In its written instructions, the Bureau states that any evidence of possible violations of the treason statute should receive "immediate, continuous, and preferred" investigation as treason is the "highest crime known to this country" and is the only crime mentioned in the Constitution.

For the period prior to World War II, most cases reflect concern with alleged radicals and related activities. Typical cases concern anarchists, Bolsheviks, and the Communist Party of the United States of America. During the war the Bureau refocused its attentions, pursuing investigations relating to Germany, Japan, and other wartime enemies. Beginning in 1944 the FBI began looking into treasonous activities committed by foreigners in overseas theaters of operations. The Bureau also investigated allegations that Americans aided in the escape of prisoners of war from internment camps. During the Korean War, the major investigative topic was allegations of U.S. prisoners of war collaborating with Chinese Communists. These investigations led to jurisdictional conflicts with the armed services, which often ran parallel investigations. In 1954 a "delimitation agreement" clarified jurisdictional lines. In it, all parties agreed that investigative jurisdiction over treason offenses committed by individuals, active or retired, while in the armed services, would be vested in the intelligence office of the appropriate branch of the service. In addition to virtually unknown cases of peacetime radical activities and wartime collaboration, this classification contains files on Tokyo Rose* (Iva Ikuko Toguri D'Aquino), Axis Sally (Mildred Gillars), and Ezra Pound,* for example, and on the twenty-one U.S.

prisoners of war who refused repatriation from China at the end of the Korean War. There are also files relating to the National Negro Congress* and its efforts to get a Federal antilynching bill passed; the admission of Albert Einstein* to the United States; the National Association for the Advancement of Colored People* and what the Bureau termed its "radical activities"; the Highlander Folk School* in Monteagle, Tennessee, which the Bureau investigated from the 1930s to the 1960s for suspected subversive activities; Jane Addams* and the Women's International League for Peace and Freedom; the Sacco and Vanzetti* case; some information on the Rosenberg case; and the New Left* in the 1960s.

Volume HQ: 11,595 cases. FIELD: 11,497 cases. Fifty-one field offices reported opening cases. There has been substantial destruction.

Dates 1921 to present

Location FBI

NARA Disposition Recommendation HQ: All records—Permanent. FIELD: All records—Permanent.

Access To gain access to the records in this classification a researcher must file a Freedom of Information Act request with the FBI.

Related Records Records of the Office of the Secretary of Defense, Record Group 330, Records of the Office of the Secretary of the Air Force, Record Group 340, Records of the United States Marine Corps, Record Group 127, and General Records of the Department of the Navy, Record Group 80, all in the National Archives. See also Department of Justice Classifications 51 Bribery and Perjury and 146 World War II (Internal Security).

CLASSIFICATION 62

Administrative Inquiry
(Miscellaneous Subversive and Nonsubversive)

The Bureau opened this classification about 1921 as a location for records on subjects that could not be filed in more specific file designations. There is a great deal of subversive documentation dating until 1953 in this classification. With the change of this classification's name at headquarters to Miscellaneous Nonsubversive, such nonsubversive files were also placed here. In the field, Classification 62 is used for both subversive and nonsubversive files.

This classification has been dynamic since its creation, primarily as a result of the establishment of new classifications to handle material originally filed here. Examples of these types of files are those concerning security informants that are now filed in Classification 134, those on criminal informants that are now in Classification 137, Freedom of Information requests, which now form Classification 190, and civil suits against the government, which now constitute Classification 197. Other subjects once filed here and now filed elsewhere include liaison activities with other parts of the U.S. government and other governments, so-called nut files, congressional mail (including constituent referrals), General Accounting Office reviews of operations, and congressional studies and investigations of the Bureau or Bureau-related activities. This classification may also have served as the predecessor for early domestic security files now found in Classification 100. It is important to note that closed cases and some pending cases did not get transferred to the new categories and are still found in Classification 62.

The Bureau's early 1980s *Manual of Investigative Operations and Guidelines* lists sixteen major types of files to include in this classification:

1) misconduct investigations of FBI employees and officers, and of employees of the Department of Justice and the Federal judiciary;
2) census matters;
3) domestic police cooperation;
4) Contract Work Hours and Safety Standards Act;
5) Fair Credit Reporting Act;
6) Federal Cigarette Labeling and Advertising Act;
7) Federal judiciary investigations;
8) Kickback Racket Act;
9) Lands Division matters;
10) other violations and/or matters;
11) civil suits—miscellaneous;
12) Soldiers' and Sailors' Civil Relief Act of 1940;
13) Tariff Act of 1930;
14) unreported interstate shipment of cigarettes;
15) Fair Labor Standards Act of 1938; and
16) conspiracy.

In addition, the classification contains files on Bureau liaison with foreign governments and international organizations, with congressional committees, and with presidential committees, commissions, and boards, and on publicity about the Bureau. Early files for categories established at later times will also be found in this classification.

The records in this classification contain information relating to a variety of famous cases or people. For example, there is material relating to Justice Hugo Black* and the Ku Klux Klan, the House Select Committee on Assassinations,* Howard Hughes,* the Osage Indian murders,* the assassination of John F. Kennedy,* the Saint Valentine's Day massacre,* the *Hindenburg* disaster,* Kate (Ma) Barker,* the Warren Commission,* Nelson Rockefeller,* Huey P.

Long,* Charles (Pretty Boy) Floyd* and the Kansas City massacre, the Dillinger gang,* Alvin Karpis,* and the Moorish Science Temple of America.*

Volume HQ: 118,947 cases. FIELD: 234,191 cases. All field offices reported opening cases. There has been substantial destruction.

Dates 1921 to present

Location FBI

NARA Disposition Recommendation HQ: Misconduct investigations—Permanent; census matters, multisectional cases—Permanent; liaison with agencies of the Federal government, states, and local institutions—Permanent; Contract Work Hours and Safety Standards Act, multisectional cases—Permanent; fair credit reporting—Permanent; Federal Cigarette Labeling and Advertising Act, multisectional cases—Permanent; Federal judiciary investigations—Permanent; Kickback Racket Act—Permanent; lands division matters—Destroy; civil suits, multisectional cases–Permanent; Soldiers' and Sailors' Civil Relief Act of 1940, multisectional cases—Permanent; Tariff Act of 1930, multisectional cases—Permanent; unreported interstate shipment of cigarettes, multisectional cases—Permanent; Fair Labor Standards Act of 1938, multisectional cases—Permanent; conspiracy, multisectional cases—Permanent; Freedom of Information and Privacy Act—Permanent; all other records—Disposal not authorized. FIELD: Misconduct investigations, multisectional cases—Permanent; census matters—Destroy; liaison with agencies of the Federal government, states, and local institutions—Permanent; Contract Work Hours and Safety Standards Act—Destroy; fair credit reporting—Destroy; Federal Cigarette Labeling and Advertising Act—Destroy; Federal judiciary investigations—Permanent; Kickback Racket Act—Permanent; lands division matters—Destroy; civil suits, multisectional cases—Permanent; Soldiers' and Sailors' Civil Relief Act of 1940, multisectional cases—Permanent; Tariff Act of 1930, multisectional cases—Permanent; unreported interstate shipment of cigarettes, multisectional cases—Permanent; Fair Labor Standards Act of 1938—Destroy; conspiracy—Destroy; Freedom of Information and Privacy Act—Permanent; all other records—Disposal not authorized.

Access To gain access to the records in this classification a researcher must file a Freedom of Information Act request with the FBI.

Related Records FBI Classifications 100 Domestic Security, 134 Foreign Counterintelligence Assets, 137 Informants, 190 Freedom of Information/Privacy Acts, 197 Civil Actions or Claims against the Government.

CLASSIFICATION 63

Miscellaneous—Nonsubversive

When this classification opened formally in 1924 the Bureau titled it Supervision of Accountants. At that time, it contained records dated as early as 1921; the extant records in this classification, however, date back only as far as 1953. In that year the Bureau shifted most accounting records to other classifications and destroyed the rest. At headquarters this classification was given the name it carries today. Files that fell under that rubric that had been placed in Classification 62 were now included in this "new" classification. As a result, there is some overlap of subjects between the two classifications. In the field, these matters remain a part of Classification 62.

Since its 1953 redesignation, this classification has seen many additions and deletions to the subjects covered, and its purview continues to change today. In 1958, for example, case files relating to investigations by the Lands Division of the Department of Justice were added. Cases under the Veterans Readjustment Assistance Act were shifted to Classification 17 in 1955, and in 1978 cases under the Federal Revenue Sharing Act were moved to Classification 204. Other broad categories of subjects covered by case files in this classification include fraud against the government; unreported interstate shipment of cigarettes; civil suits; relations with professional associations of police officials and lawyers, such as the National Conference of Police Associations and the Criminal Law and Criminal Justice sections of the American Bar Association; the Bureau's internal employee benefits programs (life insurance, flu-vaccine program, and unemployment compensation); Top Hoodlum Program cases; investigations of racketeering; cases concerning labor leader Jimmy Hoffa; Crimdel (Current Developments in Criminal Matters, Central Research Section) reports; and lawsuits alleging Bureau violations of citizens' rights by electronic surveillance, harassment, and improper maintenance of derogatory information.

This classification also contains cases that do not fall under the broad categories outlined above. Examples include files on Assistant Attorney General Warren Olney and a 1965 Department of Justice investigation of the exclusion of African-Americans from juries, criminal influence in labor unions, the Defense Atomic Support Agency, and the appointment of the FBI director in the years 1962 to 1978. Many of the files found in this classification are closely related to cases found in other classifications including, for example, those concerning top hoodlums and racketeering.

Volume HQ: 17,765 cases. FIELD: NA

Dates 1953 to present

Location FBI

NARA Disposition Recommendation HQ: All records—Disposal not authorized. FIELD: NA

Access To gain access to the records in this classification a researcher must file a Freedom of Information Act request with the FBI.

Related Records FBI Classifications 17 Fraud against the Government— Veterans Administration, 62 Administrative Inquiry, 92 Racketeering Enterprise Investigations, 122 Labor Management Relations Act, 143 Interstate Transportation of Gambling Devices, 159 Labor-Management Reporting and Disclosure Act of 1959, 166 Interstate Transportation in Aid of Racketeering, 182 Illegal Gambling Business, 183 Racketeer Influenced and Corrupt Organizations, 195 Hobbs Act—Labor Related, and 204 Federal Revenue Sharing. See also Department of Justice Classifications 46 Fraud against the Government, 164 Interstate Transmission of Wagering Information, 165 Interstate or Foreign Travel in Aid of Racketeering Organizations, 156 Labor Management Relations, 159 Gambling Device Controls, 123 Anti-Racketeering Act, and 191 Bribery by Multinationals.

CLASSIFICATION 64

Foreign Miscellaneous

This control file, arranged by country, is used by the Bureau to report intelligence information on foreign countries. It was originally called Latin American Matters. In most cases the Bureau simply provides assistance to the foreign government in identification and job applicant matters by checking its files and those of other Federal agencies for pertinent information. Included is a file relating to Ernest Hemingway* and his desire to serve as an informant in Cuba during the 1940s. Hoover rejected Hemingway's offer and the writer later criticized the Bureau for supporting Fulgencio Batista. There is also information relating to Justice Hugo Black.*

Volume HQ: 50,000 cases (700 cu. ft.). FIELD: 12,000 cases.

Dates Not given

Location FBI

NARA Disposition Recommendation HQ: All cases opened prior to 1951— Permanent; multisectional cases—Permanent; systematic sample of post-1951 cases—Permanent; all others—Destroy. FIELD: Multisectional cases—Permanent; all others—Destroy.

Access To gain access to the records in this classification a researcher must file a Freedom of Information Act request with the FBI.

Related Records See FBI Classification 163 Foreign Police Cooperation.

CLASSIFICATION 65

Espionage

The Bureau opened this classification in the early 1920s; when listed in Director Hoover's July 28, 1924, memorandum on filing it was called Japanese Activities. The Bureau uses this classification for files generated as the result of investigations of individuals alleged to have unlawfully obtained information affecting national defense or to have unlawfully disclosed such information to a foreign government. The FBI jurisdiction in this area is rooted in both law and presidential directives, including the passage of the Espionage Act of 1917 and, during World War II, the 1939 and 1943 promulgations of presidential directives assigning to the Bureau responsibility for the investigation of espionage and subversion.

This classification remained relatively unused until the period of World War II (1939–1945). Although the bulk of the cases deal not with actual espionage but with individuals suspected of sympathy with the Axis, the Bureau's major World War II-era espionage investigations are also found in this classification. For example, there is a file relating to Axel Wenner-Gren,* a Swedish arms merchant and friend of the Duke of Windsor* who provided munitions and aviation equipment on the U.S. blacklist through Mexico to the Axis powers, and a file on William Rhodes Davis,* who sold Mexican oil to Germany despite the blacklist. Included here also are files relating to Albert Einstein,* Adolf Hitler,* and Errol Flynn.* There is even a file for the period relating to UFOs.*

After the war, emphasis shifted to investigations of individuals suspected of working on behalf of the Communist bloc and of foreigners coming to the United States, to determine if they were foreign agents. Again, as with the wartime files, many of the cases detail relatively minor investigations in which no espionage was proven. This classification, however, also includes the files on such major espionage investigations as the cases of Julius and Ethel Rosenberg,* Alger and Priscilla Hiss,* Nathan Silvermaster,* Dusko Popov,* Adam von Trott zu Solz,* and Amy Elizabeth Thorpe Pack Brousse.* For the 1960s there is a file relating to the Soviet spy Colonel Rudolf Abel. Since the 1970s, this classification has also been used for files on investigations of the unauthorized disclosure of classified information. There is a file, however, relating to Andrew Lee and Christopher Boyce (nicknamed the Falcon and the Snowman), who were convicted in 1977 of selling U.S. military secrets to the Soviet Union and one relating to the FBI's COINTELPRO.*

Most cases in this classification were opened in the period from 1939 to 1945. For example, at FBI headquarters, of the 77,258 extant cases only about 1,900 were opened before 1939. The Bureau opened approximately 55,000 cases at headquarters between 1939 and 1945, with the remainder opened since that date. The establishment of other classifications, particularly Classification 105 Foreign Counterintelligence, may account for the fewer number of cases opened after the war.

Volume HQ: 77,258 cases. FIELD: 162,024 cases. All field offices reported opening cases. There has been substantial destruction.

Dates 1920s to present

Location FBI

NARA Disposition Recommendation HQ: All cases with six or more serials— Permanent; all cases opened before 1939—Permanent; all others—Destroy. FIELD: All cases opened before 1939—Permanent; all cases with six or more serials—Permanent; all others—Destroy.

Access To gain access to the records in this classification a researcher must file a Freedom of Information Act request with the FBI.

Related Records FBI Classifications 100 Domestic Security, 105 Foreign Counterintelligence, 200–203 Foreign Counterintelligence Matters, and Department of Justice Classification 146 World War II (Internal Security).

CLASSIFICATION 66

Administrative Matters

As with all government entities, the FBI creates and maintains files relating to its own administration. Consequently, the Bureau established this classification about 1921 to serve as the central repository for this type of documentation. As to be expected, these files are a mixture of the significant and the ephemeral. Morever, the classification has changed over time; for example, in 1952 informant files were moved from this classification to Classification 134 Foreign Counterintelligence Assets and Classification 137 Informants.

The main subjects covered by this classification at FBI Headquarters are:

1) control files on each field office and legal attaché;
2) control files on each administrative unit in headquarters, including the director's office, each division, branch, section, and school;
3) minutes of the Executive Conference;
4) the Bureau's annual reports;

5) annual appropriations;
6) procurement and supplies;
7) manuals, instructions, bulletins, memorandums to all officials and supervisors, Special-agent-in-charge (SAC) letters, forms, and other procedural and operational issuances;
8) Bureau motor vehicle maintenance and operation;
9) accidents involving Bureau personnel;
10) administration and accounting of funds;
11) proposed legislation;
12) surveys of field offices;
13) statistics and accomplishments;
14) control files on informants and individual files on informants and sources;
15) space and maintenance;
16) periodic reporting from Bureau units;
17) law enforcement, police, and other conferences;
18) employee services such as the flower fund, savings bonds, and campaigns;
19) special applicants;
20) security and protective services;
21) publicity;
22) history of the Bureau including organizational charts;
23) records management and disposition;
24) visitors, callers, and tours;
25) personnel-related files; and
26) policy files on investigative techniques.

The *Manual of Administrative Operations and Procedures* indicates that the following matters should be incorporated in Classification 66 in the field: accomplishments, addressograph, administrative report, ammunition, arraignment, arrests, automobiles, bills of lading, charity campaigns, check circulators, use of coordinators, credit bureau, duplicating and reproduction equipment, employee compensation, films, firearms, forms, household goods, identification orders, imprest fund, inspections, Internal Revenue Service data, interviews, inventory, jails, copies of the *Law Enforcement Bulletin*, leave information, mailing lists, office memoranda, personnel, photographic equipment, property, radio, recreation association, registers, report writing, resident agencies, retirement, SAC letters, salary matters, searches and seizures, space, supplies, surveillance, technical equipment, technical and microphone surveillance, telephones and teletypes, transmittal letters, visiting employees, vouchers, wanted fliers, and weekend and night duty. Many offices maintain files on other subjects as well as part of this classification. Typical of these are security, liaison with foreign governments, other Federal agencies, and state and local organizations; SAC confidential fund; codes; and early Freedom of Information and Privacy Act cases.

Volume HQ: 19,248 cases. FIELD: 175,327 cases. All field offices reported opening cases. There has been substantial destruction.

Dates 1920s to present

Location FBI

NARA Disposition Recommendation HQ: All records—Disposal not authorized. FIELD: All records—Disposal not authorized.

Access To gain access to the records in this classification a researcher must file a Freedom of Information Act request with the FBI.

Related Records See the various FBI classifications relating to the various subjects.

CLASSIFICATION 67

Personnel Matters

The Bureau established this classification in 1924. It is maintained separately from other classifications and contains three basic types of files. The first are the Official Personnel Files (OPFs) maintained for all out-of-service and in-service employees of the Bureau. These files contain routine employment information. The second are employment applications. The third type of files are the so-called Special and General Files. The OPF file contains information, for example, relating to J. Edgar Hoover,* Clyde A. Tolson,* Hoover's assistant director and close friend, and Special Agent Melvin Purvis,* the FBI agent who shot John Dillinger.

The Special and General Files relate to specific personnel subjects rather than to individuals and are arranged by subject. The Special Files are set up by name of the field office, legal attaché, or headquarters division to which they relate. In general, these files include information on the functioning of the various units of the Bureau, including assignments, transfers, promotions, censure, commendations, salary, organization, and investigative priorities. There are main and subfiles for each field office, legal attaché, or headquarters division. The main files cover general personnel matters. The subfiles include documentation on inspections, including inspection summaries, inspection reports, findings, recommendations, and implementation of inspectors' recommendations and instructions; 1950s personnel guidance programs; civil service and eligible applicant rosters; and proposals for establishing and classifying positions.

The General Files document the more routine personnel matters of the Bureau. There are files for the Standard Form 278, Executive Personnel

Financial Disclosure Report; participants in the Bureau's alcoholism program; tabulations of work-related injuries; grievance, disciplinary, and adverse action files; employee housing requests; Equal Employment Opportunity official discrimination complaint files; personnel counseling records; and blood donation records. Documentation on the oversight and direction of the alcoholism program is found in Classification 62 Administrative Inquiry.

Volume HQ: Unknown. Some records have been microfilmed. FIELD: Unknown. All field offices reported opening cases.

Dates 1924 to present

Location FBI

NARA Disposition Recommendation HQ: See the FBI Task Force Appraisal Report. FIELD: See the FBI Task Force Appraisal Report.

Access To gain access to the records in this classification a researcher must file a Freedom of Information Act request with the FBI.

Related Records NA

CLASSIFICATION 68

Alaskan Matters
(Obsolete)

The Bureau established this classification in 1938 to delineate peculiar problems of jurisdiction and investigation in the territory of Alaska. Although the Bureau has been involved in all violations of Federal territorial law, in 1946 the Justice Department reduced its jurisdiction to only major crimes. In 1948 with the codification of Alaskan territorial law, the Bureau further limited its area of jurisdiction. Until this time the Bureau had been the major law enforcement agency in Alaska and territorial governor Ernest Gruening objected to the reduced FBI role and activity, but Hoover closed the FBI offices in the territory nonetheless. The Bureau closed the classification at the time Alaska became a state in 1959.

Volume HQ: 852 cases (826 on microfilm). FIELD: Only eleven field offices reported opening cases. There are no extant cases from Anchorage.

Dates 1924 to 1958

Location FBI

NARA Disposition Recommendation HQ: All records—Permanent. FIELD: All records—Destroy.

Access To gain access to the records in this classification a researcher must file a Freedom of Information Act request with the FBI.

Related Records See state records in Anchorage and the Records of the Alaskan Territorial Government, Record Group 348, National Archives.

CLASSIFICATION 69

Contempt of Court

The Bureau established this classification in 1924 to replace an obsolete classification previously used by the Department of Justice (Classification 16 Violation of Federal Injunction). At the time that the new classification was created, cases carried in Classification 16 were incorporated into it. According to the law the FBI may be called in at the request of a Federal judge, a U.S. Attorney, or another Federal agency. Investigations under this classification cover jury tampering, perjury, contempt of court and threats to, intimidation of, or assaults on witnesses. There are also investigations relating to officers of the court who commit improprieties while on official business or who were derelict in carrying out their duties.

The violations covered by the cases actually opened include leaks of grand jury testimony, union violations of restraining orders issued by the courts, attempted harassment of witnesses, improper use of Fifth Amendment rights, and improper handling of Federal prisoners, as well as instances of contempt of court. There is also some information relating to Alphonse (Al) Capone.*

Volume HQ: 848 cases (5 rolls of microfilm). FIELD: Unknown. Fifty-two field offices reported opening cases. There has been substantial destruction.

Dates 1924 to present

Location FBI

NARA Disposition Recommendation HQ: Multisectional cases—Permanent; microfilm—Permanent; all others—Destroy. FIELD: All records—Destroy.

Access To gain access to the records in this classification a researcher must file a Freedom of Information Act request with the FBI.

Related Records Department of Justice Classification 16 Strikes.

CLASSIFICATION 70

Crime on Government Reservation

Hoover established the Bureau's authority to conduct the investigations filed in this classification in 1924. This classification has also been used to cover crimes on Indian reservations, acts of inducing conveyance of Indian Trust Land, and embezzlement or theft of Indian property. Also included are crimes committed on military reservations and in Federal prisons. Generally, the files cover crimes such as murder, rape, child abuse, auto theft, assaults, homosexual activities, trespassing, and writing bad checks. In 1977 the Bureau established Classification 198 for investigations of crimes on Indian reservations. In this classification, however, there remains some information relating to the 1973 occupation of Wounded Knee, South Dakota, and the prosecution of Indian activist Leonard Peltier for the 1977 killings of two FBI agents on an Indian reservation.

Volume HQ: 72,814 cases (205 rolls of microfilm). FIELD: 235,809 cases. Fifty-seven field offices reported opening cases. There has been substantial destruction.

Dates 1924 to present

Location FBI

NARA Disposition Recommendation HQ: Systematic informational sample of 1,500 cases—Permanent; multisectional cases—Permanent; microfilm—Permanent; cases in which the subject or victim was an American Indian—Permanent; all others—Destroy. FIELD: Cases in which the subject or victim was an American Indian—Permanent; all others—Destroy.

Access To gain access to the records in this classification a researcher must file a Freedom of Information Act request with the FBI.

Related Records FBI Classification 198 Crime on Indian Reservations and Department of Justice Classification 90 Lands.

CLASSIFICATION 71

Bills of Lading Act

This classification dates from 1924. It is now used for investigations involving falsely made, altered, forged, or counterfeited bills of lading used in interstate commerce with intent to defraud. Through October 1953, however, this classification was also used to file investigations of false entries in records of interstate carriers, illegal use of railroad passes, interstate transportation of gambling devices, interstate transportation of lottery tickets, interstate transportation of obscene matter, and interstate transportation of prison-made goods. In early October 1953 the Bureau established Classifications 141 through 146 for each of these offenses, leaving only cases concerning bills of lading in Classification 71.

Volume HQ: 6,175 cases (31 rolls of microfilm). FIELD: 17,894 cases. Fifty-six field offices reported opening cases. There has been substantial destruction.

Dates 1924 to present

Location FBI

NARA Disposition Recommendation HQ: Microfilm—Permanent; multisectional cases—Permanent; all cases predating 1953 and relating to Interstate Transportation of Gambling Devices, Lottery Tickets, and Obscene Matter—Permanent; all others—Destroy. FIELD: All records—Destroy.

Access To gain access to the records in this classification a researcher must file a Freedom of Information Act request with the FBI.

Related Records FBI Classifications 141–146 and Department of Justice Classifications 64 Lottery, 97 Obscene Literature, 131 Interstate Transportation of Prison-Made Goods, and 159 Gambling Device Controls.

CLASSIFICATION 72

Obstruction of Criminal Investigations

The Bureau formally opened this classification in 1924, although it contains documentation from an earlier date. The FBI originally investigated jury tampering, bribes of witnesses, and threats against judges and witnesses either at the request of a Federal judge or of U.S. Attorneys. In the 1940s and 1950s, when other agencies pressed the Bureau to take responsibility for bribery, Hoover resisted, successfully arguing that those agencies had their own investigative staffs and sought only to dump difficult cases on the FBI. In 1947 the Bureau rejected a proposal that it investigate intimidation of witnesses called before congressional committees. A law passed in 1960 gave the FBI the power to investigate the obstruction of criminal investigations from the beginning of a case through the end of a trial. The Bureau, however, has remained selective about which cases it undertakes, maintaining its position that its primary concern is with the integrity of Federal court proceedings. Typical cases involve threats to witnesses, government officials, and judges; attempts to influence juries; suborning perjury; and withholding information. There is a case file on the murder of John Rosselli.

Volume HQ: 2,725 cases. FIELD: 6,047 cases. All field offices reported opening cases. There has been substantial destruction.

Dates 1924 to present

Location FBI

NARA Disposition Recommendation HQ: All records—Permanent. FIELD: All records—Destroy.

Access To gain access to the records in this classification a researcher must file a Freedom of Information Act request with the FBI.

Related Records Department of Justice Classification 51 Bribery and Perjury.

CLASSIFICATION 73

Application for Pardon

The Bureau established this classification in the early 1920s. It contains two types of investigations: The first covers individuals seeking presidential pardons after completing prison sentences received as a result of Federal offenses. The second covers persons convicted of Federal offenses who are seeking executive clemency. The Bureau rarely conducts investigations of the latter type. Investigations typically include interviews with an applicant's friends, neighbors, and employers, as well as checks with law enforcement agencies and credit organizations. The FBI's activities in this area are in support of the Office of the Pardon Attorney, which has primary jurisdiction in pardon matters.

Volume HQ: 19,566 cases (46 rolls of microfilm). FIELD: 44,503 cases. All field offices reported opening cases.

Dates 1920s to present

Location FBI

NARA Disposition Recommendation HQ: Systematic evidential sample of 500 cases—Permanent; multisectional cases—Permanent; microfilm—Permanent; all others—Destroy. FIELD: All records—Destroy.

Access To gain access to the records in this classification a researcher must file a Freedom of Information Act request with the FBI.

Related Records Records of the Office of the Pardon Attorney, Record Group 204, National Archives.

CLASSIFICATION 74

Perjury

The FBI established this classification in 1924 upon an order from Hoover concerning investigations of perjury and subornation of perjury. In 1971, as a result of the Organized Crime Control Act of 1970, the Bureau added investigations of violations that include false declaration before a grand jury or court.

In general, the Bureau does not investigate perjury charges arising from cases under the primary jurisdiction of the Secret Service, the Internal Revenue Service, the Immigration and Naturalization Service, the Bureau of Customs, the Drug Enforcement Administration, the Bureau of Alcohol, Tobacco and Firearms, and the U.S. Postal Service. An order from FBI headquarters, however, can lead to an investigation involving those agencies. Similar prior headquarters authority is required before proceeding in matters under the jurisdiction of departments, agencies, and committees, and in those incidental to court action such as affidavits and statements made by defendants in order to obtain representation paid for by the government. Given the severe limitations placed on Bureau involvement in perjury matters, it is not surprising that the FBI has opened relatively few cases in this classification. There are some important files here, however, including the primary file relating to Alger Hiss* and his perjury trial, the Hatch Act investigation of William W. Remington,* whom Elizabeth Bentley identified as a Communist and whom the Bureau suspected of being a party member engaging in un-American activities, and a file on the investigation of Spiro Agnew.

Volume HQ: 2,765 cases. FIELD: 6,026 cases. All field offices reported opening cases. There has been substantial destruction.

Dates 1924 to present

Location FBI

NARA Disposition Recommendation HQ: Systematic evidential sample—Permanent; multisectional cases—Permanent; all others—Destroy. FIELD: All records—Destroy.

Access To gain access to the records in this classification a researcher must file a Freedom of Information Act request with the FBI.

Related Records Records of the United States Secret Service, Record Group 87, Records of the Immigration and Naturalization Service, Record Group 85, Records of the Bureau of Alcohol, Tobacco, and Firearms, in General Records of the Department of the Treasury, Record Group 56, Records of the U.S. Postal Service, Record Group 28, all in the National Archives, and Department of Justice Classification 51 Bribery and Perjury.

CLASSIFICATION 75

Bondsmen and Sureties

The Bureau established this classification in early 1925 to cover investigations of fraudulent criminal bail bonds regardless of the Federal criminal statute violated. Investigations may determine if persons forfeiting bonds have property that can be seized, but the FBI does not investigate forfeited bail bonds or the issuance of immigration bonds furnished in regard to control and regulation of admission and deportation of aliens. Prosecutions are usually brought under the perjury and conspiracy statutes.

Volume HQ: 1,786 cases (7 rolls of microfilm). FIELD: 1,879 cases. Forty-four field offices reported opening cases. There has been substantial destruction.

Dates 1925 to present

Location FBI

NARA Disposition Recommendation HQ: Systematic evidential sample— Permanent; all others—Destroy. FIELD: All records—Destroy.

Access To gain access to the records in this classification a researcher must file a Freedom of Information Act request with the FBI.

Related Records Records of the Immigration and Naturalization Service, Record Group 85, National Archives, and Department of Justice Classification 51 Bribery and Perjury.

CLASSIFICATION 76

Escaped Federal Prisoners

The Bureau formally opened this classification in 1937 for cases involving escaped Federal prisoners and parole and probation violators. In 1979 the

Bureau transferred all such fugitive cases to the U.S. Marshals Service for investigation. The typical file consists of a form announcing the escape of a prisoner or a parole violator and a teletype announcing the apprehension and return to custody of the subject. There is a large amount of biographical information in these files as well. Taken as a whole the files demonstrate the standard Bureau techniques for tracking felons and parole violators. Moreover, there are numerous prisoner interviews and the files are sprinkled with interesting cases, such as those related to Leonard Peltier, convicted of killing two FBI agents, the escapee from Alcatraz whose file remained open for forty years despite the fact that he was presumed drowned, and the escaped Federal prisoner who was eventually tracked down when he was over eighty years old. There is also a file relating to Ed Ramsey, a black prison escapee under a death sentence, and his extradition struggle involving Massachusetts and South Carolina, and one relating to Arthur Barker* and the Barker gang.

Volume HQ: 64,190 cases (506 cu. ft.), of which 27,547 cases have been microfilmed on 214 rolls. FIELD: 256,419 cases. All fifty-nine field offices reported opening cases in this classification. There has been substantial destruction.

Dates 1934 to 1979

Location FBI

NARA Disposition Recommendation HQ: Systematic informational sample of 2,500 cases—Permanent; microfilm—Permanent; all other records—Destroy. FIELD: All records—Destroy.

Access To gain access to the records in this classification a researcher must file a Freedom of Information Act request with the FBI.

Related Records Records of the United States Attorneys and Marshals, Record Group 118, National Archives, and Department of Justice Classifications 4 Prisons Matters, 99 Federal Escape Act, and 126 Fugitive Felon Act.

CLASSIFICATION 77

Applicants (Special Inquiry, Departmental, Other Government Agencies)

The Bureau established this classification in 1929 for its investigations of applicants for Federal employment, limited initially to the Department of Justice, and appointees to the Federal judiciary. Under the Truman administration the Bureau expanded the classification to include nominees of interest to the

White House and congressional committees; however, the Bureau shifted these special inquiries to Classification 161 in 1960. Most of the cases involve routine background checks of professional and nonprofessional applicants for a variety of Justice Department and Federal judiciary positions ranging from clerk-typist to U.S. Attorneys, correctional officials, Immigration and Naturalization Service inspectors, and Federal judges. The records contain a great deal of biographical information on individuals and their life-styles. The records also document the Bureau's investigative techniques in dealing with applicants, including, for example, credit checks; interviews with employees, colleagues, friends, and neighbors; military service records; and housing information. There is a case file relating to the Federal judicial appointment of Edward A. Tamm,* and files relating to some Bureau applicants.

Volume HQ: 139,942 cases (2040 cu. ft.). FIELD: 637,517 cases. All fifty-nine field offices reported opening cases. There has been some destruction.

Dates 1928 to present

Location FBI

NARA Disposition Recommendation HQ: Statistical sample of 1,500 cases—Permanent; multisectional cases—Permanent; all others—Destroy. FIELD: All records—Destroy.

Access To gain access to the records in this classification a researcher must file a Freedom of Information Act request with the FBI.

Related Records FBI Classification 161 Special Inquiries for White House, Congressional Committees, and Other Government Agencies.

CLASSIFICATION 78

Illegal Use of Government Transportation Requests

The Bureau established this classification in 1938 to handle cases involving the theft or misuse of government travel forms and travel claims, but the classification has been rarely used. The more serious cases investigated involved forgery or the counterfeiting of government forms and were turned over to the Secret Service for investigation.

Volume HQ: 79 cases, on 1 roll of microfilm. FIELD: 213 cases extant.

Dates 1938 to present

Location FBI

NARA Disposition Recommendation HQ: Microfilm—Permanent. FIELD: All records—Destroy.

Access To gain access to the records in this classification a researcher must file a Freedom of Information Act request with the FBI.

Related Records Records of the United States Secret Service, Record Group 87, National Archives, and Department of Justice Classification 55 Counterfeit and Forgery.

CLASSIFICATION 79

Missing Persons

The Bureau established this classification in 1933 to handle information relating to missing persons. Most of the case files consist of an initiating document requesting FBI assistance in locating a missing husband, wife, or child and a positive or a negative response from the Bureau. Any assistance the Bureau provided usually came from its Identification (Fingerprint) Division. Although there is some biographical information in the files, the researcher would make better use of the FBI's National Crime Information Center. The center, established in 1966, maintains statistical data on missing persons that has been gathered from local authorities. The Bureau's case load in this classification has steadily dropped from a high of one thousand cases in 1949 to twenty in 1980.

Volume HQ: 32,731 cases (27,304 cases on 50 rolls of poor-quality microfilm). FIELD: Although all field offices reported opening cases in this classification, few remain extant.

Dates 1933 to present

Location FBI

NARA Disposition Recommendation HQ: Systematic evidential sample of 500 cases for the pre-1978 files—Permanent; multisectional cases—Permanent; all others—Destroy. FIELD: All records—Destroy.

Access To gain access to the records in this classification a researcher must file a Freedom of Information Act request with the FBI.

Related Records Records of state and local authorities.

CLASSIFICATION 80

Laboratory Research Matters—Headquarters

This classification, established in 1932, contains records relating to the Bureau's technical laboratory. Unlike Classification 95 Laboratory Examinations, however, which documents individual laboratory analyses, this classification relates to (1) public relations activities of the Bureau, (2) forensic techniques of interest to the Bureau, and (3) files relating to the administration of the laboratory itself. Between 1932 and 1955 this classification was titled Public Relations Matters. In January 1946, Hoover ordered each of the FBI field offices to establish a Classification 80 for "various types of speech material." The files, both at headquarters and in the field, contain reports and write-ups of interesting cases and contacts with local and state police departments, newspapers and broadcasting stations, district and state attorneys' offices, and local businesses and civic leaders. There are also book manuscripts, radio and television scripts, and press clippings in the files.

As a part of its public relations program, the Bureau also encouraged its laboratory staff to prepare essays on interesting cases and techniques. Headquarters files alone contain over four hundred such write-ups between 1934 and 1940 (see files 80-101 through 80-500). Most of the files at headquarters are devoted to the development or implementation of forensic techniques. There are, for example, reference collections of items found useful in solving particular crimes that include samples of type faces, fibers, handwriting specimens, and firearms. (See Appendix VI for a complete list of these collections.) The records also document such forensic techniques as electronic surveillance and monitoring, cryptography and cryptanalysis, paper, fingerprint, handwriting analysis, and research and development in these areas. There are monthly reports from the laboratory that document its case load and a file of "outside experts" that is of some interest in documenting the Bureau's early reluctance to recognize or consult with local experts. On the local level this classification carefully documents Bureau efforts to court local civic leaders and such businesses as hotels and banks that might provide useful information in the future.

Volume HQ: 879 cases (174 cu. ft). The Bureau also maintains a list of extant cases along with a summary caption of each case. FIELD: Fifty-eight of the field offices reported opening cases in this classification. There has been some destruction.

Dates 1932 to present

Location FBI

NARA Disposition Recommendation HQ: All records—Permanent or Disposal not authorized. FIELD: Contacts with state and local law enforcement agencies and with district and state attorneys, and of the special agents in charge contacts—Permanent; all contacts with the media and local business—Destroy; all other files—Disposal not authorized.

Access To gain access to the records in this classification a researcher must file a Freedom of Information Act request with the FBI.

Related Records FBI Classification 95 Laboratory Examinations.

CLASSIFICATION 81

Gold Hoarding
(Obsolete)

When Congress in 1933 passed the Emergency Banking Relief Act, which gave the president broad discretionary powers over foreign exchange, it also prohibited gold hoarding or the export of gold. It further authorized the secretary of the treasury to call in all gold and gold certificates in the country and sharply restricted the amount of gold individuals could maintain. The FBI was given the responsibility for investigating alleged violations of the act. In 1935 the Department of Justice instructed the Bureau to end such investigations following passage of a new Gold Reserve Act in 1934, but the Bureau continued to add material to existing cases for a decade more.

The records in this classification are filed somewhat differently from the normal Bureau procedure. Case files 2 through 22 are compilations of investigations from each of the then-existing twenty-one FBI field offices. For example, Case 4 contains all the reports from Chicago, Case 19 all reports from San Francisco. Each file was opened with a letter from Hoover to the special agent in charge enclosing a list of possible gold hoarders submitted by the region's Federal Reserve Bank. The Bureau agent then approached the subject, advised him or her of potential criminal violation, and provided the subject the opportunity to turn in any hoarded gold. Only a few cases were ever turned over to U.S. district attorneys for prosecution. The records themselves, however, provide a wealth of biographical data and are unusually rich in information relating to economic conditions in urban areas in the United States during the era of the Great Depression.

Volume HQ: 28 cases on 7 rolls of microfilm. FIELD: Extant cases reported only in Portland and Butte.

Dates 1933 to 1945

Location FBI

NARA Disposition Recommendation HQ: All records—Permanent. FIELD: Multisectional cases—Permanent; all others—Destroy.

Access To gain access to the records in this classification a researcher must file a Freedom of Information Act request with the FBI.

Related Records General Records of the Department of the Treasury, Record Group 56, National Archives, and Department of Justice Classification 112 Gold Reserve Act.

CLASSIFICATION 82

War Risk Insurance
(Obsolete)

The Bureau established this classification in 1933 when it was given the responsibility for conducting investigations involving civil suits filed by U.S. veterans against the government. Prior to 1933 the Veterans Administration handled all such suits. The cases cover fraudulent insurance claims against the government and general disability claims disallowed by the Veterans Administration. One case, for example, that involved a victim of mustard gas in World War I was finally settled in 1954 when the veteran's heirs received $7,500 for a permanent disability claim. Most of the cases either settled out of court or were dismissed. Although the files contain some biographical data, the records of the Veterans Administration and the army and navy better document claims activity. The Bureau declared the classification obsolete in 1967.

Volume HQ: 14,896 cases (14,444 on microfilm). FIELD: Twenty-two field offices reported opening 18,162 cases. There has been substantial destruction.

Dates 1933 to 1967

Location FBI

NARA Disposition Recommendation HQ: Systematic evidential sample of 500 cases—Permanent; multisectional cases—Permanent; all others—Destroy. FIELD: All records—Destroy.

Access To gain access to the records in this classification a researcher must file a Freedom of Information Act request with the FBI.

Related Records Records of the Veterans Administration, Record Group 15, Records of the Office of the Secretary of the Army, Record Group 335, and General Records of the Department of the Navy, Record Group 80, all in the

National Archives. See also Department of Justice Classifications 17 War Risk Insurance and 37 Bonus Overpayment.

CLASSIFICATION 83

Claims Court

Established in 1934, this classification covers Bureau investigations of civil claims made against the government and litigated in the U.S. Court of Claims in Washington, DC. The assistant attorney general for the Civil Division of the Department of Justice must request an investigation before the Bureau will open a case in this classification. In most cases the Bureau has based its investigation on detailed accounting procedures and attempted to determine damages by estimating actual costs to the plaintiff. The investigations are carried out by special agent accountants. The cases relate to such diverse subjects as the management of alien property estates during World War I, war contracts during World War II, Japanese-American farmers suing for losses of land and crops during World War II, patent infringements involving major defense contractors, such as Lockheed and Litton Industries, and even breach of contract disputes arising from the construction of the Kennedy Center for the Performing Arts. In the early cases Hoover claimed credit for saving the government money whenever the courts dismissed a case or awarded a lower amount than the plaintiff sued. The cases document fully the FBI's extensive audit techniques and capabilities.

Volume HQ: 2,688 cases (55.5 cu. ft.), 995 cases of which are on 26 rolls of microfilm. FIELD: 8,821 cases opened. The Washington field office is the office of origin for most of these, although considerable destruction has occurred in all field offices.

Dates 1934 to present

Location FBI

NARA Disposition Recommendation HQ: Cases 83-1 to 83-10, 83-1339 to 83-1349, and 83-2678 to 83-2688—Permanent; microfilm—Permanent; all others—Destroy. FIELD: All records—Destroy.

Access To gain access to the records in this classification a researcher must file a Freedom of Information Act request with the FBI.

Related Records Records of the Court of Claims Section, Record Group 205, National Archives, and Department of Justice Classifications 154 Court of Claims and 78 Tucker Act (Claims against the United States).

CLASSIFICATION 84

Reconstruction Finance Corporation Act
(Obsolete)

In 1932, to address the growing economic crisis in the country, President Herbert Hoover advocated an economic recovery program based on government loans to banks and railroads. After passage of the act creating the Reconstruction Finance Corporation (RFC), the Bureau established this classification in 1934 to cover investigations relating to possible violations of the act. Such violations included the making of false statements on loan applications, speculating in government securities, forgery, and counterfeiting. When Franklin D. Roosevelt became president in 1933, his New Deal included the creation of the Commodity Credit Corporation, which was authorized to use RFC funds to support farm prices by enabling producers to retain commodities until they received a higher price. At the outset these loans were primarily extended to cotton farmers in the South.

In 1937 the Bureau turned over most investigations in this classification to the Secret Service. In 1938 the Bureau began to refer cases involving the Commodity Credit Corporation to the Agricultural Adjustment Administration. The Bureau declared the classification obsolete in 1949 and assigned all cases relating to Federal lending and insurance agencies to Classification 66 Administrative Matters.

Most of the extant cases involve attempts to defraud the Commodity Credit Corporation. The most common violation was misrepresenting a cotton crop for the purpose of obtaining a loan. Many cases contain extensive interviews with Southern farmers, especially blacks, which provide great detail on family life in the South. They also contain a wealth of information on sharecroppers and tenant farmers, and rural life in general, in the South during the Great Depression.

Volume HQ: 111 cases (105 on 1 roll of microfilm). FIELD: No extant cases.

Dates 1934 to 1949

Location FBI

NARA Disposition Recommendation HQ: All records—Permanent. FIELD: No extant records.

Access To gain access to the records in this classification a researcher must file a Freedom of Information Act request with the FBI.

Related Records Records of the Reconstruction Finance Corporation, Record Group 234, Records of the Agricultural Adjustment Administration, in Records of the Office of the Secretary of Agriculture, Record Group 16, and Records of the Commodity Credit Corporation, Record Group 161, all in the National Archives. See also Department of Justice Classification 105 Reconstruction Finance Corporation and FBI Classification 66 Administrative Matters.

CLASSIFICATION 85

Home Owners Loan Corporation
(Obsolete)

The Home Owners Refinancing Act of 1933 created the Home Owners Loan Corporation (HOLC) to refinance home mortgage debts for nonfarm owners during the depression. The HOLC was also empowered to furnish cash advances for the payment of taxes, repairs, and maintenance costs on homes. It terminated its activities in June 1936. The Bureau established this classification in 1934 for its investigations of violations of the criminal provisions of the act. The Bureau, as the records reflect, was reluctant to pursue such cases and generally referred the cases to the HOLC for disposition. The extant cases generally deal with attempts by bank officials to extract additional monies for processing loan requests. The Bureau declared the classification obsolete in 1952.

Volume HQ: 135 cases, on 1 roll of microfilm. FIELD: 35 cases from two field offices.

Dates 1934 to 1952

Location FBI

NARA Disposition Recommendation HQ: All records—Permanent. FIELD: All records—Destroy.

Access To gain access to the records in this classification a researcher must file a Freedom of Information Act request with the FBI.

Related Records Records of the Federal Home Loan Bank System, Record Group 195, National Archives, and Department of Justice Classification 111 Federal Home Loan Bank.

CLASSIFICATION 86

Fraud against the Government—
Small Business Administration

The Bureau established this classification in 1935 for its investigations into fraud cases in the agencies created by the Emergency Relief Act during the second phase of President Franklin D. Roosevelt's New Deal. The early cases involved the Works Projects Administration as it came under attack for being inefficient, wasteful, and corrupt. After 1953, when the Small Business Administration (SBA) was set up, the classification was devoted exclusively to investigations of SBA frauds. These cases usually involved the illegal sale of collateral used to secure a loan from the SBA, nonpayment of loans, the misrepresentation of information on loan applications, and possible kickback and bribery schemes. In one case, for example, despite the evidence provided by the FBI, the local U.S. Attorney refused to prosecute because it was a disaster loan and the business was the only grocery store in the town.

Volume HQ: 3,794 cases (38 cu. ft.) on 11 rolls of microfilm. FIELD: All field offices hold records in this classification. There has been substantial destruction.

Dates 1935 to present

Location FBI

NARA Disposition Recommendation HQ: Microfilm—Permanent; 5% evidential sample—Permanent; all others—Destroy. FIELD: All records—Destroy.

Access To gain access to the records in this classification a researcher must file a Freedom of Information Act request with the FBI.

Related Records Records of the Small Business Administration, Record Group 309, National Archives, and Department of Justice Classification 46 Fraud against the Government.

CLASSIFICATION 87

Interstate Transportation of Stolen Property

The Bureau established this classification in 1934 in connection with the passage of the National Stolen Property Act, under which the FBI was given investigative authority when the interstate transportation of stolen property valued at $5,000 or more was alleged. In 1939 the Bureau added cases involving forged securities and forged checks to this classification. In 1956 the Bureau expanded its area of investigation to include all stolen property valued at $50,000 or more regardless of whether or not it was transported across state lines.

In general, the Bureau has focused its investigations on professional burglary rings and their fence operations, but it has also examined check-kiting schemes, tax evasion attempts relating to the establishment of illegal or nonexistent trusts, counterfeit corporate bonds, stocks, international bank checks, payroll checks, and money orders, and even grain and commodity scams. The records detail FBI laboratory analysis techniques, particularly regarding handwriting and fingerprint samples, and illustrate the FBI's National Fraudulent Check File and Top Jewel-Theft Program. Cases also document major criminal rings involved in the theft of heavy-duty earth-moving equipment, new automobiles, and painting and art objects such as a Van Gogh, a Degas, and a Stradivarius violin.

In an interesting case involving the theft and sale of historic Mexican artifacts and treasures, the records detail jurisdictional conflicts between Mexican authorities and the FBI, as well as interagency competition between the special strike force set up by the Department of the Treasury to investigate the case and the FBI headquarters agents and field office working on it. In this particular case, Hoover reprimanded the field office in Dallas for allowing the Department of the Treasury to solve the case and make the arrest. There is also a file relating to Elvis Presley,* who reported his jet aircraft, a Lockheed Jetstar, stolen in 1970. Presley, a police buff, asked Hoover for a tour of FBI headquarters and subsequently met with the director. In addition, there is a file concerning (Wladziu Valentino) Liberace* and jewelry stolen from his home in Chicago, and one relating to Peter Lawford,* who reported jewelry stolen in the 1960s.

Volume HQ: 153,064 cases (2,449 cu. ft.), of which 74,000 cases are on 671 rolls of microfilm. FIELD: 1,155,073 cases. All fifty-nine field offices reported opening cases. There has been substantial destruction.

Dates 1934 to present

Location FBI

NARA Disposition Recommendation HQ: Systematic informational sample—Permanent; microfilm—Permanent; all others—Destroy. FIELD: All records except exceptional cases—Destroy.

Access To gain access to the records in this classification a researcher must file a Freedom of Information Act request with the FBI.

Related Records Department of Justice Classification 122 National Stolen Property Act.

CLASSIFICATION 88

Unlawful Flight to Avoid Prosecution

Congress passed the Unlawful Flight Act in 1934 to assist local authorities in their efforts to find fugitives. Under the act, the FBI was given primary investigative responsibility for cases of unlawful flight involving murder, kidnapping, burglary, rape, assault with a deadly weapon, and threats of violence. In the 1960s the classification expanded when the Bureau included all state felony crimes and crimes committed under the new Civil Rights Act. The Bureau usually assisted local and state agencies in this area; even if the fugitive was arrested by FBI agents the Bureau usually turned the person over to local authorities for prosecution. As might be expected, there is a large amount of biographical data present in these files, as well as information relating to the Bureau's development of its Top Ten Criminals List (included in the Top Ten Program File), relationships with foreign police organizations, especially in Canada, Mexico, and Hong Kong, and Bureau techniques used to apprehend fugitives. In addition, the files address a variety of subjects, ranging from the associates of the notorious bank robber William Francis (Willie) Sutton in the 1950s, to black extremists, Abbie Hoffman,* and the Weathermen, as well as organized crime, drug dealers, murderers, and con men.

Volume HQ: 82,429 cases (823.5 cu. ft.), of which 23,236 cases are on 380 rolls of microfilm. FIELD: 642,725. All fifty-nine field offices reported opening cases. There has been substantial destruction.

Dates 1934 to present

Location FBI

NARA Disposition Recommendation HQ: Systematic evidential sample— Permanent; multisectional cases—Permanent; all others, including the microfilm—Destroy. FIELD: Multisectional cases—Permanent; all others—Destroy.

Access To gain access to the records in this classification a researcher must file a Freedom of Information Act request with the FBI.

Related Records Department of Justice Classifications 126 Fugitive Felon Act and 127 Harboring Felons.

CLASSIFICATION 89

Assaulting or Killing a Federal Officer

The Bureau opened this classification in 1925 for its investigations into assaults on and murder of Federal officers—FBI agents, U.S. Marshals, and postal, Secret Service, Internal Revenue Service, and Immigration and Naturalization Service officials. The Bureau gradually expanded the classification to include incidents involving congressmen and elected officials, including the president and vice president, and all Federal judges. In 1972 the Bureau created Classification 175 Assaulting, Kidnapping, or Killing the President expressly for threats to the president, vice president, and members of Congress. Despite the new classification, cases relating to elected officials may still be filed in Classification 89.

The records themselves relate to a whole range of assault and murder cases, including assaults on park rangers in Yosemite National Park, threats made on the lives of Federal judges, and assaults on postal workers, police on Indian reservations, and prison guards. One case involved the rape of a female prison guard at a Federal penitentiary and resulted in a major review of prison conditions and scrutiny of the employment of female guards at all-male prisons. Another documented the investigation of the murder of an FBI agent, and the subsequent trial, and touched on racial conditions in the Bureau and in Federal prisons. Yet another file relates to the Indian activist Leonard Peltier and his indictment for the murder of two FBI agents on an Indian reservation. In the political arena there are cases pertaining to threats against President John F. Kennedy and his brothers, Governor George Wallace, and Senators Sam Ervin and John Stennis. This classification contains the primary file concerning the assassination of President Kennedy. One of the more unusual investigations in this area revolved around the murder of Representative Leo Ryan at Jonestown, Guyana, in November 1978 by members of the Reverend Jim Jones's People's Temple of Christian Disciples of God.

Volume HQ: 4,876 cases (97.5 cu. ft.), of which 319 cases through the mid-1940s are on 3 rolls of microfilm. FIELD: All fifty-nine field offices reported opening cases.

Dates 1925 to present

Location FBI

NARA Disposition Recommendation HQ: Systematic informational sample—Permanent; multisectional cases—Permanent; microfilm—Permanent; all others—Destroy. FIELD: Multisectional cases—Permanent; all others—Destroy.

Access To gain access to the records in this classification a researcher must file a Freedom of Information Act request with the FBI.

Related Records Department of Justice Classifications 125 Killing or Assaulting a Federal Officer, 70 War Transaction, and 90 Lands. See also FBI Classification 175 Assaulting, Kidnapping, or Killing the President.

CLASSIFICATION 90

Irregularities in Federal Penal Institutions

The Bureau established this classification in 1936 for its investigations involving contraband in Federal prisons. Most of the cases relate to drugs and weapons being smuggled into prisons; a few of the cases, however, vividly describe prison conditions including homosexual assaults and racial violence. The records also show Hoover's FBI inflating its statistics in order to improve its image as a major crime stopper. For example, the Bureau claimed a conviction under this classification even though the conviction was obtained under state charges and the Federal charges were dismissed. There is also a file relating to Robert Stroud, nicknamed the Bird Man of Alcatraz, and his associates.

Volume HQ: 1,901 cases, of which 108 cases are on 1 roll of microfilm. FIELD: 4,300 cases. All fifty-one field offices reported opening cases in this classification. There has been substantial destruction.

Dates 1936 to present

Location FBI

NARA Disposition Recommendation HQ: Systematic informational sample—Permanent; multisectional cases—Permanent; microfilm—Permanent; all others—Destroy. FIELD: All records—Destroy.

Access To gain access to the records in this classification a researcher must file a Freedom of Information Act request with the FBI.

Related Records Department of Justice Classification 4 Prisons Matters.

CLASSIFICATION 91

Bank Robbery

The Bureau established this classification in 1936 subsequent to Congress making the robbery of most financial establishments, including member banks of the Federal Reserve System, all banks organized under Federal statute, and all federally insured banking institutions, a Federal crime. The Bureau, however, does not have exclusive jurisdiction over bank robberies, and state and local law enforcement agencies are also involved in investigations. Few of the cases opened in Bureau files contain historically valuable information, but there is information relating to the FBI's Top Ten Criminals List and various bank robbery gangs, for example those led by Lester Joseph Gillis* (Baby Face Nelson) and John Dillinger.* There is also a case file relating to Katherine Powers, a Brandeis University student who made the FBI's Most Wanted List in 1970 on suspicion of bank robbery and murder.

Volume HQ: 85,563 cases (2,606 cu. ft.), of which 13,735 cases are on 360 rolls of microfilm. FIELD: 513,336. All fifty-one field offices reported opening cases in this classification. There has been substantial destruction.

Dates 1936 to present

Location FBI

NARA Disposition Recommendation HQ: Systematic informational sample—Permanent; multisectional cases of four or more sections—Permanent; microfilm—Permanent; all others—Destroy. FIELD: All cases that correlate with Permanent files at headquarters—Permanent; multisectional cases—Permanent; all others—Destroy.

Access To gain access to the records in this classification a researcher must file a Freedom of Information Act request with the FBI.

Related Records See state and local court records.

CLASSIFICATION 92

Racketeering Enterprise Investigations

The Bureau established this classification in 1936 for its investigations of violations of the Hobbs Act and the Lea Act. Based on the broad interstate commerce clause of the Constitution, these acts authorized the FBI to become involved in cases of violence, bribery, and extortion. Subsequent legislation broadened FBI jurisdiction into organized crime cases. The scope of Bureau investigations under this category is broad. The Bureau investigates individuals suspected of being involved in organized crime, the degree and extent of criminal infiltration of legitimate businesses, police and local political corruption by organized crime elements, and the nature of interstate gambling activities and organized crime. Since the late 1950s the Bureau has aggressively pursued antiracketeering cases as well. In 1977 the Bureau split the classification into five parts: Classifications 192–196.

The records clearly illustrate the infiltration of organized crime into a host of activities including extortion, skimming operations, kickbacks, the legal gambling industry, and narcotics. The records also illustrate the extent of organized crime influence in the gambling casinos of Las Vegas and Atlantic City, in labor unions, such as the Teamsters, and in the garment and waste collection industries. More recently the records document the rise of the black mafia, the gang wars in the major cities, and the infiltration of drug money into legitimate businesses. They also contain information on local police and local political corruption and attempts by Federal and local strike forces to break organized crime and its influence.

The records indicate a certain FBI "innocence" in the 1960s with regard to the activities of organized crime. By the 1970s, however, through the use of the investigative techniques of electronic surveillance, wiretaps, and undercover agents, the Bureau had become much more sophisticated. Information from the Criminal Intelligence Program describes the activities of Mafia figure Carlo Gambino and the Gambino family and the Bureau's efforts in the late 1960s to have him deported. The files also contain evidence of possible connections between Peter Lawford* and organized crime figures. Finally, there is some information in the records on the dispute between J. Edgar Hoover and Attorney General Robert Kennedy.*

Volume HQ: 19,146 cases, of which 2,627 cases are on 30 rolls of microfilm. FIELD: 128,000 cases. There has been some destruction of these cases.

Dates 1936 to present

Location FBI

NARA Disposition Recommendation HQ: Systematic informational sample— Permanent; multisectional cases—Permanent; microfilm—Permanent; all cases with eight or more serials—Permanent; all others—Destroy. FIELD: All cases that correlate with permanent files at headquarters—Permanent; multisectional cases—Permanent; all cases with fifteen or more serials—Permanent; all others—Destroy.

Access To gain access to the records in this classification a researcher must file a Freedom of Information Act request with the FBI.

Related Records Department of Justice Classifications 123 Anti-Racketeering Act, 165 Interstate or Foreign Travel in Aid of Racketeering Organizations, 164 Interstate Transmission of Wagering Information, 159 Gambling Device Controls, and 160 Wagering Occupational Tax. See also FBI Classifications 52 Theft or Destruction of Government Property, 192–195 Hobbs Act, and 196 Fraud by Wire.

CLASSIFICATION 93

Ascertaining Financial Ability

This classification has a tortuous history. In 1934 the Bureau assumed the responsibility for examining Federal court cases involving debt payments. The Department of Justice then informed the Bureau that this responsibility included assisting U.S. Attorneys in determining the financial ability of debtors, and, reluctantly, the Bureau agreed to cooperate. In late 1936 the Bureau was relieved of the responsibility for examining judicial offices but not from determining the financial condition of debtors. In 1944, Attorney General Tom Clark launched a major campaign to collect federal fines and ordered the Bureau to assist in the collection in all cases where the debt was $100 or more. The present limit has increased to $15,000, except for criminal fines and bank judgments which are set at $500. Bureau agents, in general, dislike such cases, referring to them as "collection agency work." Accordingly, the Bureau has assigned a low priority to such investigations. Most of the cases involve bond appearance forfeitures, court fines, Internal Revenue Service judgments and tax claims, and student loans. In many cases it is obvious that the government spent more time and money in attempting to collect the debt than the fine brought in revenues. There is some information included in these files relating to the writer Dashiell Hammett.*

Volume HQ: 40,609 cases (225 cu. ft.), of which 21,847 cases are on 160 rolls of poor-quality microfilm. FIELD: Few extant cases are reported.

Dates 1935 to present

Location FBI

NARA Disposition Recommendation HQ: Systematic evidential sample—Permanent; multisectional cases—Permanent; microfilm—Permanent; all others—Destroy. FIELD: All cases that correlate with permanent cases at headquarters—Permanent; all others—Destroy.

Access To gain access to the records in this classification a researcher must file a Freedom of Information Act request with the FBI.

Related Records Department of Justice Classification 67 Bail Bonds and Forfeitures.

CLASSIFICATION 94

Research Matters

The Bureau established this classification in 1938. At headquarters this classification has meant the filing of general correspondence with the public, organizations, law enforcement groups, and the media, Bureau speeches and press releases, and general public-relations matters—all originally filed in Classification 62. In the field offices this classification covers research matters in a much narrower sense, and general correspondence and public relations matters are found in Classification 80.

Hoover considered the creation of a positive image of the FBI as an essential and integral part of its law enforcement function. In order for the Bureau to be effective it had to be, in Hoover's words, "widely known and respected." Accordingly, the director promoted an aggressive public-relations program for the Bureau that was apparently successful: public opinion polls consistently show the Bureau with high name recognition and as respected and admired. At headquarters, Classification 94 contains materials devised to create and maintain this high recognition and admiration. The files are divided into six major subcategories, including: correspondence; movie, television, and radio scripts; parole matters; mailing lists; FBI training materials; and speeches, press releases, and other public relations materials.

The subcategory containing correspondence is by far the largest. The files contain miscellaneous correspondence from individuals and groups requesting a variety of information on the FBI and its activities. There are separate files on such groups as the American Legion, the Masons, the Boy Scouts, the Boys Clubs of America, law enforcement organizations, and other charitable groups. The letters generally document the folk hero image of Hoover and the FBI. Letters from prominent individuals, such as John F. Kennedy, Adlai Stevenson, and George McGovern, are maintained in the Special File Rooms, although they are indexed under Classification 94. There is an interesting file on the United Fund Campaign that documents the organization and collection process within the FBI. In addition, the file contains correspondence relating to public broadcasts and programs that depict the FBI and comments on various books, newspapers, and journal articles relating to the Bureau. There are also files relating to the Duke and Duchess of Windsor* and their tour of Quantico, directed by Hoover himself, in 1943; Hedda Hopper,* the columnist and a friend of Hoover; Lucille Ball;* Justice Hugo Black;* Edward A. Tamm;* John Wayne;* and Interpol,* the International Criminal Police Organization. Some information relating to Edward M. Kennedy and the Chappaquiddick* incident that resulted in the death of Mary Jo Kopechne in 1969 may also be found in this classification.

The subcategory concerning movie, television, and radio scripts contains correspondence from authors and producers on proposed scripts and programs relating to the FBI. Included are internal memoranda evaluating the materials and often copies of the scripts or manuscripts themselves. The creation of a subcategory to gather material on parole matters reflects Hoover's interest in crimes committed by people out on parole. The director ordered that separate files be maintained for such crimes. They are filed by state.

The subcategory containing mailing lists is simply a list of non-law enforcement subscribers to Bureau publications. A single subcategory contains correspondence relating to FBI training materials and requests for such materials.

The final subcategory includes requests for speaking engagements, drafts of speeches, manuscripts, and press releases. In addition, there are also some copies of Bureau publications, such as the *Law Enforcement Bulletin*, and requests and information relating to FBI tours, awards, and personnel.

Field office use of this classification differs somewhat from that of headquarters. Although they contain some public relations materials and correspondence, most of the records in field offices relate to more traditional concepts of research material. For example, in the field-office records of this classification are found Crime Survey Reports, General Investigative Intelligence Reports, juvenile offender files, lists of local law enforcement officials, and research materials on the polygraph and its operation and the Witness Protection and Maintenance Program.

Taken as a whole the records in this classification document the Bureau's continuing interest in self-promotion. The records also shed light on Bureau views regarding state and local law enforcement officials and its preoccupation with communism. For example, in one case when an individual wrote requesting information on the FBI's Top Ten Communists List, the Bureau replied that the information was restricted and then proceeded to open a investigation on the writer of the request. The investigators found a ten-year-old boy eager to obtain the material for his scrapbook on the FBI. In addition, there is information relating to the Bureau's interest in the media's portrayal of the feud between Martin Luther King, Jr., and Hoover, especially after Hoover publicly called the civil rights activist a "notorious liar," the Bureau's Disaster Squad, and the director's meetings with the president.

Volume HQ: 69,745 cases (1011 cu. ft.). FIELD: Fifty-seven field offices reported opening cases. There has been substantial destruction.

Dates 1938 to present

Location FBI

NARA Disposition Recommendation See the very complex disposition recommendations in the NARA FBI Task Force Report on this classification.

Access To gain access to the records in this classification a researcher must file a Freedom of Information Act request with the FBI.

Related Records FBI Classifications 62 Administrative Inquiry and 80 Laboratory Research Matters, Headquarters.

CLASSIFICATION 95

Laboratory Examinations

The Bureau established this classification in 1937 for files that document laboratory examinations conducted by the Bureau in response to requests from state and local law enforcement authorities. The Bureau established a technical laboratory as early as 1932 to help in its investigations. Following public criticism of its methods, in the 1970s Bureau policymakers sought to reduce drastically the Bureau's laboratory work for outside agencies. Field offices, however, recognizing the value of the laboratory in encouraging closer cooperation with local law enforcement officials, continued to use the program. Only in 1976 did the Bureau officially encourage the development of state and local crime laboratories.

The files themselves are disappointing with regard to FBI forensic techniques and the documenting of the methods of analysis employed by Bureau examiners. Most of the cases relate to fraudulent check writing and to handwriting analysis. The typical file consists of a request letter, the examiner's brief notes, a copy of the lab report, and where relevant, a field office memorandum on the ensuing trial testimony. Most of the laboratory findings were inconclusive, although there is some interesting information regarding murder cases, the analysis of clothing fibers, blood samples, DNA analysis, and ballistic tests. The Bureau returned all evidence submitted to it for examination. One case provided information on organized crime elements led by John Rosselli and their connection with the motion picture industry in Los Angeles. There is also some information relating to Howard Hughes.*

Volume HQ: 241,250 cases (2,173.5 cu. ft.). There has been substantial destruction in these files. FIELD: All fifty-nine field offices reported opening cases in this classification. There has been substantial destruction of the files.

Dates 1937 to present

Location FBI

NARA Disposition Recommendation HQ: Systematic evidential sample—Permanent; all others—Destroy. FIELD: All records—Destroy.

Access To gain access to the records in this classification a researcher must file a Freedom of Information Act request with the FBI.

Related Records None

CLASSIFICATION 96

Alien Applicants
(Obsolete)

The Bureau opened this classification in 1939 for its investigations of aliens already employed or seeking employment in defense industries. At first, the Bureau limited its investigations to the aircraft industry. By 1940 the Bureau expanded its investigations in this classification to all government contractors involved with the defense industry. In 1942 the U.S. Army's provost marshal general took charge of these investigations. When indications of subversion were found, however, the FBI was called in. The Bureau continued its investigations, primarily name searches in its indexes, for aliens engaged in classified work. Most of the cases opened involved aliens who simply failed to register under the Alien Registration Act or who falsely claimed U.S. citizenship. The Bureau declared the classification obsolete in 1945.

Volume HQ: 5,059 cases (204 cu. ft.). FIELD: Eleven Field Offices reported opening cases in this classification, a total of 128 cases. Only a few of these cases are still extant.

Dates 1939 to 1945

Location FBI

NARA Disposition Recommendation HQ: A 5% systematic evidential sample—Permanent; multisectional cases—Permanent; all others—Destroy. FIELD: Multisectional cases—Permanent; all others—Destroy.

Access To gain access to the records in this classification a researcher must file a Freedom of Information Act request with the FBI.

Related Records Records of the Office of the Provost Marshal General, Record Group 389, National Archives.

CLASSIFICATION 97

Foreign Agents Registration Act

The Bureau opened this classification in 1939 in response to the passage by Congress in 1938 of the Foreign Agents Registration Act. The act required "foreign propagandists," or "agents" of a foreign principal engaged in distributing propaganda, to register with the Department of State. In 1950, under the

Internal Security Act, the Bureau expanded its investigations in this classification to include persons who failed to register and who had knowledge of espionage, counterespionage, or sabotage methods and tactics of foreign countries or foreign governments. Theoretically, this classification should contain only investigations of individuals, as organizations are covered by Classification 102 Voorhis Act. Organizations, however, were the subject of many Classification 97 cases.

The records document the changing concerns of U.S. officials over security matters and the rapidly changing world situation. During the 1930s and 1940s, for example, the Bureau focused on pro-Axis propaganda and on German and Japanese agents. It investigated the Japanese Tourist Bureau and individuals with suspected German or Japanese sympathies. Among these early records is information on U.S. internment camps and on life in the United States for German and Japanese nationals. During the Cold War period the Bureau concentrated on Soviet agents and Soviet propaganda. Classification 65 Espionage, however, is a better source of information on communism in the United States.

The files document Bureau concern with subjects such as Cuba and Fidel Castro, the Dominican Republic and Juan Bosch, and Nicaragua and the Sandinistas. There is also information on African and Mideast radicals and their activities within the United States. In addition, the files contain information relating to the FBI and its relationships with foreign police and intelligence organizations.

Volume HQ: 5,750 cases (204 cu. ft.). FIELD: Fifty-seven field offices reported opening cases in this classification. There has been some destruction.

Dates 1939 to present

Location FBI

NARA Disposition Recommendation HQ: Systematic information sample—Permanent; multisectional cases—Permanent; all cases relating to organizations—Permanent; all others—Destroy. FIELD: Multisectional cases—Permanent; all cases with 30 or more serials—Permanent; all others—Destroy.

Access To gain access to the records in this classification a researcher must file a Freedom of Information Act request with the FBI.

Related Records Department of Justice Classifications 13 National Defense Act, 158 Internal Security Act of 1950, and 149 Foreign Agents Registration Act. See also FBI Classifications 65 Espionage, 102 Voorhis Act, 105 Foreign Counterintelligence, 109 Foreign Political Matters, and 134 Foreign Counterintelligence Assets.

CLASSIFICATION 98

Sabotage

The Bureau established this classification in 1939 as part of its increased responsibility for and involvement in investigations of potential espionage and subversive activities. Initially, the Bureau was only authorized to conduct investigations involving government property and material manufactured for the government under contract. As the possibility of war approached, however, Congress in 1940 broadened the scope of the FBI investigations to include damage to all defense plants, public utilities, and transportation systems.

The records relate to three rather distinct periods: the World War II experience, the Korean War, and the Vietnam War era. Most of the cases were opened by the Bureau during World War II. In almost all cases, however, including the Korean and Vietnam conflicts, no willful acts of sabotage were discovered. Upon investigation the Bureau usually found most of the cases revolved around labor disputes and attempts to organize unions in plants, disgruntled workers, juveniles, and greedy entrepreneurs who sought extra profits by providing the government with defective war materials. The exception was a case involving the landing of eight German saboteurs, including George Dasch (George John Davis),* the leader of the New York City team, Richard Quirin, and Ernest Peter Burger, on Long Island in 1942. All were quickly apprehended and prosecuted; except for Dasch and Burger, who were deported to Germany after the war, the members of the sabotage team were executed in August 1942. The records reflect a close working relationship in this particular incident between the Bureau, the Coast Guard, and Naval Intelligence.

For the 1950s there is some information relating to the Bureau's efforts to protect Strategic Air Command bases from sabotage. The Vietnam War era records offer an interesting view on antiwar groups in the United States and their attempts to disrupt the war effort. The cases ranged from the spray painting of peace signs on guided missiles to destroying Reserve Officers' Training Corps buildings on college campuses and the shooting, in 1970, of four students at Kent State University* by members of the Ohio National Guard.

Volume HQ: 47,000 cases. FIELD: All fifty-nine field offices reported opening cases in this classification, for a total of 76,000 cases.

Dates 1939 to present. Most of the cases were opened in the 1939–1945 period.

Location FBI

NARA Disposition Recommendation HQ: Systematic evidential sample— Permanent; all multisectional cases—Permanent; all others—Destroy. FIELD: All records—Destroy.

Access To gain access to the records in this classification a researcher must file a Freedom of Information Act request with the FBI.

Related Records Department of Justice Classifications 13 National Defense Act, 148 War Policy Classification, and 146 World War II (Internal Security). See also FBI Classifications 100 Domestic Security, 102 Voorhis Act, 65 Espionage, and 97 Foreign Agents Registration Act. See also the FBI's multivolume history of World War II located in Classification 66, case 1723.

CLASSIFICATION 99

Plant Survey
(Obsolete)

With the world situation becoming increasingly unstable and the chances of the United States becoming involved in the European war increasing daily, President Franklin D. Roosevelt in 1939 requested that the FBI assume responsibility for ascertaining the protection capabilities and security weaknesses of defense plants. Initially, the Bureau conducted very detailed surveys with descriptive and quantitative data on virtually all aspects of a particular plant—security matters, labor conditions, management attitudes. The Bureau made each plant survey a separate case file. On June 1, 1941, and January 5, 1942, the U.S. Navy and U.S. Army, respectively, assumed responsibility for the surveying of defense plants.

The records are a unique source of information relating to World War II-era attitudes of U.S. industry, business, and labor. Union officials, for example, complained often that the Bureau spied on employees. To some extent this is correct: Every defense plant had between three and thirty employees serving as Bureau confidential sources or informants, and in many of the major plants the Bureau had placed undercover agents. The Bureau relied on these sources for information concerning possible espionage or sabotage. The Bureau, at times, appeared to be on the side of management, reporting in one case that workers were lazy, unskilled, unmotivated, and spending "too much time in the toilet."

Volume HQ: 7,699 cases on 111 rolls of microfilm. (The microfilm is of very poor quality). FIELD: No extant cases.

Dates 1939 to 1942

Location FBI

NARA Disposition Recommendation HQ: All records—Permanent. FIELD: NA

Access To gain access to the records in this classification a researcher must file a Freedom of Information Act request with the FBI.

Related Records See also the Records of the Office of the Secretary of Defense, Record Group 330, and the General Records of the Department of the Navy, Record Group 80, both in the National Archives.

CLASSIFICATION 100

Domestic Security

The Federal Bureau of Investigation's jurisdiction in subversive matters evolved from the U.S. government's response to world crises. During World War I, the General Intelligence Division of the Bureau had the responsibility for investigating specific allegations of sabotage, treason, or espionage. After the Palmer Raids of 1919–1920, however, Attorney General Harlan Fiske Stone and J. Edgar Hoover abolished the division.

In response to growing worldwide crises and expanding Nazi activities, President Franklin D. Roosevelt, in 1934, asked Hoover to launch an "intensive and confidential investigation" of the Nazi movement in the United States with emphasis on its anti-American activities. In August 1936, Roosevelt restored the Bureau's mandate to engage in general intelligence investigations by requesting that the Bureau furnish information concerning the subversive activities of Nazis, Fascists, Communists, and representatives or advocates of other organizations or groups that promoted the overthrow of the government of the United States by violent or illegal methods. The President designated the FBI as the "clearing house" for national defense and general domestic intelligence matters.

Reviving the General Intelligence Division, Hoover renamed it the Security Division (later the Domestic Intelligence Division) and directed its members to focus on Nazi and Fascist activities in the United States. The FBI investigated the German-American Bund and helped to ferret out German spies operating in the United States, such as William G. Sebold and Frederick (Fritz) Duquesne. Using Sebold as a double agent, the Bureau virtually neutralized the German wartime intelligence apparatus in the United States.

Given Hoover's rabid anticommunist feelings, however, the Bureau centered most of its attention on identifying and investigating Communists and their fellow travelers. It compiled extensive files on the Abraham Lincoln Brigade, the Communist Party of the USA,* the Socialist Workers party, and a wide variety of individuals including Earl Browder,* the chief of the Communist party, Gus Hall, Whittaker Chambers,* Judith Coplon, Julius and Ethel Rosenberg,* Colonel Rudolf Abel, Alger Hiss,* William W. Remington,* and Harry Dexter White, as well as on numerous other less well-known American citizens. There are more files on Communists than on Nazis or Fascists for the period of World War II. In addition, there is some information relating to Japanese relocation centers of the time. For example, there are case files relating to Mitsuye Endo, a Japanese American from Sacramento, California, and her efforts to obtain an unconditional release from a relocation center, and Toyosaburo Korematsu, who refused to submit to orders that American citizens of Japanese ancestry evacuate designated areas during the war. Each sued the government and saw the relevant legislation declared unconstitutional by the Supreme Court.

During the Cold War period the focus is almost entirely on suspected Communists and Communist-front groups. Convinced that communism, led by the Soviet Union, threatened not only the security of the United States but the survival of the entire American way of life, Hoover drove the Bureau to investigate Communists or suspected Communists throughout the United States. During the 1950s and 1960s, Hoover assumed that all nations with Communist governments, including Eastern Europe, the People's Republic of China, and Cuba, were fundamentally hostile to the United States and intent on destroying it. For example, there are files relating to the Bureau's Emergency Detention Program and Lee Harvey Oswald.* There are also case files relating to Owen Lattimore,* Edgar Snow,* Walter G. Krivitsky,* A. Philip Randolph,* Nelson Algren,* Abbie Hoffman,* and the British Soviet spies Harold (Kim) Philby,* Guy F. Burgess, and Donald D. Maclean. In addition, there is some information relating to the Southern Christian Leadership Conference* and Malcolm X.*

In the late 1960s, Hoover expanded FBI investigations into the anti-Vietnam War movement, the New Left, and radical black militants. Setting up a counterintelligence program (COINTELPRO),* the Bureau, at Hoover's direction, infiltrated not only the Communist party but also protest groups such as the Students for a Democratic Society (SDS),* the Student Nonviolent Coordinating Committee,* and other New Left* campus groups. The Bureau compiled voluminous files on individuals active in the war protest and black nationalist movements.

Following the Watergate scandals and the Church committee investigations into domestic spying activities of the U.S. intelligence community, the attorney general ordered that all cases opened by the Bureau under this classification be reported to the Department of Justice within ninety days. Thereafter, the number of cases opened by the Bureau radically declined: from more than 11,000 cases in 1952 to only 87 in 1977.

The records themselves are an invaluable source for materials relating to German and Japanese espionage efforts in the United States during the Second World War. There is information relating to the German-American clubs, the German-American Bund, German anti-Nazi refugees, and Japanese aliens. The files are often lengthy and detailed. In one case, the Bureau tracked a Japanese nationalist suspected of spying from his employment in a Japanese fishing fleet, through his detention and internment, the confiscation of his property, and his activities after the war, to his membership in the American Communist party and finally to his flight from the United States in 1956.

More importantly perhaps, the files document the Bureau's long preoccupation with Communists and communism. There are detailed cases on Soviet spy rings operating in the United States, from the Elizabeth Bentley case to the Rosenbergs. There is also a file relating to the International Brotherhood of Mine, Mill, and Smelter Workers and its officials because of alleged Communist influences. The records reveal the extraordinary investigative techniques the Bureau utilized in these endeavors and the enormous resources committed to even minor cases. The Bureau often followed a relatively unimportant figure for years in an unsuccessful investigation of suspected Communist activities. In addition to Bureau papers, the files contain newspaper clippings, copies of Communist leaflets and publications, and information relating to the Bureau's Security Informant Program, Custodial Detention List, and Security Index.

The records contain a rich gathering of information on such organizations as the Socialist Workers party, the Labor Youth League, and the W. E. B. DuBois Clubs. In the 1960s and 1970s the Bureau opened internal security files on a host of anti-Vietnam War groups and organizations and on the SDS, New Left, Weathermen, Black Panthers, Nation of Islam, and Black Muslims, and on such individuals as Stokely Carmichael and Abbie Hoffman.* In addition, it maintained a regional status report on antiwar and radical activities at every college and university within the jurisdiction of each field office. There is also some information relating to the 1976 assassination of the former Chilean ambassador to the United States, Orlando Letelier. In short, the records are a unique and extremely valuable resource on U.S. domestic developments from World War II through the Cold War and U.S. involvement in Vietnam.

Volume HQ: 487,113 cases (7,656 cu. ft.). FIELD: All fifty-nine field offices reported opening cases in this classification, for a total of 1,303,078 cases (14,685 cu. ft.).

Dates 1939 to present

Location FBI

NARA Disposition Recommendation HQ: Systematic informational sample—Permanent; multisectional cases—Permanent; all cases with 18 or more serials—Permanent; all cases with an institution or organization as the subject—Permanent; all informant cases—Permanent; all others—Destroy. FIELD: Systematic informational sample from New York, Los Angeles, and Chicago—Permanent; multisectional files—Permanent; all cases that correlate with HQ multisectional cases—Permanent; all cases that correlate with HQ files with 18 or more serials—Permanent; all cases that correlate with the HQ informational sample—Permanent; all informant cases—Permanent; all cases with an institution or organization as the subject—Permanent; all others—Destroy.

Access To gain access to the records in this classification a researcher must file a Freedom of Information Act request with the FBI.

Related Records Records of the Federal Bureau of Investigation, Record Group 65, National Archives, and Department of Justice Classifications 158 Internal Security Act of 1950, 95 Miscellaneous Criminal Cases, and 146 World War II (Internal Security). See also FBI Classifications 65 Espionage, 105 Foreign Counterintelligence, and 200–203 Foreign Counterintelligence Matters.

CLASSIFICATION 101

Hatch Act
(Obsolete)

One of the provisions of the Hatch Act, passed by Congress in 1939, made it illegal for Federal employees and contractors to be a member of any political party or organization advocating the overthrow of the American form of government. In 1941 the Bureau received a special appropriation of $100,000 to investigate subversive activities in the government under the provisions of the Hatch Act. Hoover believed that such activity was one of the more important aspects of the FBI's work during World War II. Until 1949 the FBI undertook an investigation only after requested to do so by the Department of Justice or the agency employing an alleged subversive and then only if information considered "derogatory" existed. In 1947, Executive Order 9835 established another loyalty security program that surpassed all previous U.S. government programs in scope and numbers of investigations. FBI records concerning that program are filed in Classification 121 Loyalty of Government Employees. At the time that the new program was established, Classification 101 became inactive: no new cases were added, but files on persons initially investigated under the Hatch Act remained active under the later program. The Bureau declared Classification 101 obsolete in 1973.

The files in this classification reveal little subversive activity on the part of Federal employees. Some files, however, contain valuable documentation on pro-German and leftist activity in the United States. Other files were opened because employees voiced criticism of President Franklin D. Roosevelt or opposed U.S. government policies.

Volume HQ: 7,000 cases. FIELD: Unknown. Almost all field office records in this classification have been destroyed.

Dates 1939 to 1973

Location FBI

NARA Disposition Recommendation HQ: Systematic informational sample of 2.500 cases—Permanent; multisectional cases—Permanent; all others—Destroy. FIELD: All records—Permanent.

Access To gain access to the records in this classification a researcher must file a Freedom of Information Act request with the FBI.

Related Records FBI Classification 121 Loyalty of Government Employees and Department of Justice Classification 35 Civil Service Act.

CLASSIFICATION 102

Voorhis Act

The Bureau opened this classification in June 1942 for files resulting from investigations under the Voorhis Act of 1939. The act required organizations subject to foreign control and advocating the overthrow of the U.S. government to register with the Department of Justice. Until October 1942 the Bureau opened a new case for each organization investigated. After that date, a new case was opened in this classification only if there was no other file on the organization in another FBI classification. The Bureau opened only one new case after 1945, although material in the files dates to 1974. There is documentation concerning organizations such as the German-American Bund, the Young Communist League, the Dante Alighieri Society, and the Japanese Prefectural Association.

Volume HQ: 195 cases. FIELD: 300 cases. Forty field offices reported opening cases. There has been substantial destruction.

Dates 1942 to present

Location FBI

NARA Disposition Recommendation HQ: All records—Permanent. FIELD: All records—Permanent.

Access To gain access to the records in this classification a researcher must file a Freedom of Information Act request with the FBI.

Related Records FBI Classifications 65 Espionage, 97 Foreign Agents Registration Act, 100 Domestic Security, and 107 Denaturalization Proceedings. See also Department of Justice Classification 158 Internal Security Act of 1950.

CLASSIFICATION 103

Interstate Transportation of Stolen Cattle

The Bureau opened this classification in 1941. It contains investigations of the theft of cattle, including cows, bulls, oxen, steers, heifers, and calves. This classification covers a relatively minor investigative area; moreover, FBI involvement with investigations of this kind declined during the 1950s, when U.S. Attorneys expressed a desire to have state and local authorities prosecute these crimes.

Volume HQ: 1,042 cases. FIELD: 4,750 cases. Fifty-seven field offices reported opening cases. There has been substantial destruction.

Dates 1941 to present

Location FBI

NARA Disposition Recommendation HQ: 5% systematic evidential sample—Permanent; multisectional cases—Permanent; all others—Destroy. FIELD: All records—Destroy.

Access To gain access to the records in this classification a researcher must file a Freedom of Information Act request with the FBI.

Related Records See state and local records.

CLASSIFICATION 104

Servicemen's Dependents Allowance Act of 1942
(Obsolete)

The Bureau opened this classification in January 1944 for files relating to investigations of the Servicemen's Dependents Allowance Act of 1942. Case files for investigations opened before that date will be found in Classification 46 Fraud against the Government or Classification 62 Administrative Inquiry (Miscellaneous Subversive and Nonsubversive). Investigations under Classification 104 focused on the illegal claims to and receipt of the dependent allowance of a serviceman by a woman not his legal wife. Usually the cause of the problem was bigamy on the part of the man or woman. U.S. Attorneys often declined to prosecute such cases because the amount of money was small or because the subject agreed to make restitution. Files contain significant biographical data and information on women, family conditions, and social and moral attitudes.

Payments under the act were terminated in 1952, at which time this classification was closed.

Volume HQ: 7,666 cases (41 rolls of microfilm). FIELD: 5,543 cases. Sixteen field offices reported opening cases. There has been substantial destruction.

Dates 1944 to 1952

Location FBI

NARA Disposition Recommendation HQ: All records—Permanent. FIELD: All records—Destroy.

Access To gain access to the records in this classification a researcher must file a Freedom of Information Act request with the FBI.

Related Records FBI Classifications 46 Fraud against the Government and 62 Administrative Inquiry (Miscellaneous Subversive and Nonsubversive). See also Department of Justice Classification 151 World War II Veterans Matters.

CLASSIFICATION 105

Foreign Counterintelligence
(Formerly: Internal Security, Foreign Intelligence)

The files in this classification are a unique resource for documenting not only foreign subversive activities in the United States but also the activities of domestic political and social groups. The records illustrate Bureau techniques and procedures in carrying out such investigations, including the use of electronic surveillance and informants. The FBI's authority in the field of counterintelligence rests largely on vaguely formulated executive orders and has never been formally codified in the statute books. Using the authority of presidential directives and executive orders issued over the years, the Bureau has assumed near-complete responsibility for investigation of subversive activities and counterintelligence in the United States.

Although the files in this classification relate primarily to FBI investigations of Soviet and Soviet-bloc espionage activities in the United States, the travel of Communist aliens, and other internal security issues, the records contain additional documentation of a wide variety of cases not specifically related to Soviet activities. There is, for example, a file with photographs and news clippings relating to Adolf Hitler* and his reported escape to Argentina and files relating to the Bureau's investigations of the Ku Klux Klan, various anti-Semitic groups, and fringe racial hate groups in the 1950s. In 1959 investigations of these types of cases were transferred to Classification 157 Civil

Unrest. In the late 1950s investigations of Puerto Rican nationalist groups and pro- and anti-Castro organizations began finding their way into this classification. During the 1960s the Bureau's increased surveillance of Chinese Communist activities ended up in this classification.

In 1971 the Bureau changed the title of this classification to Internal Security (Nationalistic Tendency, Foreign Intelligence) in an attempt to narrow its focus. Despite that change, however, investigations filed in this classification continued to cover topics beyond the activities of foreign intelligence services operating in the United States. Included were files on organizations with foreign political ties, such as the Irish Republican Army, the Jewish Defense League, Yugoslav émigré groups,* and Cuban and Arab nationalist groups. In September 1977 this classification was limited strictly to foreign counterintelligence investigations directed at activities of the Soviet Union in the United States. The Bureau established five new classifications for other investigations that had been included: Classification 199 Foreign Counterintelligence—Terrorism; Classification 200 Foreign Counterintelligence—People's Republic of China; Classification 201 Foreign Counterintelligence—Satellites; Classification 202 Foreign Counterintelligence—Cuba; and Classification 203 Foreign Counterintelligence—All Other Countries.

The files maintained in the field offices reflect the regional aspect of certain types of investigations. The Atlanta and Miami offices, for example, opened a large number of cases relating to the Nation of Islam, revolutionaries from the Dominican Republic, Cuban anti-Castro groups, and Third World intelligence operations. The Los Angeles office has a large number of cases on Black Muslims, radical Hispanic groups, and the Congress of Racial Equality.

A sampling of the extant cases reveals the great diversity of this classification. There are records relating to Wallace D. Fard (Wali Farad),* who, although white, was the founder of the Black Muslims, and Elijah Muhammad, who became his chief apostle and prophet; the American Indian Movement* and its occupation of the Bureau of Indian Affairs in Washington, DC, in 1972, as well as its confrontations in 1973 at Wounded Knee and in 1977 at Pine Ridge, South Dakota; COINTELPRO* operations against black extremist groups; Ethel and Julius Rosenberg*; Errol Flynn* and his connections with Cuban gambling activities and Fidel Castro; the Black Panther party of North Carolina* and Huey Newton; the assassination of Malcolm X*; COINTELPRO operations against violence-prone Yugoslav émigrés* in the United States and against the Puerto Rican Independence party*; as well as files containing information relating to Marilyn Monroe* (Norma Jean Baker), Wernher von Braun,* Lee Harvey Oswald,* Arthur Rudolph,* and John Steinbeck.* There is also a case file relating to COINTELPRO operations involving the organization Clergy and Laity Concerned about Vietnam.*

Volume HQ: 334,910 cases. FIELD: 936,285 cases. All field offices reported opening cases.

Dates 1938 to present

Location FBI

NARA Disposition Recommendation HQ: Pre-1978 systematic evidential sample of 500—Permanent; pre-1978 multisectional cases—Permanent; pre-1978 cases with ten or more serials—Permanent; all pre-1978 informant cases—Permanent; all other pre-1978 cases—Destroy; Post-1978 systematic evidential sample—Permanent; post-1978 multisectional cases—Permanent; post-1978 cases with ten or more serials—Permanent; all post-1978 informant cases—Permanent; all other post-1978 cases—Destroy. FIELD: Multisectional cases—Permanent; all cases with 15 or more serials—Permanent; all others—Destroy.

Access To gain access to the records in this classification a researcher must file a Freedom of Information Act request with the FBI.

Related Records FBI Classifications 157 Civil Unrest, 199 Foreign Counterintelligence—Terrorism, 200–203 Foreign Counterintelligence Matters. See also Department of Justice Classification 158 Internal Security Act of 1950 and the U.S. Congress, Senate Select Committee to Study Government Operations with Respect to Intelligence Activities (Church committee), *Final Report*, 7 vols., 94th Cong., 2d Sess., 1976, Report 94-755.

CLASSIFICATION 106

Alien Enemy Control

The FBI opened this classification in 1940 for its files relating to investigations of violators of the Alien Registration Act of 1940. The Immigration and Naturalization Service held primary responsibility under the act, but the Bureau investigated certain types of cases, such as failure to register, violation of travel restrictions, and the possession of contraband.

After the United States entry into World War II, the Bureau used this classification for investigations of escapees from prisoner-of-war (POW) camps in the United States. Activity in this area increased after a 1943 agreement with the Department of War that the FBI would apprehend escapees, a role the Bureau assumed because it considered escaped prisoners of war to be potential spies and saboteurs. An April 1945 law making it a crime to aid an escaped prisoner of war expanded the Bureau's involvement even further. Although the Immigration and Neutralization Service expected to handle all POW cases once the war ended, the Bureau continued to keep open those cases it had begun. As late as 1963, two cases still remained active. The records contain information on FBI surveillance of Germans in the United States before and during World

War II, conditions in POW camps, and relations between the camps and the communities in which they were located.

Volume HQ: 3,677 cases. FIELD: Unknown. Massive destruction has occurred in these records.

Dates 1940 to present; however, few cases have been opened since 1945.

Location FBI

NARA Disposition Recommendation HQ: All records—Permanent. FIELD: All records—Permanent.

Access To gain access to the records in this classification a researcher must file a Freedom of Information Act request with the FBI.

Related Records Records of the Immigration and Naturalization Service, Record Group 85, and the Records of the Office of the Secretary of Defense, Record Group 330, National Archives. See also the Department of Justice Classifications 126 Fugitive Felon Act, 127 Harboring Felons, 146 World War II (Internal Security), and 148 War Policy Classification.

CLASSIFICATION 107

Denaturalization Proceedings
(Obsolete)

The Bureau established this classification in June 1944 as an outgrowth of its World War II activities. It contains investigations of citizens of the United States allegedly engaged in activities that indicated that they were loyal to another government. At the request of the attorney general, the Bureau's field offices submitted names and information concerning persons believed to be potential candidates for denaturalization proceedings. Cases were opened based on allegedly unpatriotic remarks, renunciation of citizenship, or attendance at meetings of organizations such as the German-American Bund. As might be expected, most cases were opened during the last months of the war and during the immediate postwar period and involved persons who were allegedly pro-Japanese or pro-German. Also included, however, is a case involving William Schneiderman, who was a Communist at the time he took the citizenship oath, and one relating to the poet Ezra Pound* and his wartime activities. The Bureau declared this classification obsolete in 1952.

Volume HQ: 1,523 cases. FIELD: 127 cases. Six field offices reported opening cases; all have been destroyed.

Dates 1944 to 1952

Location FBI

NARA Disposition Recommendation HQ: All records—Permanent. FIELD: No extant cases.

Access To gain access to the records in this classification a researcher must file a Freedom of Information Act request with the FBI.

Related Records Department of Justice Classification 38 Naturalization.

CLASSIFICATION 108

Foreign Travel Control

The Bureau opened this classification in July 1944 as another outgrowth of its World War II intelligence activities. In cooperation with military intelligence, the FBI attempted to interview all persons entering the United States as part of an effort to restrict spies, saboteurs, subversives, and other dangerous persons. Many of the persons interviewed were U.S. citizens repatriated from Germany and Japan during the war. At the time this classification opened, the Bureau assumed all responsibility for the program. After 1945, FBI headquarters filed travel control investigations in Classification 100 Domestic Security. Field offices, however, continue to use this classification for such investigations.

Volume HQ: 2,353 cases. FIELD: Unknown. Forty-seven field offices reported opening cases. There has been substantial destruction.

Dates This classification opened in 1944, but some files date from as early as 1942. Headquarters files stop in 1945. The classification remains active in the field.

Location FBI

NARA Disposition Recommendation HQ: 5% evidential sample—Permanent; multisectional cases—Permanent; all others—Destroy. FIELD: All records—Destroy.

Access To gain access to the records in this classification a researcher must file a Freedom of Information Act request with the FBI.

Related Records FBI Classification 100 Domestic Security.

CLASSIFICATION 109

Foreign Political Matters

The Bureau opened this classification during World War II for information it received about political matters in various foreign countries. In addition to general political information, these records contain information relating to investigations concerning individuals who were potential political leaders of other countries, leaders of foreign revolutionary groups and organizations operating in the United States or abroad, and events bearing on the Bureau's responsibilities abroad.

Volume HQ: 708 cases with a large number of subfiles for individual countries. FIELD: 2,903 cases. Fifty-five field offices reported opening cases. There has been substantial destruction.

Dates 1940 to present

Location FBI

NARA Disposition Recommendation HQ: All records—Permanent. FIELD: All records—Permanent.

Access To gain access to the records in this classification a researcher must file a Freedom of Information Act request with the FBI.

Related Records See the General Records of the Department of State, Record Group 59, National Archives.

CLASSIFICATION 110

Foreign Economic Matters

The Bureau opened this classification in 1944 for files containing information on economic conditions in foreign countries. The classification is divided into subsections pertaining to individual countries. The files are informational in nature, not investigative, and collect data from a variety of sources, including Bureau legal attachés, the Department of State, and the Central Intelligence Agency. The records relate to such concerns as anti-American sentiments among foreign businesses, smuggling activities, efforts by businesses to circumvent the Proclaimed List during World War II, and the flight of German capital abroad at the end of the war.

Volume HQ: 172 cases, each with a large number of subfiles for individual countries. FIELD: 233 cases.

Dates 1940 to present

Location FBI

NARA Disposition Recommendation HQ: All records—Permanent. FIELD: All records—Permanent.

Access To gain access to the records in this classification a researcher must file a Freedom of Information Act request with the FBI.

Related Records See the General Records of the Department of State, Record Group 59, the General Records of the Department of Commerce, Record Group 40, the Records of the Foreign Economic Administration, Record Group 169, and the Records of the Bureau of Foreign and Domestic Commerce, Record Group 151, all in the National Archives.

CLASSIFICATION 111

Foreign Social Conditions

The FBI opened this classification in 1944 for files containing miscellaneous documentation of social conditions in foreign countries. Included is information on population statistics, health conditions, educational and scientific matters, and welfare programs. These files are informational files, not investigative ones, and include documentation, from agencies such as the Department of State and the Central Intelligence Agency, that is passed to the Bureau for its use, as well as field office reports of interviews with refugees and defectors.

Volume HQ: 6 cases with numerous subfiles for individual countries. FIELD: Unknown. Ten field offices reported opening cases.

Dates 1944 to present

Location FBI

NARA Disposition Recommendation HQ: All records—Destroy. FIELD: All records—Destroy.

Access To gain access to the records in this classification a researcher must file a Freedom of Information Act request with the FBI.

Related Records See the General Records of the Department of State, Record Group 59, Records of the United States Information Agency, Record Group 306, and the Records of the Agency for International Development, Record Group 286, all in the National Archives.

CLASSIFICATION 112

Foreign Funds

The Bureau opened this classification in 1944. It includes a large control file of intelligence information on foreign funds of interest to the FBI, as well as Bureau investigations of suspicious activities in this area. The main file in this classification contains no investigative records, and is broken into subfiles for individual countries. Typical subjects within it include the tracing of German funds to Latin America after World War II, unusual transfers of funds from U.S. banks to other countries, and the sale of U.S. dollars on the black market. The investigative files document the use of mail intercepts and informants by the Bureau.

Volume HQ: 49 cases with numerous subfiles for individual countries. FIELD: 37 cases. Eighteen field offices reported opening cases. There has been substantial destruction.

Dates 1944 to present

Location FBI

NARA Disposition Recommendation HQ: All records—Permanent. FIELD: All records—Destroy.

Access To gain access to the records in this classification a researcher must file a Freedom of Information Act request with the FBI.

Related Records See the General Records of the Department of State, Record Group 59, National Archives.

CLASSIFICATION 113

Foreign Military and Naval Matters

The Bureau opened this classification during World War II for information it received about foreign military and naval affairs. The main file in this classification contains no investigative records and is a large file broken into subfiles for individual countries. The records include documentation of possible sales of military equipment to other countries, visits of foreign military officers to the United States, and counterespionage activities.

Volume HQ: 54 cases. FIELD: 102 cases. Thirty field offices reported opening cases.

Dates 1941 to present

Location FBI

NARA Disposition Recommendation HQ: All records—Permanent. FIELD: Multisectional cases—Permanent; all others—Destroy.

Access To gain access to the records in this classification a researcher must file a Freedom of Information Act request with the FBI.

Related Records See the General Records of the Department of State, Record Group 59, the Records of the Office of the Secretary of Defense, Record Group 330, the General Records of the Department of the Navy, Record Group 80, and the Records of the Office of the Secretary of the Air Force, Record Group 340, all in the National Archives.

CLASSIFICATION 114

Alien Property Custodian Matters
(Obsolete)

The Bureau opened this classification in 1945 when the Department of Justice directed it to investigate cases brought against the alien property custodian under the Trading with the Enemy Act of 1917 and the first War Powers Act, passed in 1941. The Bureau provided the results of the investigations to the Department of Justice. Most of these cases involved investigations of the ownership and control of unvested property and of vested property subject to claims and litigation. The Bureau also investigated reports of misuse or misapplication by private citizens of property under the jurisdiction of the Office of Alien Property. This classification was declared obsolete in 1972. All subsequent alien property investigations will be found in Classification 63 Miscellaneous—Nonsubversive.

Volume HQ: 565 cases. FIELD: Unknown

Dates 1945 to 1972

Location FBI

NARA Disposition Recommendation HQ: All records—Destroy. FIELD: All records—Destroy.

Access To gain access to the records in this classification a researcher must file a Freedom of Information Act request with the FBI.

Related Records FBI Classification 63 Miscellaneous—Nonsubversive and Department of Justice Classification 9 European War Matters.

CLASSIFICATION 115

Bond Default

The Bureau opened this classification in 1946 for cases involving FBI investigations of bond defaulters. Over time, it expanded to include cases involving bail-bond jumpers. The Bail Reform Act of 1966 gave the Bureau jurisdiction over investigations of all persons who willfully failed to appear before judicial bodies as required. Some cases in this classification cover probation violations as well. In 1979 most of the Bureau's responsibilities in this area ended when the Department of Justice assigned responsibility for apprehending such fugitives to the U.S. Marshals Service.

Volume HQ: 6,766 cases. FIELD: 31,000 cases. All fifty-nine field offices reported opening cases. There has been some destruction.

Dates 1946 to present

Location FBI

NARA Disposition Recommendation HQ: All records—Destroy. FIELD: All records—Destroy.

Access To gain access to the records in this classification a researcher must file a Freedom of Information Act request with the FBI.

Related Records Records of the United States Attorneys and Marshals, Record Group 118, National Archives, and Department of Justice Classification 67 Bail Bonds and Forfeitures.

CLASSIFICATION 116

Department of Energy, Applicant

The Bureau opened this classification in 1946 for investigations of applicants and employees under the Atomic Energy Act of 1946 and its amendments. Under provisions of the act, the FBI held primary responsibility for investigating not only employees and applicants of the Atomic Energy Commission (AEC), but also the employees of contractors and licensees with access to restricted data (information on the manufacture and utilization of atomic weapons, on the production of fissionable material, and on its use in the production of power). The Bureau was charged with determining a subject's true allegiance to the United States or sympathies with a foreign government or ideology. The Bureau could halt an investigation if it found proved past or present membership in the Communist party or another organization declared subversive by the attorney general; recent "continuous criminal activity" or conviction for a serious felony within the previous ten years; chronic alcoholism during the previous five years; traits that indicated mental instability, including perversion; membership by a close blood relative in the Communist party; or recent proved breach of trust, a major security violation, or other facts overwhelmingly demonstrating that a person had become a security risk.

In 1947 the Bureau agreed to investigate the congressional staff of the Joint Committee on Atomic Energy and to investigate whole companies and their top officials at the request of the AEC. As might be expected, this created a large volume of work for the Bureau. As a result, the FBI decided to investigate only top scientists and certain top officials beginning on January 1, 1947, and to refer only synthesized reports to headquarters. This latter practice remained in effect from November 1947 to September 1948, when detailed reports were again sent forward. Despite the changes, the work load became so great that in 1951 the Bureau began lobbying for changes in the law. In 1952 its efforts were successful and Congress transferred responsibility for most cases to the AEC. The Bureau, however, continued its investigations of persons of importance or sensitivity or when other agencies discovered evidence of disloyalty. Included here are files relating to Walter Koski,* the Johns Hopkins physicist who worked at Los Alamos and testified at the Rosenberg trial, and German rocket scientist Wernher von Braun.*

Volume HQ: 483,833 cases. FIELD: Unknown. All fifty-nine field offices reported opening cases. There has been substantial destruction.

Dates 1946 to present

Location FBI

NARA Disposition Recommendation HQ: Systematic evidential sample of cases containing ten or more serials that involve scientists—Permanent; multisectional cases—Permanent; all others—Destroy. FIELD: NA

Access To gain access to the records in this classification a researcher must file a Freedom of Information Act request with the FBI.

Related Records Records of the Atomic Energy Commission, Record Group 326, National Archives.

CLASSIFICATION 117

Atomic Energy Act

The Bureau established this classification in 1946 to contain investigations of violations of the Atomic Energy Act of that year. FBI jurisdiction covered violations such as the release of information about nuclear weapons with the intent to injure the United States. Included are investigations of the media, in cases where information the government considered classified was released to the public, and of suspected Communist activities relating to atomic energy matters. In addition, there is information relating to the 1979 nuclear accident at the Three Mile Island reactor and the Love Canal cleanup.

Volume HQ: 2,967 cases. FIELD: 6,154 cases. All fifty-nine field offices reported opening cases. There has ben substantial destruction.

Dates 1946 to present

Location FBI

NARA Disposition Recommendation HQ: All records—Permanent. FIELD: Multisectional cases—Permanent; all others—Destroy.

Access To gain access to the records in this classification a researcher must file a Freedom of Information Act request with the FBI.

Related Records Records of the Atomic Energy Commission, Record Group 326, and General Records of the Department of Energy, Record Group 434, both in the National Archives, and Department of Justice Classification 90 Lands.

CLASSIFICATION 118

Applicant, Central Intelligence Group
(Obsolete)

The Bureau opened this classification in 1946 to gather background investigations of persons under consideration for employment by the Central Intelligence Group (CIG), a predecessor to the Central Intelligence Agency (CIA). The FBI's Executive Conference recommended that the Bureau assume this responsibility in order to "prevent the Central Intelligence Group from having any justification for an investigative unit operating within the United States" and to ensure that it had access to the identities of CIG personnel. Investigating agents were instructed to concentrate on developing information concerning the applicants' reliability, reputation, patriotism, and loyalty. Within a year of assuming responsibility for investigating these applicants, the Bureau began negotiating a release from that line of work. Its efforts finally succeeded in June 1950. This classification was declared obsolete in 1952, at which time the CIA assumed full responsibility for its own background security investigations.

Volume HQ: 899 cases. FIELD: Unknown. Fifteen field offices reported opening cases. Virtually all of those cases have been destroyed.

Dates 1946 to 1952

Location FBI

NARA Disposition Recommendation HQ: Systematic informational sample of 1,500 cases—Permanent; multisectional cases—Permanent; all others—Destroy. FIELD: NA

Access To gain access to the records in this classification a researcher must file a Freedom of Information Act request with the FBI.

Related Records Records of the Central Intelligence Agency, Langley, Virginia.

CLASSIFICATION 119

Federal Regulation of Lobbying Act

The Bureau opened this classification in 1946 for investigations of alleged violations of the Federal Lobbying Act of 1946. The law requires that all lobbyists involved in matters pending before Congress register and file quarterly statements of receipts and expenditures relating to their efforts to affect pending legislation. The FBI's responsibilities have changed somewhat over time. In 1952 the U.S. District Court suspended certain provisions of the law, and in 1977, Congress made further modifications. Because the Bureau considers investigations under this classification to be "delicate," it requires agents to follow special procedures. Typical cases involve persons and groups who have failed to submit reports as required or to register as lobbyists; the files also contain documentation on the interest of the White House and congressional opposition in some investigations. One case found in these files relates to President Jimmy Carter's brother Billy and his lobbying activities.

Volume HQ: 75 cases. FIELD: 170 cases. Thirty-four field offices reported opening cases.

Dates 1946 to present

Location FBI

NARA Disposition Recommendation HQ: All records—Permanent. FIELD: All records of Washington field office—Permanent; all others—Destroy.

Access To gain access to the records in this classification a researcher must file a Freedom of Information Act request with the FBI.

Related Records Department of Justice Classification 149 Foreign Agents Registration Act.

CLASSIFICATION 120

Federal Tort Claims Act

The Bureau established this classification in 1946 to gather investigations undertaken when the U.S. government is involved in a civil suit concerning alleged negligence or liability. Such cases usually result from accidents of one type or another. The FBI's involvement comes only at the direction of the Department of Justice if a claim exceeds $1,000. In the case of a "major disaster," the Bureau becomes involved immediately. Typical cases involve vehicular accidents, malpractice at military and Veterans Administration hospitals, and accidents at government facilities.

Volume HQ: 11,828 cases. FIELD: 46,472 cases. All fifty-nine field offices reported opening cases.

Dates 1946 to present

Location FBI

NARA Disposition Recommendation HQ: Systematic evidential sample—Permanent; multisectional cases—Permanent; all others—Destroy. FIELD: All records—Destroy.

Access To gain access to the records in this classification a researcher must file a Freedom of Information Act request with the FBI.

Related Records Department of Justice Classification 157 Federal Tort Claims Act.

CLASSIFICATION 121

Loyalty of Government Employees
(Obsolete)

The Bureau opened this classification in 1947 for investigations carried out under Executive Order 9835, issued by President Harry S. Truman and dated March 22, 1947, which required investigation of the loyalty of all Federal employees and future applicants. The President issued the order as a result of early Cold War anti-Communist hysteria. Under the order, a loyalty review board was established to make final determinations; it fell to the FBI to conduct the initial investigations. If further investigation was found to be warranted, the Bureau retained jurisdiction over all civilian agencies while the military investigated its civilian employees.

Initial Bureau directions to the field called for an evenhanded approach that recognized that "there is a distinction between Liberalism and Communism." Later, agents were also required to report on "loose morals" in addition to criminal activity. A person might be investigated for membership in organizations such as the National Lawyers Guild, personal friendships with alleged Communists, and membership of members of the family in the Communist party. Considerable criticism of the loyalty program led Hoover to argue that the FBI should make no recommendations, only report its findings to the employing agency so that the agency and the loyalty review board could make the final decision. The Federal Employees Loyalty Act, passed in 1953, further broadened the loyalty program. Bureau investigations under the new program were filed under Classification 140 Security of Government Employees. The Bureau declared Classification 121 obsolete in 1953, although it continued to add material to cases already opened.

Volume HQ: 44,850 cases. FIELD: 51,970 cases. Twenty-four field offices reported opening cases.

Dates 1947 to 1953

Location FBI

NARA Disposition Recommendation HQ: Systematic informational sample— Permanent; multisectional cases—Permanent; all others—Destroy. FIELD: NA

Access To gain access to the records in this classification a researcher must file a Freedom of Information Act request with the FBI.

Related Records FBI Classification 140 Security of Government Employees and Department of Justice Classification 158 Internal Security Act of 1950.

CLASSIFICATION 122

Labor Management Relations Act

The Bureau opened this classification in 1947 for investigations of violations of the Taft-Hartley Act. The section of the act that prohibited members of the Communist party from holding union office provided the Bureau with most of its investigative work in this area. The law required that all union leaders, including local officials, sign affidavits stating that they were not members of the Communist party and that they did not advocate the violent overthrow of the U.S. government. The result was that most party members resigned their membership in a union before having to sign an affidavit.

In 1959 the affidavit provisions of the law were repealed. Thereafter, the Bureau concentrated on enforcing those provisions of the act prohibiting strikes that endangered public health and safety and payoffs from union employees to union officials. In 1965 the designation of this classification was changed from "security" to "criminal." Cases include files on investigations of efforts of the Teamsters Union to subvert the farm workers union, the Jimmy Hoffa jury-tampering conspiracy, allegations of illegal payoffs, kickbacks, and extortion, and the misuse of union funds. This classification also contains information relating to Bureau policy regarding the Internal Security Act of 1950.

Volume HQ: 5,185 cases. FIELD: Unknown. Fifty-eight field offices reported opening cases. There has been substantial destruction.

Dates 1947 to present

Location FBI

NARA Disposition Recommendation HQ: Systematic evidential sample— Permanent; multisectional cases—Permanent; all case files with eleven or more serials—Permanent; all others—Destroy. FIELD: Multisectional cases—Permanent; all cases with eleven or more serials—Permanent; all others—Destroy.

Access To gain access to the records in this classification a researcher must file a Freedom of Information Act request with the FBI.

Related Records General Records of the Department of Labor, Record Group 174, National Archives, and Department of Justice Classification 156 Labor Management Relations.

CLASSIFICATION 123

Special Inquiry—Department of State, Voice of America
(Obsolete)

The Bureau opened this classification in 1948 as a result of that year's enabling legislation for the Voice of America (VOA), which specified that the FBI should investigate all employees and applicants of VOA to determine their loyalty to the United States. At the time that the legislation was passed, VOA was a part of the Department of State, the victim of a great deal of suspicion on the part of Congress and the media for harboring disloyal employees. Applicants to VOA did not submit loyalty oaths; instead, they completed a personal questionnaire that the Bureau then reviewed as part of its investigation. Extended investigations of individuals were undertaken on the grounds of organizations to which the persons belonged and their personal and family associations. The FBI forwarded the results of its investigations to the Department of State and a loyalty review board, which made final decisions. The Bureau's responsibility for investigating personnel and applicants to VOA narrowed over the years and this classification was finally declared obsolete in 1963.

Volume HQ: 15,870 cases. FIELD: Unknown. Twenty-one field offices reported opening cases. There has been substantial destruction.

Dates 1948 to 1963

Location FBI

NARA Disposition Recommendation HQ: Systematic informational sample of 1,500 cases—Permanent; multisectional cases—Permanent; all others—Destroy. FIELD: NA

Access To gain access to the records in this classification a researcher must file a Freedom of Information Act request with the FBI.

Related Records General Records of the Department of State, Record Group 59, National Archives.

CLASSIFICATION 124

European Recovery Program
(Obsolete)

The Bureau opened this classification in 1948 pursuant to provisions of the Foreign Assistance Act of 1948. That act required the Bureau to investigate all applicants for positions with the Economic Cooperation Administration (ECA), which held primary responsibility for the European Recovery Program (the Marshall Plan). This classification eventually held investigations for applicants to the ECA and its successor agencies, the Foreign Operations Administration, the International Cooperation Administration, and the Agency for International Development. Primary concern was given to an applicant's potential pro-Communist attitudes, activities, and associations. The Bureau's responsibility was modified in 1952. Beginning in that year, the Civil Service Commission (CSC) assumed responsibility for all such cases and the FBI entered cases only where the initial investigation by the CSC revealed questionable details about an individual's background. The result is that over 90 percent of all cases opened in this classification are dated prior to 1953. Eventually, the FBI's responsibility ended and the Bureau declared this classification obsolete in 1963.

Volume HQ: 8,989 cases. FIELD: Unknown. There has been massive destruction of these records.

Dates 1948 to 1963

Location FBI

NARA Disposition Recommendation HQ: 5% systematic evidential sample—Permanent; multisectional cases—Permanent; all others—Destroy. FIELD: NA

Access To gain access to the records in this classification a researcher must file a Freedom of Information Act request with the FBI.

Related Records Records of the United States Civil Service Commission, Record Group 146, Records of the Economic Cooperation Administration, the Foreign Operations Administration, and the International Cooperation Administration, all part of Records of U.S. Foreign Assistance Agencies 1948–1961, Record Group 469, and the Records of the Agency for International Development, Record Group 286, all in the National Archives.

CLASSIFICATION 125

Railway Labor Act

The Bureau opened this classification in 1948 for investigations of provisions of the Railway Labor Act of 1946. Despite its title, cases in this classification cover both railroads and airlines. Until 1949 the FBI began an investigation only with the authority of the Criminal Division of the Department of Justice. Before 1955 this classification included only investigations under the criminal provisions of the act. In 1955, Congress passed the Employee Liability Act covering workers' injuries and other accident-related investigations. The Bureau's jurisdiction over accidents was removed in 1980.

Volume HQ: 198 cases. FIELD: Unknown. Forty-nine field offices reported opening cases. There has been substantial destruction.

Dates 1948 to present

Location FBI

NARA Disposition Recommendation HQ: All records—Permanent. FIELD: All records—Destroy.

Access To gain access to the records in this classification a researcher must file a Freedom of Information Act request with the FBI.

Related Records Department of Justice Classification 124 Railroad Labor Act.

CLASSIFICATION 126

National Security Resources Board
(Obsolete)

In 1947, as a reaction to increasing Cold War tensions between the Soviet Union and the United States, Congress created the National Security Resources Board (NSRB) to deal with civil defense and economic mobilization issues in case of a war emergency. In 1949 the Bureau agreed to provide security investigations to all board employees or applicants. The Bureau ceased such investigations in 1950 and declared the classification obsolete. There is considerable biographical data in these files; the one case that stands out, however, involves not NSRB hiring practices or security investigations but the hiring practices of the FBI itself, especially its reluctance to hire Jews.

In 1953 the newly created Office of Civil Defense Mobilization absorbed the NSRB's functions.

Volume HQ: 779 cases (12 cu. ft). FIELD: Seventeen field offices reported extant cases, totaling 986. There has been substantial destruction.

Dates 1949 to 1950

Location FBI

NARA Disposition Recommendation HQ: Multisectional cases—Permanent; 5% systematic evidential sample—Permanent; case 126–725—Permanent; all other cases—Destroy. FIELD: All records—Destroy.

Access To gain access to the records in this classification a researcher must file a Freedom of Information Act request with the FBI.

Related Records Records of the Office of Civil and Defense Mobilization, Record Group 304, and Records of the National Security Resources Board, Record Group 304, National Archives.

CLASSIFICATION 127

Sensitive Positions in the United States Government
(Obsolete)

As part of increasing Cold War tension and fear of communism after World War II, Congress in August 1949 authorized the FBI to initiate investigations into the loyalty of people accepting employment or fellowships for work in sensitive governmental areas. The Bureau opened its first case under this law in April 1950, and conducted complete investigations of individuals from April to June of that year. After that time, however, the Bureau checked only applicant fingerprints, while maintaining that the work load was too great to undertake more comprehensive investigations. The classification is now obsolete. Although small in number the extant cases in this classification contain a wealth of biographical data on individuals and help document the Bureau's almost obsessive concern over possible Communist activities in the government. Included in the records are studies of State Department officials and some judicial appointments.

Volume HQ: 22 cases. FIELD: 19 cases.

Dates April to June 1950

Location FBI

NARA Disposition Recommendation HQ: All records—Permanent. FIELD: All records—Destroy.

Access To gain access to the records in this classification a researcher must file a Freedom of Information Act request with the FBI.

Related Records Department of Justice Classifications 145 Federal Service Act and 158 Internal Security Act of 1950. See also FBI Classifications 65 Espionage, 100 Domestic Security, and 140 Security of Government Employees.

CLASSIFICATION 128

International Development Program
(Obsolete)

Part of President Harry S. Truman's Point Four Program as passed by Congress called for the FBI to conduct security investigations of all applicants for positions with the then Technical Cooperation Administration (TCA) (later the Foreign Operations Administration and then the Agency for International Development). The Bureau established this classification in 1950 for its security investigations in this area. The Bureau conducted over 18,000 investigations for the TCA but after 1953 opened very few cases in this classification. The Bureau declared the classification obsolete in 1962.

In general, the cases involved the referral to the FBI of a security applicant questionnaire and then a general background investigation by the Bureau. If the investigation produced no derogatory information, the Bureau merely furnished the requesting agency a copy of its investigation report. The files, as could be expected, contain substantial biographical data on individuals and reflect FBI investigative procedures such as in-depth interviews and name checks of the Bureau's subversive indexes.

Volume HQ: 5,253 case (61.5 cu. ft.). FIELD: No extant cases.

Dates 1950 to 1962

Location FBI

NARA Disposition Recommendation HQ: Multisectional cases—Permanent; 5% systematic evidential sample of 500 cases—Permanent; all others—Destroy. FIELD: NA

Access To gain access to the records in this classification a researcher must file a Freedom of Information Act request with the FBI.

Related Records General Records of the Department of State, Record Group 59, and Records of the Foreign Operations Administration, part of Record Group 469, National Archives.

CLASSIFICATION 129

Evacuation Claims
(Obsolete)

In legislation passed in 1949, Congress permitted Japanese Americans interned during World War II to file claims against the Federal government for loss of property seized during the crisis. Although reluctant to become involved, the Bureau established this classification in 1950 to handle its investigations in this area. Most of the cases are simply name-check requests from the Department of Justice. The field office files in Los Angeles, however, contain the first Japanese-American claims to reach the courts. The plaintiffs asked for more than $1 million to offset the loss of their farm when they were interned. The final award in the case was for $300,000. Although not the primary source for documenting the treatment of Japanese Americans during the war, the FBI files supplement Federal court records and Department of Justice records in this area. The Bureau declared the classification obsolete in 1966.

Volume HQ: 15 cases. FIELD: 4 cases.

Dates 1948 to 1966

Location FBI

NARA Disposition Recommendation HQ: All records—Permanent. FIELD: All records—Permanent.

Access To gain access to the records in this classification a researcher must file a Freedom of Information Act request with the FBI.

Related Records Records of District Courts of the United States, Record Group 21, National Archives. See also Department of Justice Classifications 78 Tucker Act (Claims against the U.S.) and 146 World War II (Internal Security), as well as various hearings of the U.S. Congress and FBI field office records in Los Angeles under Classifications 65 Espionage, 100 Domestic Security, 105 Foreign Counterintelligence, and 66 Administrative Matters.

CLASSIFICATION 130

Special Inquiry—Armed Forces Security Act
(Obsolete)

After World War II, attempts to consolidate the cryptologic agencies of the military services resulted in the creation of the Armed Forces Security Agency in May 1949. This super-sensitive agency became the National Security Agency in 1952. The FBI had the responsibility for the security investigations of employee applicants until 1951, when the agency itself assumed the task and the FBI classification became obsolete. Most of the cases opened by the FBI under this classification were investigations of applicants seeking clerk-typist positions. The file appears not to contain any records relating to high-level or professional applicants.

Volume HQ: 226 cases (3 cu. ft.). FIELD: 220 cases from thirteen field offices. There has been substantial destruction.

Dates 1949 to 1952

Location FBI

NARA Disposition Recommendation HQ: Systematic evidential sample of 20 cases—Permanent; all others—Destroy. FIELD: All records—Destroy.

Access To gain access to the records in this classification a researcher must file a Freedom of Information Act request with the FBI.

Related Records Records of the National Security Agency, Record Group 457, National Archives.

CLASSIFICATION 131

Admiralty Matters

The Bureau established this classification in 1950 to investigate litigation cases involving ships and waterways. Usually the U.S. government was the defendant and the Department of Justice requested an FBI investigation. The cases themselves relate primarily to injury claims. For example, one case involved an individual who was injured in the course of a Coast Guard rescue and who subsequently sued the U.S. government. Other cases in this classification document shipping accidents involving U.S. vessels or relate to pollution clean-up costs and efforts in the 1970s to collect damages from tanker companies for oil spills. The records also reflect early U.S. efforts at drug interdiction and enforcement and document jurisdictional disputes between the FBI, the Coast Guard, and the Maritime Administration. For the 1950s there is information on Greek shipping magnates such as Aristotle Onassis.

Volume HQ: 1,859 cases. FIELD: 6,952 cases opened. There has been substantial destruction.

Dates 1933 to present

Location FBI

NARA Disposition Recommendation HQ: 5% systematic evidential sample—Permanent; multisectional cases—Permanent; all others—Destroy. FIELD: All records—Destroy.

Access To gain access to the records in this classification a researcher must file a Freedom of Information Act request with the FBI.

Related Records Department of Justice Classification 61 Admiralty Act. See also the Records of the United States Coast Guard, Record Group 26, and the Records of the Maritime Administration, Record Group 357, both in the National Archives.

CLASSIFICATION 132

Special Inquiry—Office of Defense Mobilization
(Obsolete)

The Bureau established this classification in 1951 in order to handle investigations of applicants for positions with the Office of Defense Mobilization. The Bureau was reluctant to undertake this responsibility and declared the classification obsolete in 1952 when the Department of Defense agreed to take over the security investigations.

Volume HQ: 50 cases (1.5 cu. ft.). FIELD: No extant cases.

Dates 1951

Location FBI

NARA Disposition Recommendation HQ: Systematic evidential sample of 20 cases—Permanent; all others—Destroy. FIELD: NA

Access To gain access to the records in this classification a researcher must file a Freedom of Information Act request with the FBI.

Related Records Records of the Office of Civil and Defense Mobilization, Record Group 304, and Records of the Office of the Secretary of Defense, Record Group 330, both in the National Archives.

CLASSIFICATION 133

National Science Foundation Act Applicant
(Obsolete)

The Bureau established this classification in 1951 for its investigations of National Science Foundation (NSF) civilian employees and outside consultants who had access to classified materials. Investigations of grant applicants were added to the classification in 1962. The Bureau was reluctant to pursue investigations of grant applicants, claiming that they were too time-consuming; a special request from the NSF was necessary before the Bureau would initiate a full field security investigation. The records themselves contain a large amount of biographical data including past political, educational, and social activities of highly educated, professional individuals.

Volume HQ: 272 cases (6 cu. ft.). FIELD: None

Dates 1951 to 1962

Location FBI

NARA Disposition Recommendation HQ: Systematic evidential sample of 20 cases—Permanent; all others—Destroy. FIELD: NA

Access To gain access to the records in this classification a researcher must file a Freedom of Information Act request with the FBI.

Related Records Records of the National Science Foundation, Record Group 307, National Archives. FBI Classification 116 Department of Energy, Applicant, and Department of Justice Classification 158 Internal Security Act of 1950.

CLASSIFICATION 134

Foreign Counterintelligence Assets

From the time of its creation the Bureau has used informants as part of its intelligence-gathering operations. As early as 1922, for example, an agent in El Paso, Texas, requested permission from headquarters to pay "4 Four Hundred" dollars per day for reports on "new revolutionary activities in Mexico." In 1928, Director Hoover instructed the field offices to forward all names of confidential informants to headquarters in a separate letter marked "Personal and Confidential." At this time, apparently, many field offices filed their records on informants in Classification 62 Administrative Inquiry (Miscellaneous Subversive and Nonsubversive). Some, however, filed them with the classification about which the informant was providing information, while others maintained a confidential informant file separate and distinct from the central file. With Hoover's 1928 directive, Bureau clerks created a master administrative file for informants in Classification 66 Administrative Matters. They also continued to maintain individual files for informants in Classification 62 and in the classification on which the informants were providing information.

In 1948, Hoover further directed the field offices to index and to serialize each confidential informant file, to maintain separate files for each paid or regular highly confidential informant, and to place in those files all correspondence and data pertaining to payments. Hoover addressed the question of informant files again in 1949, instructing the field offices to identify information provided by highly confidential sources by separate letter with an inner envelope marked "June" and an outer envelope marked "Personal and Confidential" and addressed to the director. Both headquarters and the field offices by this time maintained separate, classified files on informants.

It was not until 1952, however, that the Bureau established Classification 134 for all files on security informants. Beginning in that year, each informant was given an administrative file and a subfile. The administrative file contained the results of any background investigations conducted on the individual, records of Bureau contacts with the person, records of payments, copies of status reports, and the real identity of the source. The subfile contained information furnished by the informant.

During the 1950s Classification 134 included files for informants who provided information on extremist matters and suspected subversive organizations, primarily the Communist party. In 1959 the Bureau began to include files for informants on racial hate groups in Classification 137 Informants. In 1960 the Bureau established Classification 170 Extremist Informants and shifted relevant files to it. Files already opened in Classification 134, however, remained in that location. Included is a file on Hollywood newspaper columnist Hedda Hopper,* a close friend of Hoover, who provided information to the Bureau and to the House Un-American Activities Committee in 1961. During the latter part of the 1960s the Bureau focused its informant program on student radicals, the New Left, anti-Vietnam War protesters, and black militants. Files on most of these newly recruited informants and their information were placed in Classification 134.

By 1967 the Bureau began to limit the use of Classification 134, instructing the field offices to use Classification 105 Foreign Counterintelligence for security sources and Classification 65 if espionage was involved. Files on all potential informants or double agents remained in Classification 134.

In 1974 the Bureau refocused Classification 134 toward foreign counterintelligence. The Bureau replaced all references to informants in the counterintelligence area with references to operational assets or informational assets.

In 1976 the Bureau discontinued the use of extremist informants, Protection of Strategic Air Command Bases informants, and paid and confidential sources, files on all of which were included in Classification 134, and established a Classification 66 Administrative Matters dead file for continuing information. In the same year, with intensified Bureau focus on foreign counterintelligence, a number of informant files at headquarters were reclassified into Classification 137 Informants.

In 1978 headquarters reverted completely to the filing of informant files according to the subject of the information that they were providing. Thus, data on informants and informant information is now found in any number of files, although particularly in Classifications 65 and 105, and Classification 100 Domestic Security. The field offices, nevertheless, continued to concentrate informant files in Classifications 134 and 137.

The records themselves contain a wealth of information on the FBI's recruitment and development of informants, who ranged from students to bank clerks, foreign nationals, and public officials. The information provided covers such topics as the growth of the Ku Klux Klan in the 1950s, organized crime in the early 1960s, student protests and antiwar activities later in that decade, the black power movement, and, of course, the Bureau's main targets throughout, the American Communist party and Soviet espionage.

Volume HQ: 29,695 cases. FIELD: 126,400 cases in fifty-six field offices. There has been substantial destruction.

Dates 1952 to 1978 at headquarters; 1952 to present at field offices.

Location FBI

NARA Disposition Recommendation HQ: All records—Permanent. FIELD: Statistical sample of 2,500 cases each from New York, Washington, Los Angeles, San Francisco, St. Louis, and Chicago—Permanent; multisectional cases—Permanent; all files with subfiles—Permanent; all files with nonhuman sources (such as electronic surveillance)—Permanent; all other records—Destroy.

Access To gain access to the records in this classification a researcher must file a Freedom of Information Act request with the FBI.

Related Records FBI Classifications 62 Administrative Inquiry (Miscellaneous Subversive and Nonsubversive), 65 Espionage, 66 Administrative Matters, 100 Domestic Security, 105 Foreign Counterintelligence, 137 Informants, and 170 Extremist Informants.

CLASSIFICATION 135

Protection of Strategic Air Command Bases
of the U.S. Air Force (PROSAB)
(Obsolete)

The Bureau established this classification in 1953 when it reinstituted its informant program in U.S. defense manufacturing plants and at Strategic Air Command bases. The Plant Informant Program was terminated in 1969 and the Bureau discontinued the PROSAB program in 1971. There are no extant cases for this classification; only the 00 file remains.

Volume HQ: NA. FIELD: NA

Dates NA

Location FBI

NARA Disposition Recommendation HQ: 00 File—Permanent. FIELD: All records previously destroyed.

Access NA

Related Records Records of the United States Air Force Commands, Activities, and Organizations, Record Group 342, National Archives.

CLASSIFICATION 136

American Legion Contact
(Obsolete)

The Bureau opened this classification in 1952 specifically for information it obtained from American Legion members. Prior to 1952 the Bureau filed such information in Classification 66 Administrative Matters. Director Hoover encouraged all field offices to establish and to maintain contacts with legion officials to gain information on local conditions, especially with regard to domestic security concerns. After 1954, however, the program appeared to amount to little more than official annual contacts with the national officers, state officers, and members of the legion's Americanism Committee. During the 1960s there was a brief period of activity in this classification as Bureau agents attempted to gain information on the anti-Vietnam War protest movement and on racial violence in American cities. The Bureau declared the classification obsolete in 1965.

Volume HQ: None. The one extant case was reclassified into Classification 66, case 9330. FIELD: See Classification 66.

Dates 1952 to 1965

Location FBI

NARA Disposition Recommendation NA

Access NA

Related Records FBI Classification 66 Administrative Matters.

CLASSIFICATION 137

Informants

The Bureau established this classification in 1953 for its cases related to the use of criminal informants. Prior to 1953 the Bureau filed such information in Classifications 62 Administrative Inquiry (Miscellaneous Subversive and Nonsubversive) and 66 Administrative Matters. To protect informant identities headquarters stopped filing such information separately in 1976. Information supplied by informants is presently filed in the classification appropriate to the nature and subject of the information.

Although the Bureau has used criminal informants since its inception, few have ever been paid for their information. Most are minor figures on the fringes of the criminal world who promise more than they can deliver. In fact, most informant files are opened and closed within a six-month period. The records, however, taken as a whole, well document how the Bureau recruited informants and evaluated the information given by them and illustrate the development of the FBI's Top Echelon Criminal Informant Program and its White Collar Crime Informant Program. Moreover, although the records provide information on crime in America, such as bookmaking, sports betting, prostitution, theft rings, drug use, and organized crime activities, they also contain information on racial matters, the New Left, black militants, and Cuban exile activities in the United States.

Volume HQ: 48,719 cases. FIELD: Fifty-six field offices reported 291,971 cases opened in this classification. The largest numbers of cases were reported in New York (22,318), Newark (11,099), and Detroit (10,526). There has been substantial destruction in this classification.

Dates 1953 to 1976

Location   FBI

NARA Disposition Recommendation   HQ: All records—Permanent. FIELD:
Systematic informational sample of 2,500 cases each from New York, Newark,
St. Louis, Los Angeles, Chicago, and Detroit—Permanent; all cases relating to
Top Echelon Criminal Informant Program and the White Collar Crime Informant Program—Permanent; cases open for more than one year—Permanent;
cases with subfiles—Permanent; cases in which the informant has received more
than three payments—Permanent; cases in which informants have testified in
court proceedings—Permanent; cases involving nonhuman sources (such as
electronic surveillance)—Permanent; all others—Destroy.

Access   To gain access to the records in this classification a researcher must file
a Freedom of Information Act request with the FBI.

Related Records   FBI Classifications 62 Administrative Inquiry (Miscellaneous Subversive and Nonsubversive), 66 Administrative Matters, and 134
Foreign Counterintelligence Assets.

CLASSIFICATION 138

Loyalty of Employees of International Organizations

The Bureau opened this classification in 1953 for its investigations relating to
the loyalty of U.S. citizens employed by the United Nations and other international organizations. When the United Nations was first established in 1949,
Secretary General Trygve Lie called for security clearances for all its employees
over the objections of the Soviet Union, Canada, and UN employee groups.
Nothing came of this call until in 1953, President Dwight Eisenhower, responding
to increasing charges that the United Nations was heavily infiltrated by
Communists, issued Executive Order 10422 providing for investigations of U.S.
citizens working for the organization. Many international agencies, however,
including the International Monetary Fund and the World Health Organization,
refused to permit the FBI to interview their employees or to review their files.
    In 1958 the Bureau of the Budget recommended that the Civil Service
Commission (CSC) conduct the initial investigations, allowing that if it found
any derogatory information the FBI would be called in to take over the investigation. In 1966, President Lyndon Johnson complained publicly of the poor
quality of the CSC investigations but did not restore the full investigative
function to the FBI. Neither the Bureau nor the CSC found many U.S. citizens
associated with subversive groups, and in 1975 the Bureau declared that the
major security problem at the United Nations was not with American citizens
but with the Communist bloc and its nationals, who were using the United

Nations for espionage purposes. Presently, security checks for American employees of the United Nations consist of a brief check by the National Information Agency and then a full FBI investigation if needed.

Most of the cases the FBI has investigated have concerned derogatory information relating to a person's sexual habits and excessive drinking problems rather than to Communist activities. The records themselves contain biographical data and in-depth interviews that provide insight into American family life in the 1950s and illustrate how the Bureau went about conducting security investigations.

Volume HQ: 5,155 cases (168 cu. ft.). FIELD: Fifty-six field offices reported opening cases in this classification. There has been substantial destruction.

Dates 1953 to present

Location FBI

NARA Disposition Recommendation HQ: Systematic informational sample—Permanent; multisectional cases—Permanent; all others—Destroy. FIELD: All records—Destroy.

Access To gain access to the records in this classification a researcher must file a Freedom of Information Act request with the FBI.

Related Records Records of the United Nations, New York, and the Records of the United States Civil Service Commission, Record Group 146, National Archives.

CLASSIFICATION 139

Interception of Communications

The Bureau originally established this classification in 1953 as Unauthorized Publication or Use of Communications. It was designed primarily for espionage cases involving secure U.S. communications and grew out of the Federal Communications Act of 1934. Until 1953 the Federal Communications Commission investigated allegations of unlawful interception and/or disclosure of wire communications. During the height of the Cold War in the 1950s, however, the FBI assumed responsibility for such investigations and with the passage of the Omnibus Crime Control and Safe Streets Act in 1968, which provided Federal penalties for the willful and unauthorized interception of communications, changed the name of the classification to its present form.

Despite the original intent, most of the cases opened under this classification relate to domestic divorce proceedings where a telephone tap was used, employers listening to the telephones of their employees, towing companies monitoring police radio bands for business, and the sale of surveillance and counterintelligence devices. Hoover took a personal interest in the use of wire taps by private detectives and the files show that many such cases were referred to him for his personal observation. In addition, the records contain information on the Ku Klux Klan and its ability to monitor police radio frequencies, phone taps on Teamster Union officials relating to the disappearance of Jimmy Hoffa, and efforts by the Bureau to discourage the monitoring of Drug Enforcement Agency communications by drug traffickers. Included also is a file relating to the Watergate break-in* and one relating to Howard Hughes.*

Volume HQ: 6211 cases (95 cu. ft.). FIELD: Fifty-seven field offices reported opening 13,000 cases.

Dates 1953 to present. The highest volume of cases has occurred in the post-Watergate period (1974–1980).

Location FBI

NARA Disposition Recommendation HQ: Systematic evidential sample—Permanent; multisectional cases—Permanent; all cases involving prosecution—Permanent; all others—Destroy. FIELD: All records—Destroy.

Access To gain access to the records in this classification a researcher must file a Freedom of Information Act request with the FBI.

Related Records Records of the Federal Communications Commission, Record Group 173, and Records of the Drug Enforcement Agency, Record Group 170, both in the National Archives. Department of Justice Classification 82 Communications Act and 177 Interception of Communications. See also FBI Classifications 65 Espionage, 100 Domestic Security, and 105 Foreign Counterintelligence.

CLASSIFICATION 140

Security of Government Employees

The Bureau established this classification in 1953 in response to President Dwight Eisenhower's Executive Order 10450, which provided for Federal investigations of employees suspected of being risks to the national security. Under a broad interpretation by the Bureau justification for suspicion included "dishonesty, immorality, excessive drunkenness, financial irresponsibility, and mental instability." Hoover rejected Department of Justice suggestions that the Bureau sharply limit its investigations in this classification. Until the 1956

Supreme Court decision in *Cole v. Young*, which restricted such investigations to government employees in sensitive security positions, the Bureau vigorously investigated all charges involving security risks. The basis of most of the investigations was an allegation of membership in a subversive organization, support for Communist party candidates, or association with known radicals.

In addition to containing a wealth of biographical data on federal workers— there are, for example, personal histories, employment records, descriptions of educational backgrounds, neighborhood references, credit checks, and criminal records present in the files—the records document the use by the Bureau of extraordinary investigative techniques, including electronic surveillance and "black-bag" activities. The cases also provide detailed information on the American Communist party, Black Muslims, the Progressive Labor party, the Socialist Labor party, Students for a Democratic Society, and the Venceremos Brigade (student activists who went to Cuba to help in the sugar harvest).

Volume HQ: 43,901 cases (1,183.5 cu. ft.). FIELD: Fifty-six field offices reported opening cases in this classification. The Washington field office, for example, opened over 30,000 cases. There has been substantial destruction.

Dates 1953 to present

Location FBI

NARA Disposition Recommendation HQ: Systematic informational sample— Permanent; multisectional cases—Permanent; all others—Destroy. FIELD: All records—Destroy.

Access To gain access to the records in this classification a researcher must file a Freedom of Information Act request with the FBI.

Related Records Department of Justice Classifications 145 Federal Service Act and 158 Internal Security Act of 1950. See also FBI Classification 121 Loyalty of Government Employees.

CLASSIFICATION 141

False Entries in Records of Interstate Carriers

The Bureau established this classification in 1953 when it split Classification 71 Bills of Lading Act into seven new classifications. It covers investigations involving the falsification or destruction of records of interstate carriers such as railroads, trucking firms, bus lines, pipeline companies, and telephone, tele- graph, and radio companies. The Bureau frequently coupled investigations in this classification with more serious violations such as theft from interstate shipments. Also included in this classification are cases involving the Interstate Commerce Commission and the illegal releasing of information from its inspectors. Most of the cases opened under this classification involve relatively minor matters such as the filing of false claims for reimbursement, fraudulent Western Union money orders, false ticket sales on rail lines, and the charging of repair costs for work not completed.

Volume HQ: 83 cases. FIELD: Forty-six field offices reported 376 cases.

Dates 1953 to 1958

Location FBI

NARA Disposition Recommendation HQ: Systematic evidential sample—Permanent; multisectional cases—Permanent; all others—Destroy. FIELD: All records—Destroy.

Access To gain access to the records in this classification a researcher must file a Freedom of Information Act request with the FBI.

Related Records Records of the Interstate Commerce Commission, Record Group 134, National Archives. Department of Justice Classifications 59 Railroads, Transportation, ICC Acts and 63 Warehouse Act.

CLASSIFICATION 142

Illegal Use of Railroad Pass

The Bureau established this classification in 1953 for its investigations involving the unlawful use of rail, air, or bus passes to avoid payment of fares or the use of such passes to obtain favors. The classification was originally intended to document the use of such passes in influencing political elections and in freight rate-setting cases. Prior to 1953 the Bureau filed such cases in Classification 71 Bills of Lading Act.

Volume HQ: 26 cases. FIELD: 110 cases.

Dates 1953 to present

Location FBI

NARA Disposition Recommendation HQ: Systematic evidential sample—Permanent; multisectional cases—Permanent; all others—Destroy. FIELD: All records—Destroy.

Access To gain access to the records in this classification a researcher must file a Freedom of Information Act request with the FBI.

Related Records FBI Classification 71 Bills of Lading Act.

CLASSIFICATION 143

Interstate Transportation of Gambling Devices

In 1951, Congress passed the Johnson Act, which made it illegal to transport gambling devices across state lines. It also established registration and reporting procedures for the manufacture of such devices in the United States. The Bureau established this classification in 1953 for its investigations into violations of this law, filed prior to 1953 under Classification 71 Bills of Lading Act. Under a series of court decisions in 1953 and 1954, the Johnson Act was narrowly defined to cover only slot machines, pinball machines, and roulette wheels. With the Gambling Devices Act of 1962, Congress, in response, extended the definition of gambling devices to include any machine or mechanical device designed primarily for gambling.

During the 1950s slot machines were a major source of income for organized crime and the Bureau was active in pursuing these cases. The Bureau also aggressively sought the registration of the manufacturers of these devices. By 1973, however, Bureau agents filed few cases under this classification and it was virtually abandoned although not officially declared obsolete. The records document the Bureau's intense interest in these cases and the problems it had with the legal definitions of gambling devices that were produced by frequent court decisions, many of which declared machines "antiques" and their owners exempt from prosecution.

Volume HQ: 1,462 cases (33 cu. ft.). FIELD: 8,890 cases reported opened. Chicago opened twice as many as any other field office. There has been substantial destruction.

Dates 1953 to 1973

Location FBI

NARA Disposition Recommendation HQ: 5% systematic evidential sample—Permanent; multisectional cases—Permanent; all others—Destroy. FIELD: Multisectional cases—Permanent; all others—Destroy.

Access To gain access to the records in this classification a researcher must file a Freedom of Information Act request with the FBI.

Related Records Department of Justice Classification 159 Gambling Device Controls and FBI Classification 71 Bills of Lading Act.

CLASSIFICATION 144

Interstate Transportation of Lottery Tickets

The Bureau established this classification in 1953 for its investigations of the violation of laws that prohibited the interstate transportation of tickets of chance dependent on a lottery. Prior to 1953 the Bureau filed such cases under Classification 71 Bills of Lading Act. In 1975, in response to the growth of official state lotteries, Congress exempted such games from the law. The records primarily illustrate the extensive illegal sale of Irish Sweepstakes tickets and the importation and sale of lottery tickets from Puerto Rico, the West Indies, and Mexico into the United States during the 1950s and early 1960s. In one case the Bureau seized in New York over 3.2 million sweepstakes tickets, whose sellers had targeted U.S. churches, synagogues, and American Legion posts as their major markets. The files also document a close working relationship between the Bureau and the Internal Revenue Service on this issue.

Volume HQ: 482 cases. FIELD: 2,855 cases reported from fifty-seven field offices. There has been substantial destruction.

Dates 1953 to 1975

Location FBI

NARA Disposition Recommendation HQ: 5% systematic evidential sample— Permanent; multisectional cases—Permanent; all others—Destroy. FIELD: All records—Destroy.

Access To gain access to the records in this classification a researcher must file a Freedom of Information Act request with the FBI.

Related Records Department of Justice Classification 64 Lottery and FBI Classification 71 Bills of Lading Act.

CLASSIFICATION 145

Interstate Transportation of Obscene Matter

The Bureau established this classification in 1953, when it divided Classification 71 Bills of Lading Act into several classifications, and added to it in the 1970s investigations of obscene language being broadcast over the airwaves. Reporting procedures laid down by Director Hoover required the field offices to submit to headquarters all exhibits seized in such investigations. The FBI laboratory reviewed all such materials to determine whether or not they were indeed obscene and sought to identify major distributors by maintaining a special fingerprint file on them.

The records reflect America's continued concern with the definition of pornographic materials and with changing social attitudes and mores. For example, during the 1950s the Bureau investigated *Playboy* magazine, rock-and-roll lyrics such as those in the song "Louie Louie," and books such as Henry Miller's *Tropic of Cancer*. In the 1960s and 1970s the Bureau increasingly focused its investigations on major pornography producers and distributors and their connections with organized crime, adult book stores and movie theaters, and video tapes. The Bureau confiscated such video tapes and movies as *Behind the Green Door*, *Deep Throat*, and *The Devil and Miss Jones*. In the 1980s the Bureau concentrated its efforts in this area on the sexual exploitation of children and on child pornography cases. First Amendment issues continue to be a major concern in the definition of pornographic literature in the United States and the Bureau, as reflected in its investigations in this classification, is often frustrated by continually changing court interpretations.

Volume   HQ: 6,087 cases (100.5 cu. ft.). FIELD: Fifty-nine field offices reported opening 37,631 cases in this classification. There has been substantial destruction.

Dates   1953 to present

Location   FBI

NARA Disposition Recommendation   HQ: Systematic evidential sample—Permanent; multisectional cases—Permanent; all others—Destroy. FIELD: Multisectional cases—Permanent; all others—Destroy.

Access   To gain access to the records in this classification a researcher must file a Freedom of Information Act request with the FBI.

Related Records   Records of the United States Postal Service, Record Group 28, National Archives. Department of Justice Classification 97 Obscene Literature and FBI Classification 71 Bills of Lading Act. See also the extensive collection of pornographic literature at the Library of Congress.

CLASSIFICATION 146

Interstate Transportation of Prison-Made Goods

The Bureau established this classification in 1953 when it divided Classification 71 Bills of Lading Act. The investigations under this classification relate to products or goods that are produced in Federal prisons (other than agricultural goods or products produced for the Federal government such as shelving and furniture) and which are transported across state lines to be sold on the commercial market. The Bureau opened only a few cases in this classification and they relate to minor violations. In one such case a prison guard sold purses and belts made by inmates to out-of-state friends, but no prosecution took place.

Volume HQ: 36 cases. FIELD: 120 cases.

Dates 1953 to present

Location FBI

NARA Disposition Recommendation HQ: Systematic evidential sample— Permanent; multisectional cases—Permanent; all others—Destroy. FIELD: All records—Destroy.

Access To gain access to the records in this classification a researcher must file a Freedom of Information Act request with the FBI.

Related Records Records of the Bureau of Prisons, Record Group 129, National Archives. Department of Justice Classification 131 Interstate Transportation of Prison-Made Goods and FBI Classification 71 Bills of Lading Act.

CLASSIFICATION 147

Fraud against the Government—Department of Housing and Urban Development

The Bureau opened this classification in 1954 for its investigations involving fraud in Federal housing programs. Most of the cases involved minor violations, such as making false statements on Federal Housing Administration (FHA) loan applications, attempting to bribe appraisers, and renting houses purchased with Federal loans that prohibited such practices. Some of the cases, however, detail major kickback and influence-peddling schemes in the housing industry, corruption in the awarding of low-income housing projects, and fraud in obtaining Veterans Administration mortgages. The records also reflect poor, noncooperative relations between FHA officials and the FBI.

Volume HQ: 22,607 cases (531 cu. ft.). FIELD: Fifty-eight field offices reported opening 46,200 cases. There has been substantial destruction.

Dates 1953 to present

Location FBI

NARA Disposition Recommendation HQ: Systematic evidential sample— Permanent; multisectional cases—Permanent; all others—Destroy. FIELD: Multisectional cases—Permanent; all others—Destroy.

Access To gain access to the records in this classification a researcher must file a Freedom of Information Act request with the FBI.

Related Records General Records of the Department of Housing and Urban Development, Record Group 207, and Records of District Courts of the United States, Record Group 21, both in the National Archives. See also Department of Justice Classification 130 Federal Housing Act.

CLASSIFICATION 148

Interstate Transportation of Fireworks

The Bureau established this classification in 1954 for its investigations of violations of Federal statutes that barred the transportation of fireworks into any state in which their sale or use was contrary to state law. As of 1963 the Bureau had developed 154 cases concerning bootleg fireworks, including one against the so-called Cherry Bomb King of the east coast. Of these, only four reached the courts; all were thrown out on technicalities by the judges. In general, the Bureau has been unsuccessful in securing prosecution of major manufacturers and distributors of fireworks. One interesting case developed by the Bureau involved illegal fireworks on Indian reservations.

Volume HQ: 355 cases. FIELD: Fifty-four field offices reported opening approximately 1,300 cases.

Dates 1954 to present

Location FBI

NARA Disposition Recommendation HQ: Systematic evidential sample— Permanent; multisectional cases—Permanent; all others—Destroy. FIELD: All records—Destroy.

Access To gain access to the records in this classification a researcher must file a Freedom of Information Act request with the FBI.

Related Records See state and local records.

CLASSIFICATION 149

Destruction of Aircraft or Motor Vehicles

The Bureau established this classification in 1956 for its investigations of threats to destroy commercial aircraft and motor vehicles carrying passengers. In almost all cases no actual bombing occurred and the perpetrator was an "unknown subject." Most cases concerned telephoned bomb threats to commercial airlines. In one case the Bureau was brought in to help identify victims of an airplane crash.

Volume HQ: 12,849 cases. FIELD: Fifty-seven field offices reported opening 30,850 cases. There has been substantial destruction.

Dates 1953 to present

Location FBI

NARA Disposition Recommendation HQ: Systematic evidential sample—Permanent; multisectional cases—Permanent; all others—Destroy. FIELD: Cases that correlate with headquarters cases—Permanent; multisectional cases—Permanent; all others—Destroy.

Access To gain access to the records in this classification a researcher must file a Freedom of Information Act request with the FBI.

Related Records Department of Justice Classifications 88 Air Traffic Act—Civil Aeronautics and 80094 Traffic and Motor Safety.

CLASSIFICATION 150

Harboring of Federal Fugitives, Statistics
(Obsolete)

The Bureau established this classification in 1957 for administration purposes. It contained statistics on the types of persons who harbored fugitives. The Bureau declared the classification obsolete in 1960.

Volume HQ: No extant cases. FIELD: NA.

Dates 1957 to 1960

Location FBI

NARA Disposition Recommendation HQ: NA. FIELD: NA

Access NA

Related Records Department of Justice Classification 127 Harboring Felons.

CLASSIFICATION 151

Referral Cases from Office of Personnel Management—Applicant Loyalty

The Bureau established this classification in 1958 for investigations relating to applicant cases referred to it by the Civil Service Commission (CSC). The CSC investigates applicants for many U.S. agencies, as well as official U.S. representatives to certain international organizations, and was required to refer all cases in which questions about an applicant's loyalty to the U.S. government arose. That is, the FBI investigated cases in which the initial CSC review of an individual's background indicated the need for a further and more intensive security check. The Bureau furnished any resulting new information to the agency considering the applicant. If the FBI did produce so-called derogatory information, the agency receiving the reports retained responsibility for evaluating the information and for taking necessary action.

Individuals might receive particular scrutiny because they, members of their family, their friends, or their associates were alleged members of the Communist party, took part in antiwar activities during the Vietnam War era, or had alleged sympathy for or membership in groups such as the Black Panthers or the Ku Klux Klan. Generally these referrals involve applicants to the Peace Corps, ACTION Inc., the Department of Energy, the National Aeronautics and Space Administration, the Nuclear Regulatory Commission, the Arms Control and Disarmament Agency, the United States Information Agency, the Agency for International Development, the National Science Foundation, the World Health Organization, and the International Labor Organization. There is also a case file relating to Arthur Rudolph.*

Volume HQ: 5,068 cases. FIELD: 28,568 cases. Most field offices opened cases. There has been substantial destruction.

Dates 1958 to present

Location FBI

NARA Disposition Recommendation HQ: Systematic informational sample—Permanent; multisectional cases—Permanent; all others—Destroy. FIELD: NA

Access To gain access to the records in this classification a researcher must file a Freedom of Information Act request with the FBI.

Related Records See Records of the Department of Energy, Record Group 434; Records of the Nuclear Regulatory Commission, Record Group 431; Records of the Arms Control and Disarmament Agency, Record Group 383; Records of the United States Information Agency, Record Group 306; Records of the Agency for International Development, Record Group 286; Records of the National Science Foundation, Record Group 307; and Records of the National Aeronautics and Space Administration, Record Group 255; all in the National Archives. See also Department of Justice Classification 158 Internal Security Act of 1950.

CLASSIFICATION 152

Switchblade Knife Act

The Bureau established this classification in 1958 for investigations of the Switchblade Knife Act. The law prohibited the introduction or manufacture for introduction into interstate commerce of switchblade knives over three inches in length. The legislation was aimed primarily at about twenty Italian manufacturers and about thirty domestic makers of such knives. In practice, however, the Bureau conducted few investigations under this classification.

Volume HQ: 78 cases. FIELD: 886 cases. Fifty-two field offices reported opening cases. Almost all such files have been destroyed.

Dates 1958 to present

Location FBI

NARA Disposition Recommendation HQ: Systematic evidential sample of 20 cases—Permanent; all others—Destroy. FIELD: All records—Destroy.

Access To gain access to the records in this classification a researcher must file a Freedom of Information Act request with the FBI.

Related Records See the General Records of the Department of Commerce, Record Group 40, National Archives.

CLASSIFICATION 153

Automobile Information Disclosure Act

The Bureau set up this classification in 1958 for investigations of violations of the Automobile Information Disclosure Act, which required that automobile dealers make a full disclosure of pertinent information such as the make and model of a car, assembly point, retail price, and transportation costs. The investigations in this classification focus on relatively minor issues such as dealers turning back odometers, failing to display price information, and altering manufacturer's labels. The investigation rarely led to prosecution, either because no violation of the law was uncovered or because insufficient evidence was collected.

Volume HQ: 974 cases. FIELD: All fifty-nine field offices reported opening a total of 4,143 cases. There has been substantial destruction.

Dates 1958 to present

Location FBI

NARA Disposition Recommendation HQ: 5% systematic evidential sample— Permanent; multisectional cases—Permanent; all others—Destroy. FIELD: All records—Destroy.

Access To gain access to the records in this classification a researcher must file a Freedom of Information Act request with the FBI.

Related Records See Department of Justice Classification 183 Automobile Standards.

CLASSIFICATION 154

Interstate Transportation of Unsafe Refrigerators

The Bureau established this classification in 1958 for investigations of violations of the Department of Commerce standards and regulations relating to refrigerators. The Bureau has very limited responsibility in this area and will undertake an investigation only after a formal complaint and at the direction of a U.S. Attorney.

Volume There are no extant case files in this classification.

Dates 1958 to present

Location NA

NARA Disposition Recommendation HQ: NA. FIELD: NA

Access NA

Related Records General Records of the Department of Commerce, Record Group 40, National Archives.

CLASSIFICATION 155

National Aeronautics and Space Act of 1958

The Bureau established this classification in 1958 for investigations relating to its responsibilities regarding the newly created National Aeronautics and Space Administration (NASA). From the beginning, NASA was responsible for the protection of its own facilities and for investigating routine violations of the 1958 act. The FBI's jurisdiction in this area was limited. In 1974 the Department of Justice clarified the Bureau's responsibility as including investigations of the "more serious violations" of secure areas, bribery, perjury, conflict of interest, and sabotage.

Volume There are no extant files in this classification.

Dates 1958 to present

Location NA

NARA Disposition Recommendation HQ: NA. FIELD: NA

Access NA

Related Records See the Records of the National Aeronautics and Space Administration, Record Group 255, National Archives.

CLASSIFICATION 156

Employee Retirement Income Security Act

The Bureau established this classification in 1958 for cases resulting from investigations of violations of the Welfare and Pension Plan Disclosure Act of 1958. That law required that all pension plans be filed with the Department of Labor. In 1962 legislation expanded the Department of Labor's authority to include examinations of the financial records of pension and welfare plans. The Bureau's responsibility is to investigate instances of embezzlement and kickbacks uncovered by the department. The 1975 passage of the Employment Retirement Income Security Act and subsequent agreements with the Department of Labor led to expanded FBI responsibility to investigate kickbacks, false statements, embezzlements, interference with rights, and prohibitions against holding positions. The Department of Labor investigates all other matters. The files include investigations of failure to submit annual reports, embezzlement, kickbacks, and bribery.

Volume HQ: 211 cases. FIELD: 2,334 cases. Fifty-seven field offices reported opening cases. There has been substantial destruction.

Dates 1958 to present

Location FBI

NARA Disposition Recommendation HQ: Multisectional cases—Permanent; cases with five or more serials—Permanent; all others—Destroy. FIELD: Multisectional cases—Permanent; all others—Destroy.

Access To gain access to the records in this classification a researcher must file a Freedom of Information Act request with the FBI.

Related Records See the General Records of the Department of Labor, Record Group 174, National Archives.

CLASSIFICATION 157

Civil Unrest

The Bureau established this classification in 1959 for its investigations of civil disorders and demonstrations. The FBI has the responsibility for investigating criminal violations relating to civil disturbances and for assisting the Secret Service by providing, upon request, information concerning actual or potential civil disorders that might require the use of Federal troops and information relating to planned demonstrations that require the Federal government to provide health and safety measures. This classification was initially called Racial Matters/Bombing Matters and focused on the Ku Klux Klan. During the early 1960s, Bureau investigations of bombings and bomb threats against racial, religious, and educational institutions were included in this classification. It was also during this period that the Bureau began to include investigations of the American Nazi party, anti-Semitic and other hate groups, and attacks on civil rights workers in this classification.

With the onset of major urban riots in the middle and late 1960s, the Bureau began to include in this classification investigations of groups such as the Black Panthers, as well as the Weathermen. The Black Panthers* and other black extremist groups* were a particular preoccupation of Hoover and there are large files on these groups in both headquarters and field-office files. The Bureau also monitored the movement of various radical leaders such as Abbie Hoffman* and Stokely Carmichael. In 1971 this classification was renamed Extremist Matters/ Civil Unrest and investigations of the American Indian Movement* and the Symbionese Liberation Army were opened. In 1976, Attorney General Edward H. Levi issued new guidelines that sharply narrowed the FBI's authority to monitor the movements and political activities of American citizens. As a result, the number of cases opened under this classification dropped off dramatically.

Investigations focused on both individual members and organizations. Full field investigations were prepared for both local and national offices of organizations such as the Ku Klux Klan and the National Association for the Advancement of Colored People (NAACP). The Bureau justified opening cases on major civil rights groups such as the NAACP* and the Congress of Racial Equality not so much because the general purpose of the organization was in question, but "to determine the degree of subversive influence." Hoover believed that many of these left-leaning and radical groups were merely fronts for Communists or had been compromised by Communist infiltration. The files also contain information relating to many COINTELPRO operations.*

Volume HQ: 35,130 cases. FIELD: Fifty-nine field offices reported opening a total of 303,826 cases. There has been some destruction.

Dates 1959 to present

Location FBI

NARA Disposition Recommendation HQ: Systematic informational sample— Permanent; multisectional cases—Permanent; cases with fifteen or more serials—Permanent; all informant cases—Permanent; all cases in which the subject is not an individual—Permanent; all others—Destroy. FIELD: Systematic informational sample of cases from Jackson, Mississippi, New Orleans, and New York—Permanent; multisectional cases—Permanent; all cases in which the subject is not an individual—Permanent; all others—Destroy.

Access To gain access to the records in this classification a researcher must file a Freedom of Information Act request with the FBI.

Related Records See Department of Justice Classification 158 Internal Security Act of 1950 and the Records of the United States Secret Service, Record Group 87, National Archives.

CLASSIFICATION 158

Labor-Management Reporting and Disclosure Act of 1959
(Obsolete)

The Bureau established this classification in 1959 for investigations of violations of the Labor-Management Reporting and Disclosure Act of that year. One part of that legislation prohibited members of the Communist party from holding certain offices or employment in the labor sector. During the first two years of investigations under this authority, the Bureau opened 370 cases. During the period 1962 to 1965, it opened only 70 additional cases because of constitutional questions. Typical investigations include allegations of membership in the Communist party and reports on the structure and activities of various unions. In late 1965 the Supreme Court held as unconstitutional the anti-Communist provisions of the 1959 act, and all investigations ceased. The Bureau then declared the classification obsolete.

Volume HQ: 440 cases. FIELD: Twenty-two field offices reported opening a total of 74 cases. There has been substantial destruction.

Dates 1959 to 1965

Location FBI

NARA Disposition Recommendation HQ: Multisectional cases—Permanent; all others—Destroy. FIELD: Multisectional cases—Permanent; all others—Destroy.

Access To gain access to the records in this classification a researcher must file a Freedom of Information Act request with the FBI.

Related Records See Department of Justice Classification 156 Labor-Management Relations.

CLASSIFICATION 159

Labor-Management Reporting and Disclosure Act of 1959

The Bureau established this classification in 1959 for its investigations under the provisions of the Labor-Management Reporting and Disclosure Act of 1959 that did not involve Communist activities in the labor movement. The Bureau shared responsibility under the law with the Department of Labor, which is responsible for the reporting and disclosure provisions of the act. The department makes requests for FBI investigations through the Criminal Division of the Department of Justice. The FBI's areas of responsibility include investigations of embezzlement of union funds, employer payment of fines imposed upon unions, prohibitions against felons holding positions as union officials, and picketing for purposes of extortion.

Volume HQ: 4,879 cases. FIELD: Fifty-seven field offices reported opening a total of 10,342 cases.

Dates 1959 to present

Location FBI

NARA Disposition Recommendation HQ: 5% systematic evidential sample—Permanent; multisectional cases—Permanent; all others—Destroy. FIELD: Multisectional cases—Permanent; all others—Destroy.

Access To gain access to the records in this classification a researcher must file a Freedom of Information Act request with the FBI.

Related Records See Department of Justice Classification 156 Labor-Management Relations and the General Records of the Department of Labor, Record Group 174, National Archives.

CLASSIFICATION 160

Federal Train Wreck Statute

In 1940, Congress passed legislation that made wrecking trains a Federal offense. Twenty years later, new legislation broadened and clarified the earlier law. The Bureau established this classification in 1960 for investigations conducted under the newer legislation. During World War II, investigations of alleged sabotage against railroad property and trains were filed in Classification 98 Sabotage. Files in this classification include investigations of collisions, the destruction of railroad bridges, the destruction of railroad track, and blackmail threats against railroads.

Volume HQ: 2,772 cases. FIELD: Fifty-seven field offices reported opening a total of 9,000 cases.

Dates 1960 to present

Location FBI

NARA Disposition Recommendation HQ: 5% systematic evidential sample—Permanent; multisectional cases—Permanent; all others—Destroy. FIELD: All records—Destroy.

Access To gain access to the records in this classification a researcher must file a Freedom of Information Act request with the FBI.

Related Records See FBI Classification 98 Sabotage.

CLASSIFICATION 161

Special Inquiries for the White House, Congressional Committees, and Other Government Agencies

The Bureau established this classification in 1960 for its investigations of prospective employees at the White House, including candidates for positions at all levels from nonprofessionals to such senior staff as the naval aide to the president, the general counsel, and the head of the Office of Management and Budget. Under the authority of a 1961 letter from President John F. Kennedy, the Internal Revenue Service (IRS) provided tax information on applicants. After congressional investigations resulting from alleged misuse of IRS information during the Watergate affair, the IRS told the Bureau only if an applicant owed taxes rather than providing an exact dollar amount. The Tax Reform Act of 1976 required that an applicant provide a waiver identifying the agency to receive the information. In addition to White House applicants, there are files on applicants for the Peace Corps, the Church committee (1974–1975), and the House Select Committee on Assassinations (1976–1977).

The Bureau began this type of investigation even before this classification was established. As early as 1953, it investigated the permanent staffs of the Senate and House Appropriations Committees, the Senate's Armed Services and Foreign Relations Committees, and the Joint Committee on Atomic Energy. The FBI also investigated Gerald Ford and Nelson Rockefeller when each was appointed vice president.

Volume HQ: 15,126 cases. FIELD: Fifty-nine field offices reported opening a total of 115,000 cases.

Dates 1960 to present

Location FBI

NARA Disposition Recommendation HQ: All records—Permanent. FIELD: All records—Destroy.

Access To gain access to the records in this classification a researcher must file a Freedom of Information Act request with the FBI.

Related Records See the Records of the Senate Select Committee on the Study of Intelligence (Church committee), the Records of the House Select Committee on the Study of Intelligence (Pike committee), and the Records of the House Select Committee on Assassinations. All of these records are still in the legal custody of the U.S. Senate and the U.S. House of Representatives.

CLASSIFICATION 162

Interstate Gambling Activities

The Bureau established this classification in 1961 for information on the nature and scope of gambling activities taking place throughout the country. The main purpose of these files was to collect general information for possible use in prosecutions of Federal gambling laws. The files cover subjects such as horse-race wire-service facilities, numbers games, and activities that facilitate the corruption of legitimate gambling institutions. By the late 1960s, FBI headquarters noticed that field offices were opening files in this classification that more properly belonged in those classifications relating to specific gambling statutes, such as Classification 165 Interstate Transmission of Wagering Information, Classification 168 Interstate Transportation of Wagering Paraphernalia, and Classification 182 Illegal Gambling Business. As a result, the Bureau reminded its special agents in charge that only cases on individual gamblers developed as a result of the information-gathering efforts documented in Classification 162 should be opened in Classification 162.

Volume HQ: 3,641 cases. FIELD: Unknown. All fifty-nine field offices reported opening cases. There has been substantial destruction.

Dates 1961 to present

Location FBI

NARA Disposition Recommendation HQ: 5% systematic evidential sample—Permanent; multisectional cases—Permanent; all others—Destroy. FIELD: Multisectional cases—Permanent; all others—Destroy.

Access To gain access to the records in this classification a researcher must file a Freedom of Information Act request with the FBI.

Related Records See FBI Classifications 165 Interstate Transmission of Wagering Information, 168 Interstate Transportation of Wagering Paraphernalia, and 182 Illegal Gambling Business. See also Department of Justice Classifications 123 Anti-Racketeering Act and 164 Interstate Transmission of Wagering Information.

CLASSIFICATION 163

Foreign Police Cooperation

There is little available information concerning this classification since the Bureau deleted most of it from the profile and from the write-ups (see the Introduction for an explanation of FBI profiling procedures). The Bureau established the classification to gather files on FBI investigative procedures that result from a request by a foreign police or intelligence agency. Most of the files include requests for information from Interpol, the International Criminal Police Organization, documents demonstrating Bureau cooperation with foreign governments in locating fugitives, and security checks relating to official foreign visitors to the United States and official U.S. visitors overseas. The Bureau handles these requests carefully because, according to a Hoover memorandum, "the reputation of the Bureau within foreign agencies will be directly affected by the manner in which cooperation cases are handled." The classification contains a case file relating to the 1980 killings of American churchwomen in El Salvador.*

Volume HQ: 49,184 cases. FIELD: 46,678 cases. All field offices and all legal attaché offices reported opening cases. There has been substantial destruction.

Dates This classification remains active.

Location FBI

NARA Disposition Recommendation HQ: Systematic evidential sample—Permanent; multisectional cases—Permanent; all others—Destroy. FIELD: All records—Destroy.

Access To gain access to the records in this classification a researcher must file a Freedom of Information Act request with the FBI.

Related Records See FBI Classification 64 Foreign Miscellaneous, 200–203 Foreign Counterintelligence Matters, 246–248 Foreign Counterintelligence Matters.

CLASSIFICATION 164

Crime Aboard Aircraft

A 1961 law made air piracy, interference with flight crews, and other acts committed aboard airplanes Federal crimes, and the Bureau established this classification in that year for its investigations under the new legislation. Subsequently, the Tokyo, Hague, and Montreal conventions dealt with matters involving the hijacking of international flights. Those conventions were implemented by the United States in the Anti-Hijacking Act of 1974, which gave the Federal Aviation Administration (FAA) exclusive jurisdiction for handling in-flight hijacking matters. In 1979 another law made bringing a concealed weapon onto an airplane a Federal crime.

Within the framework of this legislation, the Bureau negotiated with other concerned agencies for jurisdictional control. In agreements reached with the FAA in 1970 and 1974, the FAA held jurisdiction during flights, while the FBI had primary jurisdiction when the aircraft were at rest on the ground or if an external door were opened. The Bureau was in conflict with the U.S. Marshals Service over jurisdiction as well. U.S. Marshals were stationed in airports and often made arrests and undertook investigations. During the early 1970s the Bureau and the Marshals both placed guards aboard flights. In 1976 the FBI agreed with the Bureau of Alcohol, Tobacco, and Firearms that it would have primary jurisdiction in cases involving the placement of bombs in checked luggage. Typical cases in this classification cover successful and attempted hijackings, the carrying of concealed weapons onto an airplane, interference with flight crews by drunk and disorderly passengers, and bomb threats at airports. There are also case files on D. B. Cooper who in 1971 hijacked a Northwest Orient Boeing 727, parachuted from the airplane with ransom money, and mysteriously disappeared; and one on hijacker Charles Tuller, who led his two sons on a bank robbery spree in the United States before fleeing to Cuba in a hijacked jet in 1975.

Volume HQ: 5,310 cases. FIELD: Fifty-eight field offices reported opening a total of 10,369 cases. There has been substantial destruction.

Dates 1961 to present

Location FBI

NARA Disposition Recommendation HQ: Multisectional cases—Permanent; cases relating to hijacking and attempted hijacking—Permanent; all others—Destroy. FIELD: Cases relating to hijacking and attempted hijacking—Permanent; all others—Destroy.

Access To gain access to the records in this classification a researcher must file a Freedom of Information Act request with the FBI.

Related Records See the Records of the Federal Aviation Administration, Record Group 237, Records of the United States Attorneys and Marshals, Record Group 118, and the General Records of the Bureau of Alcohol, Tobacco, and Firearms, in General Records of the Department of the Treasury, Record Group 56, National Archives.

CLASSIFICATION 165

Interstate Transmission of Wagering Information

In 1966, Congress passed a law making illegal the interstate transmission of wagering information by electronic means other than television and radio. This legislation was part of a continuing national effort to thwart national gambling syndicates and organized crime in the United States. The Bureau established this classification in 1966 for its investigations under this law. During the 1960s, Director Hoover pressed field offices to use this law as part of the FBI's campaign against organized crime, a major activity of the Bureau throughout its history, and investigations of gambling syndicates and attempts to halt the flow of gambling information became a focus of Bureau activity in those years. These cases include evidence of FBI use of electronic surveillance and other special investigative techniques and document the Bureau's cooperation with state and local law enforcement officials.

Volume HQ: 4,401 cases. FIELD: 50,173 cases. There has been substantial destruction.

Dates 1966 to present

Location FBI

NARA Disposition Recommendation HQ: Statistical informational sample of 1,500 cases—Permanent; multisectional cases—Permanent; all others—Destroy. FIELD: Multisectional cases—Permanent; all others—Destroy.

Access To gain access to the records in this classification a researcher must file a Freedom of Information Act request with the FBI.

Related Records See FBI Classifications 162 Interstate Gambling Activities, 168 Interstate Transportation of Wagering Paraphernalia, and 182 Illegal Gambling Business. See also Department of Justice Classifications 123 Anti-Racketeering Act and 164 Interstate Transmission of Wagering Information.

CLASSIFICATION 166

Interstate Transportation in Aid of Racketeering

This classification, established in 1961, includes files on investigations of gambling, prostitution, bribery, extortion, and arson in which interstate transportation or travel took part. The FBI's authority in these areas stems from legislation that gave the Federal government further means of acting against individuals with organized crime connections. The files reflect the Bureau's use of special investigative techniques such as informants and electronic surveillance.

Volume HQ: 7,976 cases. FIELD: Fifty-nine field offices reported opening a total of 80,000 cases. There has been some destruction.

Dates 1961 to present

Location FBI

NARA Disposition Recommendation HQ: Systematic informational sample of 2,500 cases—Permanent; multisectional cases—Permanent; all others—Destroy. FIELD: Multisectional cases—Permanent; all others—Destroy.

Access To gain access to the records in this classification a researcher must file a Freedom of Information Act request with the FBI.

Related Records See FBI Classifications 162 Interstate Gambling Activities, 165 Interstate Transmission of Wagering Information, 168 Interstate Transportation of Wagering Paraphernalia, 182 Illegal Gambling Business, and 183 Racketeer Influenced and Corrupt Organizations. See also Department of Justice Classifications 123 Anti-Racketeering Act, and 164 Interstate Transmission of Wagering Information.

CLASSIFICATION 167

Destruction of Interstate Property

Legislation passed by Congress in 1960 made it illegal to willfully destroy or damage property moving in interstate commerce while that property is under the control of common or contract carriers. The law limits coverage to property traveling by rail, motor vehicle, or airplane. The Bureau established this classification in 1961 for investigations of violations of that law. The Bureau expected that many of its investigations under this classification would be related to labor disputes and strikes. It turned out, however, that most cases involved simple acts of vandalism. The files cover cases such as trucks set on fire, shots fired at trucks and trains, and arson attacks against trucks and trains.

Volume HQ: 866 cases. FIELD: Fifty-eight field offices reported opening a total of 2,920 cases. There has been substantial destruction.

Dates 1961 to present

Location FBI

NARA Disposition Recommendation HQ: 5% systematic evidential sample— Permanent; multisectional cases—Permanent; all others—Destroy. FIELD: All records—Destroy.

Access To gain access to the records in this classification a researcher must file a Freedom of Information Act request with the FBI.

Related Records See Department of Justice Classification 80094 Traffic and Motor Safety.

CLASSIFICATION 168

Interstate Transportation of Wagering Paraphernalia

The Bureau established this classification in 1961 for files resulting from investigations under a law that made it illegal to transport across state lines records, tickets, certificates, bills, slips, tokens, papers, writings, or other paraphernalia designed for use in bookmaking or wagering pools. The law expressly excluded pari-mutuel betting equipment and materials used at race tracks or other sporting events in states with legalized betting. It also excluded newspapers and other publications containing information useful in numbers games.

Most Bureau investigations have been of fairly small gambling operations with some alleged organized crime connection, although some investigations of large operations can also be found in the files, including cases of illegal off-track betting, use of disappearing paper to avoid detection, and gambling organization. Cases include evidence of the use by the Bureau of informants, electronic surveillance, and other special investigative techniques. Earlier FBI investigations of wagering paraphernalia, justified by a statute covering lottery tickets, will be found in Classification 144 Interstate Transportation of Lottery Tickets.

Volume HQ: 1,066 cases. FIELD: Fifty-eight field offices reported opening a total of 23,735 cases.

Dates 1961 to present

Location FBI

NARA Disposition Recommendation HQ: 5% systematic evidential sample— Permanent; multisectional cases—Permanent; all others—Destroy. FIELD: Multisectional cases of five or more sections—Permanent; all others—Destroy.

Access To gain access to the records in this classification a researcher must file a Freedom of Information Act request with the FBI.

Related Records See FBI Classifications 144 Interstate Transportation of Lottery Tickets, 162 Interstate Gambling Activities, 165 Interstate Transmission of Wagering Information, 166 Interstate Transportation in Aid of Racketeering, 182 Illegal Gambling Business, and 183 Racketeer Influenced and Corrupt Organizations. See also Department of Justice Classifications 123 Anti-Racketeering Act, and 164 Interstate Transmission of Wagering Information.

CLASSIFICATION 169

Hydraulic Brake Fluid Act
(Obsolete)

Under the Hydraulic Brake Fluid Act of 1962, the Department of Commerce established standards for hydraulic brake fluid. It subsequently became illegal to transport in interstate commerce fluid that did not meet those standards. The Bureau established this classification in 1963 for investigations of criminal violations of the law and regulations. The Bureau undertook investigations only upon the direction of the Department of Justice, however. The Bureau declared the classification obsolete in 1968.

Volume There are no extant case files in this classification.

Dates This classification opened in 1963 but has been declared obsolete.

Location NA

NARA Disposition Recommendation HQ: NA. FIELD: NA

Access NA

Related Records See the General Records of the Department of Commerce, Record Group 40, National Archives.

CLASSIFICATION 170

Extremist Informants
(Obsolete)

In carrying out its investigations, the Bureau has often resorted to using informants to gather information. The Bureau established this classification in 1964 to gather documentation on policy and control of the recruitment, development, use, and payments of informants in racial groups, hate organizations, extremist organizations, and groups in racial communities. Included in the files were contacts with the Ku Klux Klan (KKK), the Minutemen, anti-Castro groups, the American Nazi party, the National States Rights party, Students for a Democratic Society, the Nation of Islam, the Black Panther party, the Socialist Workers party, the Student Nonviolent Coordinating Committee, the Republic of New Africa, the Black Liberation Alliance, the Weathermen, and the American Indian Movement. This classification also contains files on Martin Luther King, Jr., FBI informer Gary Thomas Rowe, and COINTELPRO activities directed at the KKK and the Black Panthers.

The Bureau's stated objective was to guarantee civil rights and equality under the law during the 1960s, a period of heightened racial tensions, the antiwar movement, and political activities believed to be revolutionary or potentially revolutionary. FBI headquarters tried to maintain strict control on the development, use, and payment of informants in racial and extremist investigations, using the same guidelines as those for the recruitment of security informants. In 1964 the program included 20 actual informants, with another 5,700 potential recruits. This is the only informant classification that used the so-called listening-post concept, under which informants were paid for reports of "continued calm," "no change," "nothing to report," and the like. The Bureau viewed such reports as positive information.

The FBI ceased adding new files to this classification in 1976, although material was added to already existing files as late as 1979. This classification is now obsolete.

Volume HQ: 7,900 cases. FIELD: 33,214 cases. Thirty-seven field offices reported opening cases.

Dates 1964 to 1979

Location FBI

NARA Disposition Recommendation HQ: All records—Permanent. FIELD: All records—Permanent.

Access To gain access to the records in this classification a researcher must file a Freedom of Information Act request with the FBI.

Related Records See FBI Classifications 100 Domestic Security and 105 Foreign Counterintelligence.

CLASSIFICATION 171

Motor Vehicle Seat Belt Act
(Obsolete)

The Bureau established this classification in 1963 for files it opened under the Motor Vehicle Seat Belt Act. Under that law, the Department of Commerce developed minimum standards for safety belts used in motor vehicles. It subsequently became illegal to transport in interstate commerce belts that did not meet those standards. The Bureau undertook investigations of criminal violations of the act only at the direction of the Department of Justice. The Motor Vehicle Safety Act of 1966 repealed the Motor Vehicle Seat Belt Act, and under the newer legislation the FBI no longer had any investigative responsibilities. The Bureau declared this classification obsolete in 1968.

Volume There are no extant case files in this classification.

Dates 1963 to 1966

Location NA

NARA Disposition Recommendation HQ: NA. FIELD: NA

Access NA

Related Records See the General Records of the Department of Commerce, Record Group 40, National Archives.

CLASSIFICATION 172

Sports Bribery

In 1964, Congress passed a law prohibiting bribery of sports officials and participants. Shortly thereafter, the Bureau established this classification. Director Hoover believed that the gambling on and the fixing of sporting events was controlled by organized crime, and, as a result, most files in this classification are connected to gambling on sporting events. While this area is not a major program for the FBI, the Bureau continues to investigate sports gambling and bribery. Files include investigations of horse races, college and professional football games, and professional boxing matches.

Volume HQ: 301 cases. FIELD: 2,000 cases.

Dates 1964 to present

Location FBI

NARA Disposition Recommendation HQ: All records—Permanent. FIELD: Multisectional cases—Permanent; all others—Destroy.

Access To gain access to the records in this classification a researcher must file a Freedom of Information Act request with the FBI.

Related Records See Department of Justice Classification 123 Anti-Racketeering Act.

CLASSIFICATION 173

Civil Rights Act of 1964

The Bureau established this classification in 1964 for investigations of violations under the Civil Rights Act of that year. The Bureau's work under the Civil Rights Act of 1964 focused on discrimination in public accommodations, public facilities, public education, and employment. In 1972 the area of concern was broadened when Congress amended the act to prohibit discrimination on the basis of sex in public educational institutions.

The FBI has generally conducted only preliminary and often perfunctory investigations upon receiving a complaint. Thorough investigations have come only at the request of the Civil Rights Division of the Department of Justice. That office has provided the Bureau with detailed instructions for investigatory procedures that require the forwarding of resulting information to the Department of Justice. The Bureau and Justice at times have found themselves in conflict, differing sharply on various matters of policy such as interpretation of the law on discrimination in employment.

There are case files relating to sex discrimination, racially motivated bomb threats, and racial and religious discrimination by restaurants and other public accommodations, as well as segregation in local jails. There are also case files relating to James Meredith, his efforts in 1961 to attend the University of Mississippi, and the campaign by Governor Ross Barnett to prevent him from matriculating there; the 1975 murder of Charles Parker in Charlotte, North Carolina; and the 1964 murder of three civil-rights workers—Michael Schwerner, Andrew Goodman, and James Chaney—killed near Philadelphia, Mississippi, while on their way to the site of a firebombed church.

Volume HQ: 11,945 cases. FIELD: 20,993 cases. Fifty-seven field offices reported opening cases. There has been substantial destruction.

Dates 1964 to present

Location FBI

NARA Disposition Recommendation HQ: All records—Permanent. FIELD: All records created prior to 1977—Permanent; multisectional cases—Permanent; all others—Destroy.

Access To gain access to the records in this classification a researcher must file a Freedom of Information Act request with the FBI.

Related Records See FBI Classifications 44 Civil Rights and 157 Civil Unrest; however, the records of the Department of Justice are far more extensive in this area. See Department of Justice Classifications 166 Voting Rights—Discrimination and Intimidation, 167 Desegregation of Public Accommodations, 168 Desegregation of Public Facilities, 169 Desegregation of Public Education, 170 Equal Employment Opportunity, 171 Miscellaneous Discrimination Matters, 172 Office of Law Enforcement Assistance, 173 Jury Discrimination, 174 Military Voting Discrimination, and 175 Discrimination in Housing.

CLASSIFICATION 174

Explosives and Incendiary Devices

The Bureau established this classification in 1964 for investigations of bomb threats and bombings. Bureau investigations were authorized under the Importation, Manufacture, Distribution, and Storage of Explosive Materials Act. The FBI shares jurisdiction in this area with the Bureau of Alcohol, Tobacco, and Firearms, and with state and local law enforcement agencies. The FBI handles investigations if the threat or bombing is against a federally owned or leased facility, against a foreign diplomatic establishment, against a college or university, or committed by members of terrorist or revolutionary groups. A large percentage of the cases involve unknown suspects. Most document little or no FBI activity as the cases were referred to local authorities or another Federal agency. In many cases, however, the Bureau provided laboratory assistance to those actually undertaking the investigation. There is a case file relating to the 1970 bombing at the University of Wisconsin, Madison, which killed a physics graduate student, Robert Fassnacht, and led to the arrest of David S. Fine and Karlton and Alan Armstrong, and one relating to the 1976 bombing of the car of former Chilean Ambassador Orlando Letelier and the conviction in 1983 of Michael Vernon Townley for conspiracy in the case.

Volume HQ: 8,854 cases. FIELD: 67,000 cases. All fifty-nine field offices reported opening cases. There has been some destruction.

Dates 1964 to present

Location FBI

NARA Disposition Recommendation HQ: Systematic evidential sample—Permanent; multisectional cases—Permanent; all others—Destroy. FIELD: Multisectional cases—Permanent; all others—Destroy.

Access To gain access to the records in this classification a researcher must file a Freedom of Information Act request with the FBI.

Related Records See state and local records.

CLASSIFICATION 175

Assaulting, Kidnapping, or Killing the President

The Bureau opened this classification in 1965 for its investigations of threats or assaults against the president or vice president. In 1968 the classification was expanded to include the president-elect and the vice president-elect. In 1972 members of Congress and members of Congress-elect were added. The Bureau investigates actual assaults, killings, kidnappings, and conspiracies against the persons covered. The United States Secret Service has jurisdiction over threats. In most cases, the FBI makes a preliminary investigation and then informs the Secret Service, which carries out a full investigation. Many cases are based on citizen reports or cover mentally unstable persons. Case files include information relating to Lynette (Squeaky) Fromme, who attempted to assassinate President Gerald R. Ford, and John W. Hinckley, Jr.,* who shot and wounded President Ronald Reagan.

Volume HQ: 601 cases. FIELD: 6,000 cases.

Dates 1965 to present

Location FBI

NARA Disposition Recommendation HQ: Multisectional cases—Permanent; all cases with eight or more serials except 175–458—Permanent; all others—Destroy. FIELD: Multisectional cases—Permanent; all cases with eight or more serials—Permanent; all others—Destroy.

Access To gain access to the records in this classification a researcher must file a Freedom of Information Act request with the FBI.

Related Records See the Records of the United States Secret Service, Record Group 87, National Archives.

CLASSIFICATION 176

Antiriot Laws

The Bureau established this classification in 1968 for its investigations of violations connected with the antiriot provisions of the Civil Rights Act of that year. The act made it illegal for individuals to cross national or state boundaries in order to participate in any civil disorder and for anyone or any group to teach or demonstrate the use of firearms, explosives, or incendiary devices in order to incite civil disorder. Although state and local authorities held the primary responsibility for prosecution under this act, if the U.S. attorney general determined it was in the public interest, Federal prosecution could be undertaken.

The files richly document the political and social history of the 1960s and 1970s. Of particular interest are the cases concerning the protest demonstrations at the 1968 Democratic Party National Convention in Chicago, during which violent clashes between police and peace demonstrators occurred in the streets. Hoover ordered that a case be opened on every person arrested at the confrontation. There are also case files relating to all the major New Left leaders, including William Kunstler, Rennie Davis, Jerry Rubin, David Dellinger, Tom Hayden, Bobby Seale, Cathlyn Platt Wilkerson, Mark Rudd, Bernadine Dohrn, Abbie Hoffman,* and Clyde Bellecourt. The classification also contains files on the Weathermen, the Black Panthers, Students for a Democratic Society, and many other radical groups. The records document plans by the Weathermen to disrupt the inauguration of Richard M. Nixon as president in 1969 and the trial of the Chicago Seven. In addition, there is a large case file on the 1973 battle at Wounded Knee and one on the American Indian Movement.*

Moreover, the cases in this classification illustrate administrative and jurisdictional disputes between the FBI and the Bureau of Alcohol, Tobacco, and Firearms, as well as various Bureau investigative techniques for gathering information including wiretaps, pretext interviews, informants, local police information, and the uses of its Photo Album Index and Security Index.

Volume HQ: 2,630 cases (93 cu. ft.). FIELD: 7,180 cases. All fifty-nine field offices reported extant cases. Chicago reported the most: 1,716.

Dates 1968 to present

Location FBI

NARA Disposition Recommendation HQ: All records—Permanent. FIELD: All records—Permanent.

Access To gain access to the records in this classification a researcher must file a Freedom of Information Act request with the FBI.

Related Records Department of Justice Classification 144 Civil Rights.

CLASSIFICATION 177

Discrimination in Housing

The Bureau established this classification in 1968 for its investigations involving complaints relating to the fair housing provisions of Title VIII of the Civil Rights Act of that year. In 1974, Congress added sex to race, color, religion, and national origin as categories of discrimination. At first, only federally financed housing came under the Bureau's jurisdiction. By 1969, however, virtually all housing-discrimination cases could be investigated by the FBI. The files are a rich source for researchers interested in American social habits and mores, racial concerns, and general business practices of the period. They document such real estate practices as blockbusting (trying to coerce people of one race to sell their homes by instilling fear that the entire neighborhood will soon be dominated by a different race), redlining (the refusal of mortgage companies to grant mortgages in certain designated neighborhoods), and other, more general patterns of racial discrimination. There are numerous cases of black, white, and Hispanic couples receiving differential treatment when seeking rental apartments and neighborhoods in which to locate. Anti-Semitism is evident, as are examples of harassment and racial hatred. The files also contain information on the Ku Klux Klan, cross burnings, and discrimination charges against major real estate firms both for their hiring and their business practices. The more recent cases provide examples of sex and age discrimination in the housing market.

Volume HQ: 5,680 cases (120 cu. ft.). FIELD: Fifty-nine field offices reported extant cases totaling 8,579. There has been some destruction in the early files.

Dates 1968 to present

Location FBI

NARA Disposition Recommendation HQ: All records—Permanent. FIELD: All records—Permanent.

Access To gain access to the records in this classification a researcher must file a Freedom of Information Act request with the FBI.

Related Records Department of Justice Classifications 175 Discrimination in Housing, 176 Consumer Credit Protection Act, 188 Equal Credit Opportunity Act, and 144 Civil Rights. See also FBI Classifications 44 Civil Rights, 173 Civil Rights Act of 1964, and 189 Equal Credit Opportunity Act.

CLASSIFICATION 178

Interstate Obscene or Harassing Telephone Calls

The Bureau established this classification in 1968 after Congress amended the Communications Act of 1934 to provide criminal penalties for placing obscene or harassing telephone calls in interstate or foreign commerce. The Bureau was reluctant to become involved in most of these cases and encouraged the telephone companies to handle most of the complaints administratively or asked local authorities to investigate. Nevertheless, the Bureau opened a number of cases in this classification. Most involved complaints of obscene phone calls to women, disgruntled employees making harassing calls to former bosses, and domestic disputes such as women calling a former husband's new wife, former husbands calling former mistresses, wives calling asking for reconciliation, or juveniles making crank calls. Most of the cases did not lead to prosecution.

Volume HQ: 297 cases (4.5 cu. ft.). FIELD: All fifty-nine field offices reported extant cases. There has been some destruction.

Dates 1968 to present

Location FBI

NARA Disposition Recommendation HQ: Systematic sample of 20 cases—Permanent; multisectional cases—Permanent; all others—Destroy. FIELD: All records—Destroy.

Access To gain access to the records in this classification a researcher must file a Freedom of Information Act request with the FBI.

Related Records Department of Justice Classification 97 Obscene Literature.

CLASSIFICATION 179

Extortionate Credit Transactions

The Bureau established this classification in 1968 for its investigations involving violations of the 1968 Consumer Credit Protection Act (the Truth in Lending Act), which prohibited extortionate extensions of credit. The cases richly document loan-sharking, extortion practices, and the influence of organized crime in the quick-loan industry. In one group of cases, referred to as the Juice Racket, crime syndicates from New York to Hawaii charged interest rates of 200 to 300 percent on gambling debts. FBI investigations uncovered cab companies acting as front organizations for loan-sharking operations, involvement of corrupt local police in extortion, major betting rings on professional and college football, and corruption in gambling casinos, as well as organized crime connections with major drug suppliers and traffickers. Rich in biographical data, the files detail FBI investigative techniques including the use of body recorders, phone taps, physical and electronic surveillance, informants, and the use of nationwide indexes such as the Top Thief Program. They also illustrate the close working relationship of the Bureau with local police in these matters.

Volume HQ: 2,069 cases (51 cu. ft.). FIELD: Fifty-nine field offices reported opening cases totaling 1,200. There has been some destruction.

Dates 1968 to present

Location FBI

NARA Disposition Recommendation HQ: All pre-1978 records—Permanent; post-1978 systematic informational sample—Permanent; post-1978 multisectional cases—Permanent; all other records—Destroy. FIELD: Pre-1978 multisectional cases—Permanent; post-1978 multisectional cases—Permanent; all other records—Destroy.

Access To gain access to the records in this classification a researcher must file a Freedom of Information Act request with the FBI.

Related Records Department of Justice Classifications 176 Consumer Credit Protection Act and 188 Equal Credit Opportunity Act. See also FBI Classifications 44 Civil Rights, 173 Civil Rights Act of 1964, and 189 Equal Credit Opportunity Act.

CLASSIFICATION 180

Desecration of the Flag

In 1968, at the height of the Vietnam War and peace demonstrations, Congress passed a law making it illegal to burn or desecrate the American flag. The Bureau subsequently established this classification for its investigations involving such activities. Although the Justice Department directed the Bureau to play a rather minor role in such cases—informing state or local officials of violators and providing supporting information—under Hoover's direction Bureau agents often pressed prosecution with great determination. Most cases involved antiwar rallies and the burning of the flag, although the Bureau was faced with such problems as whether or not to pursue protesters if they were merely sitting on the flag or were wearing it on the seat of their pants. The complexity of the entire issue was evident early on when FBI agents were forced to deal with flags used in art displays, in advertising, and for decoration. Despite a subsequent Supreme Court decision regarding flag burning and freedom of speech, the issue remains controversial and the Bureau continues to open new cases.

Volume HQ: 323 cases (6 cu. ft.). FIELD: 1,279 cases. There has been some destruction.

Dates 1968 to present

Location FBI

NARA Disposition Recommendation HQ: Systematic evidential sample of 20 cases—Permanent; multisectional cases—Permanent; all others—Destroy. FIELD: All records—Destroy.

Access To gain access to the records in this classification a researcher must file a Freedom of Information Act request with the FBI.

Related Records Records of the Supreme Court of the United States, Record Group 267, National Archives, and Department of Justice Classification 95 Miscellaneous Criminal Cases.

CLASSIFICATION 181

Consumer Credit Protection Act

The Bureau established this classification in 1968 for its investigations involving banking institutions or credit unions and possible violations of the Truth in Lending Act. Unlike the cases opened in Classification 179, the Bureau sharply restricted cases in this classification. Most cases were handled by other Federal agencies or by state and local officials. The cases opened by the Bureau usually involved a simple complaint against a bank or a credit union for not revealing the true interest rate being charged.

Volume HQ: 46 cases. FIELD: Thirty-two field offices reported a total of 75 cases.

Dates 1968 to present

Location FBI

NARA Disposition Recommendation HQ: All records pre-1978—Destroy; all records post-1978—Disposal not authorized. FIELD: All records—Destroy.

Access To gain access to the records in this classification a researcher must file a Freedom of Information Act request with the FBI.

Related Records Department of Justice Classifications 176 Consumer Credit Protection Act and 188 Equal Credit Opportunity Act. See also FBI Classification 179 Extortionate Credit Transactions, 44 Civil Rights, and 173 Civil Rights Act of 1964.

CLASSIFICATION 182

Illegal Gambling Business

The Bureau established this classification in 1970 for its investigations involving violations of the Organized Crime Control Act of that year. The act authorized the Bureau to conduct investigations into gambling activities which: (1) violated state or local laws, (2) involved five or more persons who financed, managed, supervised, or directed gambling operations, and (3) which were in operation continuously for more than thirty days or had a gross income of $2,000 per day. The act defined gambling as pool selling, bookmaking, slot-machine maintenance, operation of roulette wheels or dice tables, conducting of lotteries or numbers games, or selling chances therein. The statute excluded bingo games and state and local lotteries conducted by tax-exempt institutions. Originally designed to handle cases involving organized crime and its connections to gambling, the classification mostly contains cases relating to small-time bookmakers and sports-betting operations such as football pools, horse racing, and numbers games. The records reflect FBI cooperation with various city strike forces against organized crime and Bureau use of income tax and revenue records and phone company logs, as well as physical and electronic surveillance techniques, in an attempt to control organized crime and its gambling activities.

Volume HQ: 4,385 cases (151.5 cu.ft.). FIELD: All fifty-nine field offices reported extant cases, with Detroit, Chicago, Philadelphia, and New York having the most. There are more than 52,000 cases in the field offices.

Dates 1970 to present

Location FBI

NARA Disposition Recommendation HQ: Systematic evidential sample—Permanent; multisectional cases—Permanent; all others—Destroy. FIELD: Multisectional cases—Permanent; all others—Destroy.

Access To gain access to the records in this classification a researcher must file a Freedom of Information Act request with the FBI.

Related Records Department of Justice Classification 159 Gambling Device Controls. See also FBI Classification 162 Interstate Gambling Activities.

CLASSIFICATION 183

Racketeer-Influenced and Corrupt Organizations

When Congress passed the Organized Crime Control Act of 1970 the Bureau established this classification for its investigations involving violations of the act. The act itself prohibited the acquisition of a legitimate business enterprise with funds derived from illegal activities. It also prohibited the maintenance or control of a business by illegal activity and the use of a business enterprise to conduct an illegal operation. The records are a rich source of information on organized crime activities in the United States. They document organized crime influence over and participation in such activities as gambling, narcotics, pornography, prostitution, and loan-sharking. They illustrate the extent of organized crime influence and control over local unions such as the Longshoremen's Union and the Teamsters Union, the misuse of union pension funds, the ties of organized crime to the waste collection business, and links between the New York garment industry and organized crime activity.

The records also contain information on public corruption, the bribery of local police and elected officials, the connection between Las Vegas gambling casinos and organized crime, the use by organized crime of legitimate businesses to launder drug money, attempts to fix professional boxing, and the smuggling of untaxed cigarettes. They document, as well, FBI and Internal Revenue Service cooperation, FBI sting operations, and FBI investigative techniques. In addition, the records contain some information relating to the government's Witness Protection and Maintenance Program. The FBI heavily sanitized the data collection sheets for this classification, using seventeen separate exemption categories in denying large portions of the NARA Task Force comments.

Volume HQ: 4,464 cases (136.5 cu. ft.). FIELD: Fifty-nine field offices reported opening cases, totaling 35,000. Most of the cases are from the field offices in New York, Detroit, Chicago, Philadelphia, Miami, Newark, Los Angeles, San Francisco, New Haven, and Las Vegas.

Dates 1970 to present

Location FBI

NARA Disposition Recommendation HQ: Systematic informational sample of 1,500 cases—Permanent; multisectional cases—Permanent; all cases with 30 or more serials—Permanent; all others—Destroy. FIELD: Multisectional cases—Permanent; all cases with 30 or more serials—Permanent; all others—Destroy.

Access To gain access to the records in this classification a researcher must file a Freedom of Information Act request with the FBI.

Related Records Department of Justice Classification 123 Anti-Racketeering Act.

CLASSIFICATION 184

Police Killings

In November 1970, President Richard M. Nixon ordered the FBI to provide more assistance to state and local authorities whenever a police officer was killed. In response the Bureau established this classification in June 1971. FBI procedures require the field office to notify headquarters of all police killings regardless of whether FBI assistance is requested by local authorities. The data is then published in the Bureau's Uniform Crime Report publication "Police Killings," which breaks down the statistics by region and by type of killing. The Bureau does not have investigative responsibility over police killings; state and local authorities investigate this type of crime. The FBI's role is limited to providing assistance upon request from state and local officials. In most cases the Bureau is not asked to participate and when asked has provided only nominal support (for example, fingerprint or laboratory reports). Most of the files consist of a report from the field office noting a killing and the FBI's offer of assistance and condolences. When the FBI has become deeply involved, however, the files are substantial. One case, for example, richly documents FBI investigative techniques, relations with local jurisdictions, and attitudes toward state and local law enforcement officials.

Volume HQ: 731 cases (18 cu. ft.). FIELD: 2,900 cases. There has been substantial destruction.

Dates 1971 to present

Location FBI

NARA Disposition Recommendation HQ: 5% systematic evidential sample—Permanent; multisectional cases—Permanent; all others—Destroy. FIELD: All records—Destroy.

Access To gain access to the records in this classification a researcher must file a Freedom of Information Act request with the FBI.

Related Records See state and local police records.

CLASSIFICATION 185

Protection of Foreign Officials and Official Guests

The Bureau established this classification in 1972 for its investigations involving crimes committed against foreign officials or foreign guests that might adversely affect or interfere with the conduct of U.S. foreign relations. Although the Bureau has had final investigative jurisdiction, it has cooperated closely with state and local law enforcement officials, the Secret Service, and the Department of State. As a practical matter the Bureau usually has let local law enforcement officials handle minor crimes such as vandalism, traffic accidents, and robberies.

The cases range from threats against foreign dignitaries attending the funerals of Presidents Truman, Eisenhower, and Johnson, to Jewish Defense League threats and demonstrations against the visit of Egyptian president Anwar Sadat to the United States in 1977 and against the visit of Soviet leader Leonid Brezhnev to New York City in 1978. The records include information on a variety of subjects, including Mohammad Reza Pahlavi, the Shah of Iran, and the occupation of the U.S. embassy in Tehran by radical elements, attacks on the Yugoslavian mission in New York by Croatian nationalists, a takeover of the Liberian embassy by dissidents, threats against the Cuban UN mission, the murder of the Turkish consul general and vice consul by a noted Armenian engineer, an attack in 1974 on the Philippine embassy in Washington, DC, and the famous Letelier case, involving the 1976 bombing of the former Chilean ambassador's car in Washington, DC. There is also a large file on U.S. preparations for, and Bureau involvement in, the 1984 Olympic Games held in Los Angeles.

Volume HQ: 1,480 cases (46.5 cu. ft.). FIELD: Fifty-eight field offices reported extant cases, most in Washington, Los Angeles, San Francisco, and New York.

Dates 1972 to present

Location FBI

NARA Disposition Recommendation HQ: Multisectional cases—Permanent; all others—Destroy. FIELD: Multisectional cases—Permanent; all others—Destroy.

Access To gain access to the records in this classification a researcher must file a Freedom of Information Act request with the FBI.

Related Records Records of the United States Secret Service, Record Group 87, and General Records of the Department of State, Record Group 59, both in the National Archives.

CLASSIFICATION 186

Real Estate Settlement Procedure Act of 1974

In 1974, Congress passed legislation requiring mortgage lenders to disclose all mortgage terms and fees to buyers and prohibiting kickbacks and other unearned fees relating to the mortgage settlement process. The Bureau established this classification in 1975 for its investigations in this area. The Bureau regarded these offenses as minor and routine and opened very few cases in this classification. Most of the extant cases relate to kickback schemes on settlement points and other unwarranted fees charged by lenders.

Volume HQ: 23 cases (1.5 cu. ft.). FIELD: 29 cases

Dates 1975 to present

Location FBI

NARA Disposition Recommendation HQ: Systematic evidential sample—Permanent; all others—Destroy. FIELD: All records—Destroy.

Access To gain access to the records in this classification a researcher must file a Freedom of Information Act request with the FBI.

Related Records Department of Justice Classification 130 Federal Housing Act.

CLASSIFICATION 187

Privacy Act of 1974

The criminal provisions of the Privacy Act of 1974 include penalties for government employees willfully disclosing "individually identifiable information" to any person or agency not entitled to receive it, for government agencies maintaining a system of records without providing for notification in *The Federal Register,* and for a person knowingly and willfully requesting or obtaining any records concerning an individual from an agency under false pretenses. The Bureau established this classification in 1976 for its investigations involving such violations. Most of the cases opened by the Bureau under this classification involve the unauthorized destruction of official records, the release of privacy information without the individual's consent, and the misuse of the Privacy Act to gain business advantage. In one of the cases the Bureau criticized the Department of Justice for publicly releasing documents from a continuing investigation.

Volume HQ: 64 cases (1.5 cu. ft.). FIELD: 230 cases.

Dates 1976 to present

Location FBI

NARA Disposition Recommendation HQ: All records—Permanent. FIELD: All records—Destroy.

Access To gain access to the records in this classification a researcher must file a Freedom of Information Act request with the FBI.

Related Records None

CLASSIFICATION 188

Crime Resistance

The Bureau established this classification in 1976 to document its increased assistance to and cooperation with local law enforcement agencies and private corporations in response to the Omnibus Crime Control and Safe Streets Act of 1968. Prior to this time the Bureau placed such records in Classifications 1 National Academy Matters and 62 Administrative Inquiry (Miscellaneous Subversive and Nonsubversive). Using the field offices, the FBI made a large effort to increase its assistance to and cooperation with local police departments, financial institutions, other government agencies, and private corporations in order to combat increases in crime. It appointed a crime resistance coordinator for each field office and stepped up training at the national academy for local and state police officers. The records document this effort, ranging from a review of the conduct of crime-prevention programs and seminars aimed at auto theft, bank robbery, government fraud, and computer security, to security-check programs at major airports and attempts to reduce escapes at Federal prisons. The records also reflect the Bureau's effort to gain a more favorable press.

Volume HQ: 17 cases (7.5 cu. ft.). FIELD: 402 cases from fifty-three field offices.

Dates 1976 to present

Location FBI

NARA Disposition Recommendation HQ: Multisectional cases—Permanent; all others—Disposal not authorized. FIELD: Multisectional cases—Permanent; all cases with 10 or more serials—Permanent; all others—Destroy.

Access To gain access to the records in this classification a researcher must file a Freedom of Information Act request with the FBI.

Related Records FBI Classifications 1 National Academy Matters and 62 Administrative Inquiry (Miscellaneous Subversive and Nonsubversive).

CLASSIFICATION 189

Equal Credit Opportunity Act

In 1974, Congress passed the Equal Credit Opportunity Act to ensure that mortgage companies, financial institutions, and lending institutions did not discriminate against individuals because of their race, sex, or age. Although the Bureau was reluctant to pursue such investigations it established this classification in 1975 for cases involving possible violations of the act. The records document sex, age, and race discrimination problems throughout the United States for individuals attempting to obtain mortgages and credit cards. Some of the cases involved major department stores and large banks. Most, however, relate to citizen complaints about being unable to obtain credit and a lending institution response that due to the complainant's low-income status the institution was unable to provide it.

Volume HQ: 81 cases (1.5 cu. ft.). FIELD: 402 cases.

Dates 1975 to present

Location FBI

NARA Disposition Recommendation HQ: Disposal not authorized. FIELD: Disposal not authorized.

Access To gain access to the records in this classification a researcher must file a Freedom of Information Act request with the FBI.

Related Records Department of Justice Classification 176 Consumer Credit Protection Act.

CLASSIFICATION 190

Freedom of Information/Privacy Acts

The Bureau established this classification in 1976 to handle citizen requests for information under the Freedom of Information Act (FOIA) of 1966 as amended and the Privacy Act (PA) of 1974, which together provided for expungements of records upon the request of an individual. Prior to the establishment of this classification, the Bureau filed FOIA/PA requests in Classification 62 Administrative Inquiry (Miscellaneous Subversive and Nonsubversive) (case 115530). The early cases in this classification relate to FOIA training conferences held for Bureau employees, the General Accounting Office's study of the impact of the FOIA/PA on government agencies, the use of the FBI reading room, and requests in which the Bureau found no pertinent information. Most of the other cases in this classification relate to individuals' requests for files on themselves, subsequent appeals, and copies of excised and sanitized documents provided. Requestors range from journalists to historians, Congressmen targeted by the Abscam investigations, prisoners, informants, and radicals. Information released by the Bureau under FOIA is available upon request in the FBI reading room. (See Appendix VIII for the proper procedures.) Expungement cases are by law not made public. Although the records in this classification are not unique, the cases often draw together information from several classifications and make research easier.

Volume   HQ: 29,433 cases (802 cu. ft.). FIELD: Fifty-seven field offices reported 10,000 cases.

Dates   1975 to present

Location   FBI

NARA Disposition Recommendation   HQ: Systematic evidential sample (FOIA cases only)—Permanent; cases litigated before the Supreme Court—Permanent; all others—Destroy. FIELD: All records—Destroy.

Access   To gain access to the records in this classification a researcher must file a Freedom of Information Act request with the FBI.

Related Records   See Appendix V for a list of released materials and the related classifications. See also FBI Classification 62 Administrative Inquiry (Miscellaneous Subversive and Nonsubversive).

CLASSIFICATION 191

False Identity Matters
(Obsolete)

The FBI established this classification in 1977 for its investigations involving the use of false identifications. Deputy Attorney General Benjamin Civiletti directed the Bureau to discontinue investigations under this classification the following year, because there was no statutory authority for the program. In fact, the FBI had had a false identity program in place since 1973. The Bureau closed Classification 191 to new cases on November 1, 1978, and terminated all pending cases. Most of the cases opened by the Bureau involved the use of birth certificates of infants who had died in order to create false identifications for individuals. The individuals were in most cases radicals or aliens needing a change in identification. A major ring, for example, was run out of New York by a Weathermen faction. The records also document various FBI sting operations in which agents operated false-document factories. They also reflect FBI procedures in tracking such cases by use of the False Identity List and other investigative techniques.

Volume HQ: 1,191 cases (21 cu. ft.). FIELD: Fifty-eight field offices reported 3,376 cases.

Dates 1977 to 1978

Location FBI

NARA Disposition Recommendation HQ: 5% Systematic evidential sample—Permanent; multisectional cases—Permanent; all others—Destroy. FIELD: Multisectional cases—Permanent; all others—Destroy.

Access To gain access to the records in this classification a researcher must file a Freedom of Information Act request with the FBI.

Related Records FBI Classification 40 Passport and Visa Matters. This classification now contains false identity matters.

CLASSIFICATION 192

Hobbs Act—Financial Institutions, Commercial Institutions

The Bureau established this classification in 1977 for its investigations of extortion attempts involving federally insured financial institutions. Prior to 1977, Bureau investigations of this type were filed under Classification 92

Racketeering Enterprise Investigations. The records primarily relate to extortion attempts involving bomb threats or kidnapping threats against banking executives and their families. Most are isolated individual suspects; however, the files do contain some information on organized crime activities in this area. There is also a case in which an entire city—Ventura, California—was threatened by an extortionist who vowed to place LSD in its water supply unless he was given large sums of money. The extortionist wrote to the FBI demanding a payment of $1 million; otherwise, he claimed, the city would "get high."

Volume HQ: 581 cases (9 cu. ft.). FIELD: All fifty-nine field offices reported opening cases, totaling 2,048.

Dates 1977 to present

Location FBI

NARA Disposition Recommendation HQ: Multisectional cases—Permanent; all other records—Disposal not authorized. FIELD: All records—Disposal not authorized.

Access To gain access to the records in this classification a researcher must file a Freedom of Information Act request with the FBI.

Related Records FBI Classification 92 Racketeering Enterprise Investigations and Department of Justice Classifications 123 Anti-Racketeering Act and 84 Extortion and Blackmail.

CLASSIFICATION 193

Hobbs Act—Commercial Institutions

The Bureau established this classification in 1977 when it subdivided Classification 92 Racketeering Enterprise Investigations into specific criminal areas. Investigations in this classification are based on the obstruction of interstate commerce by robbery and extortion activities involving commercial establishments including restaurants and small businesses. The cases in this classification are rather eclectic. There are many cases relating to bomb threats, including threats against nuclear reactors, the hijacking of a Greyhound bus, skyjacking threats including one by a Cuban who wanted to return to Cuba (when the FBI refused to arrest him he argued that he was a spy and therefore must be returned to Cuba), bomb threats by former employees against the J. P. Stevens Company, and bomb threats against various schools.

Volume HQ: 347 cases (9 cu. ft.). FIELD: 922 cases, with New York opening the greatest number.

Dates 1977 to present

Location FBI

NARA Disposition Recommendation HQ: All records—Disposal not authorized. FIELD: All records—Disposal not authorized.

Access To gain access to the records in this classification a researcher must file a Freedom of Information Act request with the FBI.

Related Records FBI Classifications 92 Racketeering Enterprise Investigations and 192 Hobbs Act—Financial Institutions, Commercial Institutions. See also Department of Justice Classifications 84 Extortion and Blackmail and 123 Anti-Racketeering Act.

CLASSIFICATION 194

Hobbs Act—Corruption of Public Officials

The Bureau established this classification in 1977 when investigations of several Hobbs Act violations were separated from Classification 92 Racketeering Enterprise Investigations. Under this classification the Bureau has investigated public officials suspected of engaging in illegal acts that obstructed interstate commerce. Most of the cases have involved minor public officials and kickback schemes. The Bureau has required quarterly reports from its field offices on all activity in this classification. The cases, in general, involve such offices as local planning commissions, state boards of pardons and paroles, state licensing agencies, and various regulatory agencies including the Department of Energy and the Nuclear Regulatory Commission.

Volume HQ: 2,024 cases. FIELD: Fifty-eight field offices reported opening a total of 6,010 cases.

Dates 1977 to present

Location FBI

NARA Disposition Recommendation HQ: All records—Disposal not authorized. FIELD: All records—Disposal not authorized.

Access To gain access to the records in this classification a researcher must file a Freedom of Information Act request with the FBI.

Related Records Department of Justice Classifications 84 Extortion and Blackmail and 123 Anti-Racketeering Act. See also FBI Classification 92 Racketeering Enterprise Investigations.

CLASSIFICATION 195

Hobbs Act—Labor Related

The Bureau established this classification in 1977 when it divided several of the Hobbs Act violations into classifications separate from Classification 92 Racketeering Enterprise Investigations. Most of these cases opened by the Bureau relate to union violence in strikes, union election fraud, the misuse of union pension funds, and threats against nonunion workers. Although small in size, the classification is a good source for research into union activities in the United States.

Volume HQ: 203 cases (3 cu. ft.). FIELD: All fifty-nine field offices reported opening cases, totaling 976.

Dates 1977 to present

Location FBI

NARA Disposition Recommendation HQ: All cases with 10 or more serials— Permanent; all others—Destroy. FIELD: All records—Destroy.

Access To gain access to the records in this classification a researcher must file a Freedom of Information Act request with the FBI.

Related Records Department of Justice Classifications 16 Strikes, 123 Anti-Racketeering Act, 139 Interstate Transportation of Strike Breakers, 134 National Labor Relations Act, and 143 Fair Labor Standards Act. See also FBI Classification 92 Racketeering Enterprise Investigations.

CLASSIFICATION 196

Fraud by Wire

In 1977, when the Bureau subdivided Classification 87 Interstate Transportation of Stolen Property, it established this classification for Bureau investigations involving fraud by telephone, telegraph, shortwave, or microwave transmission. Most of the cases relate to attempts by individuals to defraud people in land-speculation schemes, investment opportunities in stocks and commodities, and credit-card fraud (the fastest growing segment of the file). In addition, there are cases relating to organized crime and its attempts to launder money from Las Vegas gambling casinos, a fraudulent scheme involving the sale of reservations and tickets to the 1984 Olympic Games in Los Angeles, and a major international scam involving the ship-building industry and bribes and kickbacks to foreign government officials. The records reflect the Bureau's growing concern and focus on white-collar crimes in the late 1970s and early 1980s, including an investigation of E. F. Hutton and Company Inc. for check kiting.

Volume HQ: 1,951 cases. FIELD: All fifty-nine field offices reported opening cases, totaling 32,606.

Dates 1977 to present

Location FBI

NARA Disposition Recommendation HQ: All records—Disposal not authorized. FIELD: All records—Disposal not authorized.

Access To gain access to the records in this classification a researcher must file a Freedom of Information Act request with the FBI.

Related Records FBI Classification 87 Interstate Transportation of Stolen Property, and Department of Justice Classifications 36 Mails to Defraud, 82 Communications Act, and 184 Insurance Fraud.

CLASSIFICATION 197

Civil Actions or Claims against the Government

The Bureau established this classification in 1977 to document its responses to civil cases brought against it under the Federal Tort Claims Act. Claims under this act involved allegations of negligence or wrongdoing on the part of FBI personnel or claims for damages, injury, or property loss through FBI actions. Most of the cases concern claims relating to automobile accidents involving FBI vehicles, Freedom of Information Act (FOIA) suits filed by persons seeking access to FBI records, suits by prisoners alleging improper FBI actions in their arrest, and suits by individuals or organizations alleging infringement of rights during FBI security investigations and operations such as COINTELPRO.

Prior to 1977 the Bureau filed civil actions and claims under Classification 62 Administrative Inquiry (Miscellaneous Subversive and Nonsubversive). Suits arising from FOIA requests were filed with the request in Classification 192 Hobbs Act—Financial Institutions, Commercial Institutions. Claims involving

FBI vehicles were filed in Classification 66 Administrative Matters. The claims in this classification vary widely. For example, the Avis Rental Car Company sought damages from the Bureau when an agent damaged a car in an accident. Individuals and groups such as James Earl Ray, Eldridge Cleaver, the Chicago Seven, the National Security Archive, and the Black Panthers have all sought the release of documents under the FOIA and brought suit against the Bureau for the release of additional information.

Other cases relate to individuals arrested in drug-related cases who have sought the return of vehicles seized by FBI agents. The Church of Scientology filed suit against the Bureau when agents raided its headquarters and seized its records. Victims of FBI sting operations have filed suits against the Bureau charging entrapment and false arrest. In an unusual case, prompted when the Bureau sought to recover government expenses incurred in returning more than nine hundred bodies to the United States from Guyana after the Jonestown massacre, surviving church members filed a suit requesting all documents held by the Bureau relating to its activities.

Volume   HQ: 2,409 cases (115.5 cu. ft.). FIELD: Fifty-nine field offices reported opening cases, totaling 2,736. There has been some destruction.

Dates 1977 to present

Location FBI

NARA Disposition Recommendation   HQ: Systematic evidential sample—Permanent; multisectional cases of 5 or more sections—Permanent; all others—Destroy. FIELD: All records—Destroy.

Access To gain access to the records in this classification a researcher must file a Freedom of Information Act request with the FBI.

Related Records Records of the District Courts of the United States, Record Group 21, National Archives. Department of Justice Classification 78 Tucker Act (Claims against the United States), and FBI Classifications 62 Administrative Inquiry (Miscellaneous Subversive and Nonsubversive), 66 Administrative Matters, and 192 Hobbs Act—Financial Institutions, Commercial Institutions.

CLASSIFICATION 198

Crime on Indian Reservation

The Bureau established this classification in 1977 for its investigations of crimes on Indian reservations. Specific crimes investigated by the Bureau under this classification include those committed by one Indian against another; the inducement of conveyances from Indians of trust interests in land; embezzlement and theft of the property of an Indian tribal organization; the destruction of boundary and warning signs on an Indian reservation; illegal hunting, trapping, or fishing on Indian lands; and the misrepresentation of Indian products for sale to the public.

Except as otherwise provided by law, in general the laws of the United States extend to Indian reservations, and so the Bureau acted accordingly in undertaking investigations on Indian lands. Prior to 1977 the Bureau filed cases relating to Indian reservations under Classification 70 Crime on Government Reservation. It established this separate classification in response to growing congressional interest in Indian affairs following the 1973 occupation of Wounded Knee, South Dakota. In 1980, in a memorandum of understanding between the Bureau and the Department of the Interior, the FBI's role in civil disturbances on reservations was sharply restricted. Henceforth, the Bureau would begin its investigations only after order had been restored on the reservation.

Most of the cases opened by the Bureau have involved general criminal activity on the reservations, such as burglary, assault, rape, and murder. Taken as a whole, the records reflect racial friction and tensions, tribal rivalries, and the FBI's work with Native American police and tribal authorities.

Volume HQ: 1,843 cases (21.5 cu. ft.). FIELD: Fifty-eight field offices reported opening 8,465 cases (218 cu. ft.).

Dates 1977 to present

Location FBI

NARA Disposition Recommendation HQ: Systematic informational sample—Permanent; multisectional cases—Permanent; all others—Destroy. FIELD: All records—Destroy.

Access To gain access to the records in this classification a researcher must file a Freedom of Information Act request with the FBI.

Related Records Records of the Bureau of Indian Affairs, Record Group 75, National Archives, and Department of Justice Classification 180 Indian Bill of Rights. See also FBI Classification 70 Crime on Government Reservation.

CLASSIFICATION 199

Foreign Counterintelligence—Terrorism

In general terms, the Bureau established this classification for its investigations of terrorist activities in the United States—primarily bombings, kidnappings, and the importation of weapons and explosives by suspected terrorist groups. The FBI, however, is understandably sensitive about releasing information relating to its investigative activities in this area. It removed the entire NARA Historical Synopsis from the Task Force report and rendered the data collection sheets for the cases in this classification virtually useless by deleting nearly everything of any substance from them.

Nevertheless, some information relating to this classification is available. For example, there is a file relating to David S. Fine and the bombing of the physics building at the University of Wisconsin that killed a graduate student during the anti-Vietnam War period. The files also detail FBI methods in developing intelligence sources and informants, its modern electronic surveillance techniques, and its close working relationships with foreign police and intelligence organizations. It has targeted mostly foreign nationals for attention, including Communists, Mideast groups, the Irish Republican Army, and black militants.

There is also a large case file relating to the Committee in Solidarity with the People of El Salvador (CISPES).*

Volume HQ: 3,618 cases (40.5 cu. ft.). FIELD: All fifty-nine field offices reported opening cases, totaling 13,572.

Dates Open

Location FBI

NARA Disposition Recommendation HQ: Systematic informational sample— Permanent; multisectional cases—Permanent; all cases with 20 or more serials—Permanent; all others—Destroy. FIELD: Multisectional cases— Permanent; all cases with 20 or more serials—Permanent; all others—Destroy.

Access To gain access to the records in this classification a researcher must file a Freedom of Information Act request with the FBI.

Related Records FBI Classifications 100 Domestic Security, 105 Foreign Counterintelligence, and 200–203 Foreign Counterintelligence Matters. See also Department of Justice Classification 13 National Defense Act and 146 World War II (Internal Security).

CLASSIFICATION 200

Foreign Counterintelligence—People's Republic of China

The Bureau is understandably sensitive about releasing information relating to its investigative activities in this area. It withheld from release for national security reasons the NARA Historical Synopsis from the Task Force report and all of the data collection sheets. There is, however, some information available relating to this classification.

200A—Official Representatives
200B—Diplomatic Establishments
200C—Nonimmigrant: Students
200D—Nonimmigrant: Visitors, Commercial, Cultural, Scientific, Technical
200E—Shipping Matters
200F—Nonimmigrant: Visitors, Tourists
200G—Immigrants, Refugees, Repatriates
200H—Contact Cases/Miscellaneous
200I—Republic of China

CLASSIFICATION 201

Foreign Counterintelligence—Satellites

The Bureau is understandably sensitive about releasing information relating to its investigative activities in this area. It withheld from release for national security reasons the NARA Historical Synopsis from the Task Force report and all of the data collection sheets. There is, however, some information available relating to this classification.

200A—Official Representatives
200B—Diplomatic Establishments
200C—Nonimmigrant: Students
200D—Nonimmigrant: Visitors, Commercial, Cultural, Scientific, Technical
200E—Shipping Matters
200F—Nonimmigrant: Visitors, Tourists
200G—Immigrants, Refugees, Repatriates
200H—Contact Cases/Miscellaneous

CLASSIFICATION 202

Foreign Counterintelligence—Cuba

The Bureau is understandably sensitive about releasing information relating to its investigative activities in this area. It withheld from release for national security reasons the NARA Historical Synopsis from the Task Force report and all of the data collection sheets. There is, however, some information available relating to this classification.

200A—Official Representatives
200B—Diplomatic Establishments
200C—Nonimmigrant: Students
200D—Nonimmigrant: Visitors, Commercial, Cultural, Scientific, Technical
200E—Shipping Matters
200F—Nonimmigrant: Visitors, Tourists
200G—Immigrants, Refugees, Repatriates
200H—Contact Cases/Miscellaneous

CLASSIFICATION 203

Foreign Counterintelligence—All Other Countries

The Bureau is understandably sensitive about releasing information relating to its investigative activities in this area. It withheld from release for national security reasons the NARA Historical Synopsis from the Task Force report and all of the data collection sheets. There is, however, some information available relating to this classification.

200A—Official Representatives
200B—Diplomatic Establishments
200C—Nonimmigrant: Students
200D—Nonimmigrant: Visitors, Commercial, Cultural, Scientific, Technical
200E—Shipping Matters
200F—Nonimmigrant: Visitors, Tourists
200G—Immigrants, Refugees, Repatriates
200H—Contact Cases/Miscellaneous

CLASSIFICATION 204

Federal Revenue Sharing

The Bureau established this classification in 1977 for its investigations involving civil-rights violations of a variety of Federal revenue-sharing acts, such as the State and Local Assistance Act (1972), the Crime Control Act (1976), the

Comprehensive Employment and Training Act (1973), the Housing and Community Development Act (1971), and the Railroad Revitalization Act (1976). Violations investigated by the Bureau have included discrimination in hiring practices based on age, sex, religion, and physical handicaps and complaints by the handicapped concerning access to public buildings. The FBI's Special Investigative Division of the Civil Rights Section conducted all investigations in this classification.

Volume HQ: 14 cases (1.5 cu. ft.). FIELD: 30 cases.

Dates 1977 to present

Location FBI

NARA Disposition Recommendation HQ: All records—Disposal not authorized. FIELD: All records—Disposal not authorized.

Access To gain access to the records in this classification a researcher must file a Freedom of Information Act request with the FBI.

Related Records Department of Justice Classification 144 Civil Rights.

CLASSIFICATION 205

Foreign Corrupt Practices Act of 1977

When Congress passed the Foreign Corrupt Practices Act, which prohibited American corporations or individuals from making payments to foreign government officials, political parties, or political candidates for the purpose of obtaining foreign business, the Bureau established this classification for its investigations in this area. The Bureau shares investigative responsibility with the Securities and Exchange Commission in most cases and works very closely with the U.S. Customs Service on investigations. The law itself requires that the U.S. intelligence community report annually to Congress concerning such activities of U.S. businesses abroad. Although most of the cases involve minor kickback and bribery attempts, there are cases relating to major U.S. companies, the U.S. Import/Export Bank, and the Agency for International Development. The cases range from the short-weighting of grain shipments to the Soviet Union and the sale of military hardware in the Middle East, to attempts to break into the telecommunications market in Asia and the sale of truck parts in Mexico.

Volume HQ: 37 cases (1.5 cu. ft.). FIELD: 60 cases.

Dates 1977 to present

Location　FBI

NARA Disposition Recommendation　HQ: Multisectional cases—Permanent; all cases with more than 20 serials—Permanent; all others—Destroy. FIELD: Multisectional cases—Permanent; all cases with 20 or more serials—Permanent; all others—Destroy.

Access　To gain access to the records in this classification a researcher must file a Freedom of Information Act request with the FBI.

Related Records　Records of the Import-Export Bank of the United States, Record Group 275, Records of the Bureau of Customs, Record Group 36, Records of the Securities and Exchange Commission, Record Group 266, and Records of the Agency for International Development, Record Group 286, all in the National Archives. See also Department of Justice Classification 193 Foreign Corrupt Practices Act.

CLASSIFICATION 206

Fraud against the Government—Department of Defense

The Bureau established this classification in 1978 for its investigations involving fraud charges relating to the Department of Defense. Prior to 1978 all government fraud cases were filed in Classification 46 Fraud against the Government, regardless of the agency involved. The records contain a wide variety of cases, ranging from minor crimes such as a divorcee continuing to use the military commissary and post exchange, to false travel and expense statements, fraudulent leave statements, and massive fraud charges in major weapons procurement contracts and construction projects. The major defense contractors are all represented here, including Lockheed Corporation, Northrop Corporation, General Dynamics Corporation, and General Electric Company. The records document business-government relations and interagency cooperation in fraud investigations.

Volume　HQ: 627 cases (6 cu.ft.). FIELD: Fifty-eight field offices reported opening 928 cases.

Dates　1978 to present

Location　FBI

NARA Disposition Recommendation　HQ: Systematic evidential sample—Permanent; multisectional cases—Permanent; all others—Destroy. FIELD: All records—Destroy.

Access To gain access to the records in this classification a researcher must file a Freedom of Information Act request with the FBI.

Related Records Records of the Office of the Secretary of Defense, Record Group 330, National Archives, and Department of Justice Classification 46 Fraud against the Government. See also FBI Classification 46 Fraud against the Government.

CLASSIFICATION 207

Fraud against the Government—Environmental Protection Agency, Department of Energy, National Aeronautics and Space Administration, and Department of Transportation

The Bureau established this classification in 1978 for its investigations involving fraud charges relating to the Environmental Protection Agency (EPA). Prior to 1978 the Bureau filed all government fraud cases in Classification 46 Fraud against the Government, regardless of the agency involved. At first, this classification contained only EPA cases; in 1979, however, the Bureau added Department of Energy and National Aeronautics and Space Administration (NASA) cases. In 1980 it added Department of Transportation (DOT) cases. The classification as presently constituted contains a wide variety of fraud cases involving these agencies. For example, EPA cases most often relate to overbilling of charges on contracts, false statements on gasoline ratings by the oil companies, illegal deposits of toxic waste materials in landfills, or false reports on water samples. NASA cases involve kickbacks, charges of sexual favors being exchanged for the awarding of contracts, and improper expense charges. In one case a company attempted to charge NASA $900,000 for travel expenses. After investigation the Bureau found that the company had included the purchase of an ocean-front condo in Ocean City, Maryland, a BMW automobile, clothes, and vacation trips in its expenses for a NASA equipment contract. DOT cases tend to focus on substandard materials being used by contractors in highway and sewer projects, kickback schemes, and false training reports being filed with the government.

Volume HQ: 103 cases (1.5 cu.ft.). FIELD: Fifty-five field offices reported opening 227 cases.

Dates 1978 to present

Location FBI

NARA Disposition Recommendation HQ: All records—Disposal not authorized. FIELD: All records—Disposal not authorized.

Access To gain access to the records in this classification a researcher must file a Freedom of Information Act request with the FBI.

Related Records Records of the Environmental Protection Agency, Record Group 412, Records of the Department of Energy, Record Group 434, Records of the National Aeronautics and Space Administration, Record Group 255, and the General Records of the Department of Transportation, Record Group 398, all in the National Archives, and Department of Justice Classification 46 Fraud against the Government. See also FBI Classification 46 Fraud against the Government.

CLASSIFICATION 208

Fraud against the Government—General Services Administration

The Bureau established this classification in 1978 for its investigations involving fraud charges relating to the General Services Administration (GSA). Prior to 1978 the Bureau filed all government fraud cases in Classification 46 Fraud against the Government, regardless of the agency involved. Most of the cases in this classification relate to GSA-awarded contracts for construction of Federal buildings, services, and supplies. The cases involve kickback and graft schemes, embezzlement, and the misuse of government funds. A series of GSA scandals in the 1970s resulted in the Department of Justice establishing a special GSA Task Force. By far the most prominent field office in this classification is the Washington office, which opened more than 113 cases in less than one year.

Volume HQ: 116 cases (1.5 cu. ft.). FIELD: Fifty-six field offices reported opening 422 cases, with Washington accounting for the greatest number.

Dates 1978 to present

Location FBI

NARA Disposition Recommendation HQ: All records—Disposal not authorized. FIELD: All records—Disposal not authorized.

Access To gain access to the records in this classification a researcher must file a Freedom of Information Act request with the FBI.

Related Records General Records of the General Services Administration, Record Group 269, National Archives, Department of Justice Classification 46 Fraud against the Government, and FBI Classification 46 Fraud against the Government.

CLASSIFICATION 209

Fraud against the Government—Department of Health and Human Services

The Bureau established this classification in 1978 for its investigations of fraud involving the Department of Health, Education, and Welfare (HEW). Prior to 1978 the Bureau maintained all fraud cases in Classification 46 Fraud against the Government. After Congress created a separate Department of Education in 1980 the Bureau redesignated Classification 209 for fraud cases involving the new Department of Health and Human Services (HHS). At the same time it established Classification 213 for fraud cases involving the Department of Education. Most of the cases in this classification relate to false claims for benefits, counterfeit social security cards, and kickback or bribery schemes for grant monies. The Bureau shares investigative responsibility with the HHS. Most of the cases simply document minor criminal offenses which the Department of Justice showed little interest in prosecuting.

Volume HQ: 773 cases (10.5 cu.ft.). FIELD: 3,208 cases. There has been some destruction.

Dates 1978 to present

Location FBI

NARA Disposition Recommendation HQ: Systematic informational sample—Permanent; multisectional cases—Permanent; all others—Destroy. FIELD: All records—Destroy.

Access To gain access to the records in this classification a researcher must file a Freedom of Information Act request with the FBI.

Related Records Records of the Department of Health and Human Services, Record Group 468, National Archives. Records of the Department of Health, Education, and Welfare, Record Group 235, National Archives. See also Department of Justice Classification 46 Fraud against the Government and FBI Classification 46 Fraud against the Government.

CLASSIFICATION 210

Fraud against the Government—Department of Labor

The Bureau established this classification in 1978 when it divided Classification 46 Fraud against the Government into several separate classifications for specific agencies or groups of agencies. Prior to 1978 the Bureau placed all such cases in Classification 46, regardless of the agency involved. Most of the Bureau investigations in this classification relate to alleged misuse of Comprehensive Employment and Training Act funds or unemployment benefits. Monies were, for example, paid to individuals who were not in training or retraining programs; in other cases, individuals received unemployment benefits to which they were not entitled. There is some information relating to the Occupational Safety and Health Administration.

Volume HQ: 782 cases. FIELD: Fifty-six field offices reported 2,250 cases.

Dates 1978 to present

Location FBI

NARA Disposition Recommendation HQ: Systematic informational sample— Permanent; multisectional cases—Permanent; all others—Destroy. FIELD: All records—Destroy.

Access To gain access to the records in this classification a researcher must file a Freedom of Information Act request with the FBI.

Related Records General Records of the Department of Labor, Record Group 174, National Archives, and Department of Justice Classification 46 Fraud against the Government. See also FBI Classification 46 Fraud against the Government.

CLASSIFICATION 211

Ethics in Government Act of 1978

In 1978, in the wake of the Watergate affair, Congress passed the Ethics in Government Act, which provided for the automatic appointment of a special prosecutor to investigate allegations of crimes by the president, the vice president, cabinet officers, and other high-ranking government officials. The Bureau established this classification for its investigations in this area. Under the act, the FBI must report to the attorney general within twenty-four hours any charges it receives that are based on specific information. At the attorney general's discretion, the Bureau then conducts a preliminary investigation within ninety days. If a special prosecutor is appointed, the FBI provides support at the prosecutor's direction. Since the role of the Bureau depends upon the needs and directions of each special prosecutor, no standard role for the Bureau is prescribed. There is a case file relating to Abscam and Congressman John Jenrette (D., South Carolina).

Volume HQ: 1 case (as of 1981). FIELD: 4 cases (as of 1981).

Dates 1978 to present

Location FBI

NARA Disposition Recommendation HQ: All records—Permanent. FIELD: All records—Permanent.

Access To gain access to the records in this classification a researcher must file a Freedom of Information Act request with the FBI.

Related Records See Department of Justice Classification 186 Public Integrity.

CLASSIFICATION 212

Foreign Counterintelligence—Intelligence Community Support

The Bureau is understandably sensitive about releasing information relating to its investigative activities in this area. It withheld from release for national security reasons the NARA Historical Synopsis from the Task Force report and all of the data collection sheets. There is, however, some information available relating to this classification.

The FBI established this classification for files relating to its support to other intelligence agencies of the U.S. government. These files document interagency cooperation on sensitive intelligence matters and contain information on the struggle for influence among these very same agencies, including the Department of State, the Central Intelligence Agency, the Defense Intelligence Agency, the National Security Agency, the Secret Service, the Department of Defense, and the Treasury Department. Some cases from Classification 105 Foreign Counterintelligence have been reclassified here.

Volume HQ: 50 cases. FIELD: 351 cases.

Dates Post-1977 to present

Location FBI

NARA Disposition Recommendation HQ: All records—Permanent. FIELD: All records—Permanent.

Access To gain access to the records in this classification a researcher must file a Freedom of Information Act request with the FBI.

Related Records Information relating to intelligence matters and the intelligence community is fragmented and scattered. See the General Records of the

Department of State, Record Group 59; the Records of the Central Intelligence Agency, Record Group 263; the Records of the National Security Agency, Record Group 457; Records of the Defense Intelligence Agency, Record Group 373; General Records of the Department of the Treasury, Record Group 56; Records of the Office of the Secretary of Defense, Record Group 330; and the Records of the United States Secret Service, Record Group 87; all in the National Archives. A good source for reviewing the workings of the intelligence community is the records released by the Church committee. See the U.S. Congress, Senate Select Committee to Study Government Operations with Respect to Intelligence Activities (Church committee), *Final Report*, 7 vols., 94th Cong., 2d Sess., 1976, Report 94–755.

CLASSIFICATION 213

Fraud against the Government—Department of Education

The Bureau established this classification in 1980 for files that relate to its investigations involving the newly created Department of Education. Investigations dating from the years 1978 to 1980 and involving education programs of the U.S. government will be found in Classification 209 Fraud against the Government—Department of Health, Education, and Welfare. Files covering investigations before 1978 will be found in Classification 46 Fraud against the Government. These laws prohibiting fraud are intended to protect the U.S. government from interference with its lawful functions, including pecuniary loss and misrepresentation to defeat governmental activities. The files cover such minor violations as defaults on student loans, false statements on loan applications, and embezzlement.

Volume HQ: 33 cases. FIELD: 153 cases.

Dates 1980 to present

Location FBI

NARA Disposition Recommendation HQ: All records—Disposal not authorized. FIELD: All records—Disposal not authorized.

Access To gain access to the records in this classification a researcher must file a Freedom of Information Act request with the FBI.

Related Records See FBI Classifications 46 Fraud Against the Government and 209 Fraud against the Government—Department of Health and Human Services. See also the Records of the Department of Education, Record Group

441, and the Records of the Department of Health, Education, and Welfare, Record Group 235, National Archives.

CLASSIFICATION 214

Civil Rights of Institutionalized Persons Act

The Bureau established this classification in 1980 to gather Bureau files relating to investigations of allegations that institutionalized persons were being systematically deprived of their constitutional rights. The definition of an institution included mental hospitals, retardation facilities, jails, prisons, certain types of nursing homes, and juvenile detention centers. The Bureau undertook investigations only upon receipt of a written request from the assistant attorney general in charge of the Civil Rights Division of the Department of Justice. If the field offices receive information from the public, they are expected to obtain details and send a letterhead memorandum to FBI headquarters for referral to the Department of Justice. The Civil Rights Division then determines if further investigation is called for. The files include investigations of allegations of mistreatment of patients at a state hospital and a suit brought by inmates at Attica prison against the correctional facility. They also contain information relating to advocacy groups such as the Legal Assistance Program, Mental Health Association, and parents' associations.

Volume HQ: 25 cases. FIELD: 20 cases.

Dates 1980 to present

Location FBI

NARA Disposition Recommendation HQ: All records—Disposal not authorized. FIELD: All records—Disposal not authorized.

Access To gain access to the records in this classification a researcher must file a Freedom of Information Act request with the FBI.

Related Records See state and local records.

CLASSIFICATIONS 215–229

Foreign Counterintelligence Matters

The Bureau is understandably sensitive about releasing information relating to its investigative activities in this area. It withheld from release for national security reasons the NARA Historical Synopsis from the Task Force report and all of the data collection sheets relating to these matters.

CLASSIFICATION 230

Training Received—Foreign Counterintelligence

The Bureau established this classification in 1982 in order to provide better statistical and supervisory control for its training programs in the foreign intelligence area. Prior to 1982 the Bureau reported all training under Classification 1 National Academy Matters.

Volume HQ: No cases. FIELD: NA

Dates 1982 to present

Location FBI

NARA Disposition Recommendations HQ: 00 file—Permanent. No other records. FIELD: 00 file—Permanent. No other records.

Access To gain access to the records in this classification a researcher must file a Freedom of Information Act request with the FBI.

Related Records FBI Classification 1 National Academy Matters.

CLASSIFICATION 231

Training Received—Organized Crime

The Bureau established this classification in 1982 in order to provide better statistical and supervisory control for its training programs in the organized crime area. Prior to 1982 the Bureau reported all training under Classification 1 National Academy Matters.

Volume HQ: No cases. FIELD: NA

Dates 1982 to present

Location FBI

NARA Disposition Recommendations HQ: 00 file—Permanent. No other records. FIELD: 00 file—Permanent. No other records.

Access To gain access to the records in this classification a researcher must file a Freedom of Information Act request with the FBI.

Related Records FBI Classification 1 National Academy Matters.

CLASSIFICATION 232

Training Received—White-Collar Crime

The Bureau established this classification in 1982 in order to provide better statistical and supervisory control for its training programs in the white-collar crime area. Prior to 1982 the Bureau reported all training under Classification 1 National Academy Matters.

Volume HQ: No cases. FIELD: NA

Dates 1982 to present

Location FBI

NARA Disposition Recommendations HQ: 00 file—Permanent. No other records. FIELD: 00 file—Permanent. No other records.

Access To gain access to the records in this classification a researcher must file a Freedom of Information Act request with the FBI.

Related Records FBI Classification 1 National Academy Matters.

CLASSIFICATION 233

Training Received—Antitrust and Civil Matters

The Bureau established this classification in 1982 in order to provide better statistical and supervisory control for its training programs in the antitrust and civil matters area. Prior to 1982 the Bureau reported all training under Classification 1 National Academy Matters.

Volume HQ: No cases. FIELD: NA

Dates 1982 to present

Location FBI

NARA Disposition Recommendations HQ: 00 file—Permanent. No other records. FIELD: 00 file—Permanent. No other records.

Access To gain access to the records in this classification a researcher must file a Freedom of Information Act request with the FBI.

Related Records FBI Classification 1 National Academy Matters.

CLASSIFICATION 234

Training Received—Civil Rights

The Bureau established this classification in 1982 in order to provide better statistical and supervisory control for its training programs in civil rights matters. Prior to 1982 the Bureau reported all training under Classification 1 National Academy Matters.

Volume HQ: No cases. FIELD: NA

Dates 1982 to present

Location FBI

NARA Disposition Recommendations HQ: 00 file—Permanent. No other records. FIELD: 00 file—Permanent. No other records.

Access To gain access to the records in this classification a researcher must file a Freedom of Information Act request with the FBI.

Related Records FBI Classification 1 National Academy Matters.

CLASSIFICATION 235

Training Received—Fugitives

The Bureau established this classification in 1982 in order to provide better statistical and supervisory control for its training programs in fugitive matters.

Prior to 1982 the Bureau reported all training under Classification 1 National Academy Matters.

Volume HQ: No cases. FIELD: NA

Dates 1982 to present

Location FBI

NARA Disposition Recommendations HQ: 00 file—Permanent. No other records. FIELD: 00 file—Permanent. No other records.

Access To gain access to the records in this classification a researcher must file a Freedom of Information Act request with the FBI.

Related Records FBI Classification 1 National Academy Matters.

CLASSIFICATION 236

Training Received—General Government Crime

The Bureau established this classification in 1982 in order to provide better statistical and supervisory control for its training programs in general government crime matters. Prior to 1982 the Bureau reported all training under Classification 1 National Academy Matters.

Volume HQ: No cases. FIELD: NA

Dates 1982 to present

Location FBI

NARA Disposition Recommendations HQ: 00 file—Permanent. No other records. FIELD: 00 file—Permanent. No other records.

Access To gain access to the records in this classification a researcher must file a Freedom of Information Act request with the FBI.

Related Records FBI Classification 1 National Academy Matters.

CLASSIFICATION 237

Training Received—General Property Crime

The Bureau established this classification in 1982 in order to provide better statistical and supervisory control for its training programs in general property crime matters. Prior to 1982 the Bureau reported all training under Classification 1 National Academy Matters.

Volume HQ: No cases. FIELD: NA

Dates 1982 to present

Location FBI

NARA Disposition Recommendations HQ: 00 file—Permanent. No other records. FIELD: 00 file—Permanent. No other records.

Access To gain access to the records in this classification a researcher must file a Freedom of Information Act request with the FBI.

Related Records FBI Classification 1 National Academy Matters.

CLASSIFICATION 238

Training Received—Personal Crime

The Bureau established this classification in 1982 in order to provide better statistical and supervisory control for its training programs in personal crime matters. Prior to 1982 the Bureau reported all training under Classification 1 National Academy Matters.

Volume HQ: No cases. FIELD: NA

Dates 1982 to present

Location FBI

NARA Disposition Recommendations HQ: 00 file—Permanent. No other records. FIELD: 00 file—Permanent. No other records.

Access To gain access to the records in this classification a researcher must file a Freedom of Information Act request with the FBI.

Related Records FBI Classification 1 National Academy Matters.

CLASSIFICATION 239

Training Received—Terrorism

The Bureau established this classification in 1982 in order to provide better statistical and supervisory control for its training programs in international terrorism. Prior to 1982 the Bureau reported all training under Classification 1 National Academy Matters.

Volume HQ: No cases. FIELD: NA

Dates 1982 to present

Location FBI

NARA Disposition Recommendations HQ: 00 file—Permanent. No other records. FIELD: 00 file—Permanent. No other records.

Access To gain access to the records in this classification a researcher must file a Freedom of Information Act request with the FBI.

Related Records FBI Classification 1 National Academy Matters.

CLASSIFICATION 240

Training

The Bureau established this classification in 1982 in order to provide better statistical and supervisory control for its training programs in domestic terrorism. Prior to 1982 the Bureau reported all training under Classification 1 National Academy Matters.

Volume HQ: No cases. FIELD: NA

Dates 1982 to present

Location FBI

NARA Disposition Recommendations HQ: 00 file—Permanent. No other records. FIELD: 00 file—Permanent. No other records.

Access To gain access to the records in this classification a researcher must file a Freedom of Information Act request with the FBI.

Related Records FBI Classification 1 National Academy Matters.

CLASSIFICATION 241

Drug Enforcement Agency Applicant Investigations

Because of the Federal government's increased focus on the drug war in the 1980s and the rapid expansion of the Drug Enforcement Agency (DEA), the DEA requested that the Bureau conduct applicant background investigations on a reimbursable basis. The DEA desired that these investigations be as thorough as those performed on the Bureau's own special agents. In addition, the DEA requested that all persons interviewed with regard to an applicant be specifically asked about the applicant's known or suspected drug use. On June 1, 1982, FBI Director William Webster agreed to perform this function. The only difference between the procedures for DEA and FBI applicants is that the courts have ordered all investigations of DEA applicants to be carried through to conclusion. Thus, the Bureau is required to document fully all derogatory information collected and to conduct additional investigations as necessary to provide thorough and accurate evaluation decisions. The records document in detail the Bureau's efforts in this investigative area and contain a wealth of biographical data on individuals.

Volume HQ: 2,698 cases. FIELD: 8,156 cases.

Dates 1982 to present

Location FBI

NARA Disposition Recommendations HQ: 5% systematic informational sample—Permanent; all others—Destroy. FIELD: All records—Destroy.

Access To gain access to the records in this classification a researcher must file a Freedom of Information Act request with the FBI.

Related Records Records of the Drug Enforcement Agency, Record Group 170, National Archives.

CLASSIFICATION 242

Automation Matters

The FBI established this classification in 1982 to provide for more centralized control over all matters relating to automation, computer technology, data processing, and data systems developed within the Bureau. In 1984 it extended this classification to the field offices in order for them to better document the time spent on establishing information management systems and other forms of information control and technology. Systems established at headquarters and documented under this classification include the National Crime Information Center, the Investigative Support Information System, and the system for Field Office Information Management Support.

Volume HQ: No investigative cases. FIELD: No investigative cases.

Dates 1982 to present

Location FBI

NARA Disposition Recommendations HQ: 00 file—Permanent; all other records—Disposal not authorized. FIELD: All records—Disposal not authorized.

Access To gain access to the records in this classification a researcher must file a Freedom of Information Act request with the FBI.

Related Records None

CLASSIFICATION 243

Intelligence Identities Protection Act of 1982

In 1982 legislation, Congress prohibited the unauthorized disclosure of information identifying certain U.S. intelligence officers, agents, assets, and sources. Covered under the act were "active assets" of the Bureau whose activities are in support of the FBI's foreign counterintelligence or foreign counterterrorism missions. Accordingly, the Bureau established this classification for its investigations involving violations of the new act, assigning primary responsibility for such investigations to the Terrorism Section of its Criminal Investigative Division.

Volume HQ: 14 cases. FIELD: None

Dates 1982 to present

Location FBI

NARA Disposition Recommendations HQ: All records—Disposal not authorized. FIELD: All records—Disposal not authorized.

Access To gain access to the records in this classification a researcher must file a Freedom of Information Act request with the FBI.

Related Records None

CLASSIFICATION 244

Hostage Rescue Team

During the early 1980s, following a rash of hostage-taking in the Middle East by terrorist groups and threats of the same activities in the United States, the Bureau developed the concept of a Hostage Rescue Team. This classification provides statistical and supervisory control for the time spent by the team in recruiting, training, undertaking readiness exercises and drills, and developing local and state cooperation efforts. Prior to 1982 such training was reported in Classification 1 National Academy Matters. There are no investigative files in the classification.

Volume HQ: No case files. FIELD: NA

Dates 1982 to present

Location FBI

NARA Disposition Recommendations HQ: 00 file—Permanent. No other records. FIELD: NA

Access To gain access to the records in this classification a researcher must file a Freedom of Information Act request with the FBI.

Related Records FBI Classification 1 National Academy Matters.

CLASSIFICATION 245

Drug Investigative Task Force

In the 1980s drug abuse in the United States reached epidemic proportions. To combat this national problem, President Ronald Reagan in October 1982 established a national Drug Enforcement Task Force. The program goals of the task force were to identify, investigate, and prosecute high-level drug trafficking organizations. The Drug Enforcement Agency (DEA) was given the lead in this "War on Drugs"; however, the Bureau played a significant role in it as well, establishing this classification in 1982 for its investigations involving drug trafficking in the United States. The records provide an excellent example of Bureau investigative techniques used to stop the flow of drugs into and within the United States. Techniques used by the Bureau have included undercover agents posing as major buyers, video surveillance and consensual and Title III (court-ordered) monitoring, and the application of computer technology. In addition, the records document early Bureau problems in interagency cooperation and later exemplary cooperative efforts between the Bureau, the Internal Revenue Service, the DEA, the U.S. military, and the U.S. Customs Service.

Volume HQ: 1262 cases. FIELD: 8,592 cases.

Dates 1982 to present

Location FBI

NARA Disposition Recommendations HQ: Multisectional cases— Permanent; all cases with 19 or more serials—Permanent; all other records— Destroy. FIELD: Multisectional cases—Permanent; all other records—Destroy.

Access To gain access to the records in this classification a researcher must file a Freedom of Information Act request with the FBI.

Related Records Records of the Drug Enforcement Agency, Record Group 170; Records of the Bureau of Customs, Record Group 36; Records of the Office of the Secretary of the Army, Record Group 335; Records of the Department of the Navy, Record Group 80; Records of the Office of the Secretary of the Air Force, Record Group 340; Records of the United States Coast Guard, Record Group 26; all in the National Archives. See also Department of Justice Classification 12 Narcotic Act.

CLASSIFICATIONS 246–248

Foreign Counterintelligence Matters

The Bureau is understandably sensitive about releasing information relating to its investigative activities in this area. It withheld from release for national security reasons the NARA Historical Synopsis from the Task Force report and all of the data collection sheets for these classifications.

CLASSIFICATION 249

Toxic Waste Matters

The Bureau established this classification in 1983 for its investigations involving violations of legislation governing toxic or hazardous waste. Exempted from the classification are nuclear wastes. By agreement with the Environmental Protection Agency, the Bureau investigates prosecutable violations referred to it by the agency. The few extant cases range from allegations of toxic waste dumping by small operators to major "informant files" created by the Bureau for substantial industrial polluters. There are case files, for example, relating to the nuclear accident at the Three Mile Island reactor and to Love Canal, near Niagara Falls, New York. Also included are records relating to such environmental issues as the preservation of the snail darter and the pupfish.

Volume HQ: 120 cases. FIELD: 228 cases.

Dates 1983 to present

Location FBI

NARA Disposition Recommendations HQ: All records—Disposal not authorized. FIELD: All records—Disposal not authorized.

Access To gain access to the records in this classification a researcher must file a Freedom of Information Act request with the FBI.

Related Records Records of the Environmental Protection Agency, Record Group 412, National Archives, and Department of Justice Classifications 62 Obstruction of Navigation and Pollution of Streams, 90 Lands, and 223076 Occupational Safety.

CLASSIFICATION 250

Tampering with Consumer Products

Following a nationwide series of deaths and health scares due to poisons being placed in consumer products such as candies, fruits, and over-the-counter medicines, Congress passed the Federal Anti-Tampering Act of 1983. Under this act the Bureau was given responsibility for investigating possible violations involving life-endangering tampering, tampering where extortion demands were made, and false claims resulting in serious injury to a commercial product's reputation. The Bureau has shared jurisdiction with the Food and Drug Administration and the U.S. Department of Agriculture but does not counsel manufacturers regarding the removal of products from store shelves or participate in such decisions. The extant cases in this classification range from an instance of tampering with Girl Scout cookies to one of cyanide capsules being placed in Excedrin tablet bottles.

Volume HQ: 173 cases. FIELD: 277 cases.

Dates 1983 to present

Location FBI

NARA Disposition Recommendations HQ: All records—Disposal not authorized. FIELD: All records—Disposal not authorized.

Access To gain access to the records in this classification a researcher must file a Freedom of Information Act request with the FBI.

Related Records Records of the Food and Drug Administration, Record Group 88, and the Records of the Office of the Secretary of Agriculture, Record Group 16, both in the National Archives, and Department of Justice Classifications 21 Food and Drug (Prosecution) and 22 Food and Drug (Seizure).

CLASSIFICATION 251

Controlled Substances

As part of its war on drugs, the Congress in 1983 passed the Controlled Substance Registrant Act. Under this act the Bureau was given the authority to investigate drug cases if they involve death, serious bodily harm, or large quantities of drugs, if certain Drug Enforcement Agency criteria are met, if a facility is robbed that is a manufacturer or warehouse, or if an interstate activity was involved. The introduction of the Bureau into this area was a major departure from earlier practices, in which local authorities held most of the responsibility for such investigations. In response to the 1983 legislation, the Bureau and the U.S. Attorneys drew up rather strict guidelines that limited their involvement to major cases, citing a lack of manpower and an "unwarranted thrust" of federal influence into local jurisdictional concerns. In general, the Bureau coordinates any investigations it undertakes with local authorities. The classification itself was established in 1984.

Volume HQ: 79 cases. FIELD: 286 cases.

Dates 1984 to present

Location FBI

NARA Disposition Recommendations HQ: All records—Disposal not authorized. FIELD: All records—Disposal not authorized.

Access To gain access to the records in this classification a researcher must file a Freedom of Information Act request with the FBI.

Related Records Records of the Drug Enforcement Agency, Record Group 170, National Archives, and Department of Justice Classification 12 Narcotic Act.

CLASSIFICATION 252

National Center for the Analysis of Violent Crime/
Violent Criminal Apprehension Program

In 1984, in response to the attorney general's *Task Force on Violent Crime Report*, the Bureau and the Department of Justice established the National Center for the Analysis of Violent Crime (NCAVC). The NCAVC is a nationwide clearinghouse for statistical information on unsolved serial or exceptionally violent crimes. The Bureau included in this classification such offenses as murder, rape, child molestation, arson, and bombings. The NCAVC is operated by the Bureau's Training Division, Behavioral Sciences Unit at the FBI academy in Quantico, Virginia. The Bureau divided its efforts in this area into four major functions: (1) research and development, (2) profiling and consultation, (3) training, and (4) the Violent Crime Apprehension Program. Much of the Bureau's profiling and consultation effort results from the submission of special "crime reports" by state and local agencies. Theoretically, local authorities submit such reports to FBI criminal profile coordinators in the field. From these reports a profile of the perpetrator is then developed at headquarters. In reality, however, as of 1989 the local agencies were only returning 5 percent of the report forms. According to FBI surveys they found the forms cumbersome and too time-consuming to be of any value.

Volume HQ: 312 cases. FIELD: 123 cases.

Dates 1989 to present

Location FBI

NARA Disposition Recommendations HQ: All records—Disposal not authorized. FIELD: All records—Disposal not authorized.

Access To gain access to the records in this classification a researcher must file a Freedom of Information Act request with the FBI.

Related Records See state and local police records.

CLASSIFICATION 253

Fraud and Related Activity in Connection with Identification Documents

The Bureau established this classification in 1985 for its investigations involving the unlawful production, transfer, or possession of government identification documents. The Bureau's action stemmed from the passage of the False Identification Crime Control Act of 1982 in which Congress, concerned with growing fraud in social security and alien identification cards, attempted to stiffen the penalties for the production of such false documents as drivers' licenses, military identification cards, birth certificates, social security cards, and alien green cards. The law broadened the Bureau's responsibilities in investigating such cases; however, FBI jurisdiction is nevertheless limited to the transportation of such documents in interstate and foreign commerce other than through the U.S. postal system.

Volume HQ: 17 cases. FIELD: None

Dates 1985 to present

Location FBI

NARA Disposition Recommendations HQ: All records—Disposal not authorized. FIELD: All records—Disposal not authorized.

Access To gain access to the records in this classification a researcher must file a Freedom of Information Act request with the FBI.

Related Records Records of the Immigration and Naturalization Service, Record Group 85, Records of the Social Security Administration, Record Group 47, and the Records of the U.S. Postal Service, Record Group 28, all in the National Archives. See also Department of Justice Classifications 39 Immigration, 38 Naturalization, 40 Passport and Visa, and 137 Social Security Act.

CLASSIFICATION 254

Destruction of Energy Facilities

The Bureau established this classification in 1985 for its investigations involving the destruction or damage of nonnuclear energy facilities. The term "energy facilities" has included facilities involved in the production, distribution, or transmission of electricity, fuel, or any form of energy, as well as in research and development activities in the energy field. The Bureau interpreted the Comprehensive Crime Control Act of 1984 to include demonstrations at power plant facilities and plants still under construction. The cases opened by the Bureau include bomb threats to power plants, extortion attempts, and claims of possible terrorist activities. One interesting case involved threats from environmental groups in the West to destroy a coal-using power plant.

Volume HQ: 20 cases. FIELD: None

Dates 1985 to present

Location FBI

NARA Disposition Recommendations HQ: All records—Disposal not authorized. FIELD: All records—Disposal not authorized.

Access To gain access to the records in this classification a researcher must file a Freedom of Information Act request with the FBI.

Related Records Records of the Department of Energy, Record Group 434, National Archives.

CLASSIFICATION 255

Counterfeiting of State and Corporate Securities

The Bureau established this classification in 1985 for its investigations involving the counterfeiting or forgery of all forms of securities. Under the Comprehensive Crime Control Act of 1984 the Bureau assumed investigative responsibility for cases where the extent of criminal activity was sizeable and/or where there was an interstate or international aspect. The Bureau refers all other cases to state and local law enforcement authorities for investigation. Within the Bureau, cases under this classification are assigned to the White-Collar Crimes Program, Financial Crimes Unit. Since this has been traditionally an area of state and local concern the Bureau has been reluctant to become too deeply involved and limits its activity to cases involving securities valued at $50,000 or more.

Volume HQ: 9 cases. FIELD: None

Dates 1985 to present

Location FBI

NARA Disposition Recommendations HQ: All records—Disposal not authorized. FIELD: All records—Disposal not authorized.

Access To gain access to the records in this classification a researcher must file a Freedom of Information Act request with the FBI.

Related Records See state and local police records and Department of Justice Classification 55 Counterfeit and Forgery.

CLASSIFICATION 256

Hostage Taking—Terrorism

The Bureau established this classification in 1985 in response to the Comprehensive Crime Control Act of 1984, which made it a Federal crime to engage in the taking of hostages, and the International Convention against the Taking of Hostages. The Bureau's investigative responsibility has included domestic cases in which the government is an involved party and foreign cases in which the U.S. government is involved or the perpetrator or victim(s) is an American citizen. The primary objective of the Bureau in these cases is the safe return of the hostage. Included in this classification are files on the 1985 *Achille Lauro* hijacking, in which an American citizen was murdered aboard an Italian ocean liner, and the 1976 Air Egypt hijacking in which the FBI cooperated closely with Egyptian authorities to free passengers being held on board an Egyptian commercial aircraft.

Volume HQ: 35 cases. FIELD: None

Dates 1985 to present

Location FBI

NARA Disposition Recommendations HQ: All records—Disposal not authorized. FIELD: All records—Disposal not authorized.

Access To gain access to the records in this classification a researcher must file a Freedom of Information Act request with the FBI.

Related Records See FBI Classification 199 Foreign Counterintelligence—Terrorism.

CLASSIFICATION 257

Trademark Counterfeiting Act of 1984

In 1984, Congress passed the Trademark Counterfeiting Act in an attempt to control the unauthorized use of trademarks and the flood of counterfeit goods entering the United States from Hong Kong, South Korea, and Mexico. The Bureau established this classification in 1985 to gather investigations of violations under the act.

Volume HQ: No cases (as of 1986). FIELD: No cases (as of 1986).

Dates 1985 to present

Location FBI

NARA Disposition Recommendations HQ: All records—Disposal not authorized. FIELD: All records—Disposal not authorized.

Access To gain access to the records in this classification a researcher must file a Freedom of Information Act request with the FBI.

Related Records Records of the Patent Office, Record Group 241, National Archives, and Department of Justice Classification 55 Counterfeit and Forgery. See also FBI Classifications 28 Copyright Matters and 196 Fraud by Wire.

CLASSIFICATION 258

Credit and/or Debit Card Fraud

The Bureau established this classification in 1985 for its investigations involving credit card fraud. The Bureau refers all cases that do not involve large losses or activities tied to widespread organized crime rings to the Secret Service or to local authorities for prosecution. The Bureau usually will retain cases involving the loss of more than $25,000.

Volume HQ: No cases (as of 1986). FIELD: No cases (as of 1986).

Dates 1985 to present

Location FBI

NARA Disposition Recommendations HQ: All records—Disposal not authorized. FIELD: All records—Disposal not authorized.

Access To gain access to the records in this classification a researcher must file a Freedom of Information Act request with the FBI.

Related Records Records of the United States Secret Service, Record Group 87, National Archives, and Department of Justice Classification 176 Consumer Credit Protection Act. See also FBI Classifications 29 Bank Fraud and Embezzlement and 196 Fraud by Wire.

CLASSIFICATIONS 259–278

Information concerning these classifications was not available at the time of publication. Complete information is expected to be included in the "Report on the 1991 Update to the FBI Records Schedule" (National Archives, in press).

Classification 259
Security Clearance Investigation Program

Classification 260
Industrial Security Program

Classification 261
Security Officer Matters

Classification 262
Overseas Homicide/Attempted Homicide—International Terrorism

Classification 263
Office of Professional Responsibility Matters

Classification 264
Computer Fraud and Abuse Act of 1986 and Electronic Communications Privacy Act of 1986

Classification 265
Acts of Terrorism in the United States—International Terrorist

Classification 266
Acts of Terrorism in the United States—Domestic Terrorist

Classification 267
Drug-Related Homicide

Classification 268
Engineering Technical Matters—Foreign Counterintelligence

Classification 269
Engineering Technical Matters—Non-Foreign Counterintelligence

Classification 270
Cooperative Witnesses

Classification 271
Arms Control Treaty Matters

Classification 272
Money Laundering

Classification 273
Adoptive Forfeiture Matter—Drug

Classification 274
Adoptive Forfeiture Matter—Organized Crime

Classification 275
Adoptive Forfeiture Matter—White-Collar Crime

Classification 276
Adoptive Forfeiture Matter—Violent Crime/Major Offenders Program

Classification 277
Adoptive Forfeiture Matter—Counterterrorism Program

Classification 278
President's Intelligence Oversight Board

SPECIALIZED INDEXES

An Overview of the Indexes

In the strict sense, many of these indexes would not normally be considered indexes—that is, finding aids to particular data collections. Many are instead simply lists, photograph albums, collections of wanted circulars and posters, or administrative files. The FBI has maintained these specialized indexes primarily as administrative, research, and informational aids. In some instances they duplicate information found in the Central Records System, but for convenience they are maintained separately in the operating divisions and field offices. Some allow the Criminal Investigation Division at headquarters to better coordinate its field investigations. Others are administrative tools or are maintained for statistical purposes. The Evidence Control Index, for example, enables the FBI laboratory to keep track of material sent to it for analysis. The Mail Cover Statistics Index provides a quick reference to the number of mail covers currently in effect. Several of the photograph collections, including for example the False Identity Photo Albums, are research aids used in identifying subjects of investigations. Still other indexes allow the FBI to identify and monitor subjects in organized crime or foreign counterintelligence.

Perhaps the most controversial of the indexes has been the Bureau's Security Index (SI), which evolved from a special list of potential "subversives" drawn up by the Bureau when President Franklin D. Roosevelt formally revived its internal security functions in 1939. In the early Cold War period the index was expanded to a catalog of possible wartime saboteurs who would be apprehended under the Emergency Detention Act of 1950 (later repealed) and of persons who might be a threat to the president. During the 1950s and 1960s the SI expanded again to include more than 15,000 names of individuals whom the Bureau suspected of being members of the American Communist party, terrorists, antiwar protesters, or racial agitators.

In theory, the Bureau carefully weighed the activities, associations, and ideas of anyone who was being considered for inclusion on the index. In practice, the names of many American citizens were placed there without a thorough investigation. Once a person was placed on the index, the Bureau prepared a standby warrant for his or her arrest to be executed in time of national emergency.

The SI itself consisted of 5" x 8" cards containing background information on the individual, nationalistic tendencies, a file number, and any organizational affiliations. The Bureau updated the cards periodically with new addresses. Alongside the SI the Bureau maintained a "reserve index" composed of the names of persons considered only slightly less dangerous. These individuals would be intensively investigated in time of national emergency, but not immediately detained. The Bureau officially abolished the Security Index and the reserve index in 1971. It incorporated many of the names included there, however, into an Administrative Index (ADEX), a more limited list of about 1,500 names of persons who would come under intensive investigation and scrutiny during a national emergency.

The following is a listing and brief description of all the unclassified indexes maintained by the Bureau. It provides the researcher with a brief description of the index, where it is maintained (at headquarters or in the field), where it is located, and the NARA disposition recommendation. As of 1986 the Bureau maintained six additional indexes relating to foreign counterintelligence matters or national security concerns. Because of the nature of these indexes and their sensitivity, the Bureau maintains them as classified records and even the titles are withheld.

FBI Unclassified Indexes

General Index

The General Index, which is the Bureau's primary finding aid to its records, originated in the early 1920s and parallels the development of the Bureau's case file system. The first index cards were 5" x 8". Because the cross-reference cards contained the words "See also," they became known as "see" cards. Originally, both the main index cards and the "see" cards were typed in black. In 1924, Director Hoover ordered the cards in the index changed to the now familiar 3" x 5" size. At the same time, the classifiers were instructed to mark the items on documents that were to be indexed—a blue circle denoted the main subject of the document, and a red x noted cross-reference material.[1] This practice remained in effect until the Bureau computerized its index in the 1980s. In 1935 the main parts of the "see" cards were typed in red to distinguish them more easily from the main subject cards. This practice changed again in 1953 when the entire "see" card was typed in red. Generally, few stylistic changes in the format of the cards have occurred over the years.

The content of the cards, however, has changed over time. Initially, the Bureau heavily indexed all documents, because Hoover desired that virtually all information of potential value be indexed. As a basic rule the classifiers indexed all names and subjects in the title of a document and all data in the body of the document which, in the classifiers' opinion, was of sufficient importance to warrant future reference. This system required the classifiers to read all mail in its entirety to determine what information should be indexed. This was very labor intensive and by 1944 the Bureau was indexing only the names in the title of documents in several of its classifications, especially in noncriminal classifications.

---

[1] See Appendix VII for a listing of symbols used by the FBI.

At the system's beginning, the index cards simply noted the subject matter and the case file number where relevant cross-reference material could be found. Beginning in 1941 all the cards were automatically dated by a tachometer. By the 1950s information such as race, age, date of birth, official title, and affiliation with subversive organizations and groups was noted on the cards. Starting in 1952, as a reflection of a steady trend toward less indexing, all criminal cases were indexed only by names and general subject; however, more intensive indexing in security-related classifications continued. In 1950, for example, when approximately 8,000 cards were prepared each day, 6,560 concerned subjects related to subversion.

Until 1976 there were significant differences between the General Index at headquarters and the individual general indexes maintained in the field offices. In the field the case agent made decisions on indexing; at headquarters, clerical personnel (classifiers) prepared the index cards. To minimize the differences, in 1976 the Bureau abandoned the use of clerical personnel for preparing index cards and required that the agent in charge of a case make the indexing decisions. In 1979, to help facilitate the automation of the system, the Bureau divided the headquarters General Index into active and inactive sections. The inactive section contained index cards for criminal cases closed since 1973 and security cases closed since 1958. All cards in the active section were to be entered into the automated system. By 1981 the General Index (active and inactive) contained approximately 65,500,000 cards. The Bureau purges the index cards when a case file is destroyed.[2]

Disposition Schedule HQ: Index cards for which the related case file(s) is scheduled for transfer to the National Archives—Permanent; all other index cards—Destroy. FIELD: Index cards for which the related case file(s) is scheduled for transfer to the National Archives—Permanent; all other index cards—Destroy.

Administrative Index (ADEX)

This index, maintained at headquarters and in twenty-nine field offices, consists of 3" x 5" cards with descriptive data on individuals the Bureau has designated for intensive investigation in times of a national emergency. The Bureau considered individuals in the index to constitute a potential or actual threat to the internal security of the United States. Initiated in 1971, the ADEX was compiled from information formerly contained in the Security Index and the associated "reserve index."

[2]For a more detailed description of the General Index see the NARA/FBI Task Force reports.

Disposition Schedule HQ: All records—Permanent. FIELD: All records—Destroy.

Agitator Index

Maintained at headquarters, this index was used by the Bureau to keep track of "extremist subjects" considered dangerous to the national security of the United States. The Bureau abolished this index in 1971 and incorporated its names into the ADEX.

Disposition Schedule HQ: NA. FIELD: NA

Anonymous Letter File

This file, maintained by the FBI laboratory, consists of photographs of anonymous communications and extortion transactions relating to kidnapping, extortion, threats, and terrorist activities. It is used by the laboratory in identifying possible subjects.

Disposition Schedule HQ: All materials—Destroy when no longer needed. FIELD: NA

Associates of Drug Enforcement Class I Narcotics Violators

This is a computer listing of individuals whom the Drug Enforcement Agency has identified as associating with known Class I narcotics violators. It is maintained at FBI headquarters as well as at all fifty-nine field offices. The Bureau uses the list as a ready reference and investigative aid. It is kept current but is not cumulative.

Disposition Schedule HQ: All records—Destroy when no longer needed. FIELD: All records—Destroy when no longer needed.

Background Investigation Index—Department of Justice

This index was maintained by Bureau headquarters as an administrative aid to determine the current status of background investigations for the Department of Justice. It consisted of 3" x 5" cards concerning persons who have been the subject of a full field investigation in connection with their consideration for employment in a sensitive position with the Department of Justice. It has been replaced with a computerized system.

Disposition Schedule HQ: All records—Destroy when no longer needed. FIELD: NA

Background Investigation Index—White House, Other Executive Agencies, and Congress

This index was maintained at Bureau headquarters as an administrative aid to determine the current status of background investigations undertaken for the White House, other executive branch agencies, and Congress. It originally consisted of 3" x 5" cards concerning persons who had been subjected to a full field investigation in connection with their consideration for employment in a sensitive position. The index has recently been computerized.

Disposition Schedule HQ: All records—Destroy when no longer needed. FIELD: NA

Background Investigation Index—Department of Energy

This index was maintained at Bureau headquarters as an administrative aid to determine the current status of background investigations for the Department of Energy. It consisted of 3" x 5" cards on persons who had been the subject of a full field investigation in connection with their consideration for employment in a sensitive position for the Department of Energy and the Nuclear Regulatory Commission.

Disposition Schedule HQ: All records—Destroy when no longer needed. FIELD: NA

Bank Fraud and Embezzlement Index

This index was maintained only at the New York field office and was used as an investigative aid in tracking individuals who had been the subject of a New York bank-fraud or embezzlement case.

Disposition Schedule HQ: NA. FIELD: All records—Destroy when no longer needed.

Bank Robbery Albums

These albums are maintained in forty-seven field offices and are used to develop investigative leads in bank robbery cases. Usually filed by race, height, and age, the photos are shown to witnesses for identification purposes. The albums consist of photos of known bank robbers, burglars, and larceny subjects. In some of the field offices the albums also contain pictures obtained from local police departments and the banks themselves. The albums are of current suspects and are not cumulative.

Disposition Schedule   HQ: NA. FIELD: All materials—Destroy when no longer needed.

Bank Robbery Nickname Index

Only the Washington field office maintains this form of index. The index itself consists of nicknames used by known bank robbers. The index card, since computerized, contains the nickname, real name, and method of operations of the suspects. It is filed in alphabetical order.

Disposition Schedule HQ: NA. FIELD: All records—Destroy when no longer needed.

Bank Robbery Note File

Maintained at FBI headquarters, the file is used by the FBI laboratory to assist in solving robberies in which the subject has not been identified but in which a note was left at the scene of the crime. The note is compared with samples in the index in an attempt to match the sentence structure and handwriting.

Disposition Schedule   HQ: All materials—Destroy when no longer needed. FIELD: NA

Bank Robbery Suspect Index

Maintained in thirty-three field offices, this index is used as an investigative aid in conjunction with the Bank Robbery Albums. It consists of a control file of index cards (since computerized) with photographs of known bank robbers and professional burglars. It contains only current subjects and is not cumulative.

Disposition Schedule HQ: NA. FIELD: All records—Destroy when no longer needed.

Car Ring Case Photo Albums

This type of photographic album is maintained in only three field offices as an investigative aid in stolen car ring cases. It consists of photos of subjects previously involved in large car theft ring investigations.

Disposition Schedule   HQ: NA. FIELD: All materials—Destroy when no longer needed.

Car Ring Case Photo Album and Index

Maintained only in the New York field office, this combination photo album and card index (since computerized) is used as an investigative aid. The index contains names and known addresses that have appeared on fraudulent auto titles in previous stolen-vehicle cases. Most of the names are fictitious and the titles forged.

Disposition Schedule   HQ: NA. FIELD: All materials—Destroy when no longer needed.

Car Ring Case Toll-Call Index

Used by at least two field offices, this index consists of cards (now computerized) that contain biographical information on persons who have subscribed to telephone numbers to which toll calls were placed by subjects of large auto theft ring investigations. It is maintained numerically by telephone number and is primarily used to facilitate the development of probable cause for a court-approved wiretap.

Disposition Schedule HQ: NA. FIELD: All records—Destroy when no longer needed.

Car Ring Theft Working Index

Maintained at headquarters, the index consists of 5" x 8" cards on individuals the FBI has suspected of being involved in major car ring theft cases. The index is used by the FBI laboratory as an administrative aid in keeping track of evidence relating to its examination work.

Disposition Schedule   HQ: All records—Destroy when no longer needed. FIELD: NA

Cartage Albums

Maintained as an investigative aid in three field offices, these albums consist of photographs of individuals with physical descriptions and other informational data. The individuals are convicted auto thieves and the Bureau has some reason to believe they may be repeat offenders.

Disposition Schedule HQ: NA. FIELD: All records—Destroy when no longer needed.

Channelizing Index

Maintained by nine field offices as an administrative aid in filing reports, this index contains the names and case-file numbers of persons frequently mentioned in informant records. The index is primarily used to facilitate the distribution of informant reports to the appropriate classification and case number.

Disposition Schedule HQ: NA. FIELD: All records—Destroy when no longer needed.

Check Circular File

This file is maintained at headquarters as well as in forty-three field offices. It consists of printed fliers, filed numerically in a control file, on fugitives who are notorious fraudulent check passers and who are engaged in a continuing operation of bad check passing. The fliers are used to alert business establishments, especially banks, and other FBI field offices of possible bad check schemes operating in their area. The fliers include the subject's name, a photo, a summary of the subject's method of operation, and other identifying information or characteristics. They are essentially wanted posters for fraudulent check passers.

Disposition Schedule HQ: All materials—Destroy when no longer needed. FIELD: All materials—Destroy when no longer needed.

Computerized Telephone Number File Intelligence

This is a computer listing of telephone numbers, with the subscriber's name and address, of individuals who came to the attention of the Bureau during major investigations. These numbers in turn are matched with those uncovered in future investigations to determine any connections or associations.

Disposition Schedule HQ: Destroy when no longer needed. FIELD: NA

Con Man Index

Maintained at headquarters, this index contains the names of individuals, along with any affiliations, who travel nationwide or internationally and participate in confidence schemes and swindles. Formerly on index cards, it is presently computer generated and printed in booklet form.

Disposition Schedule HQ: All materials—Destroy when no longer needed. FIELD: NA

Confidence Game (Flimflam) Albums

Used as an investigative aid in four field offices, these albums consist of photographs, with physical descriptions and other identifying information, of individuals who have previously been arrested for confidence games and related criminal activities.

Disposition Schedule HQ: NA. FIELD: All materials—Destroy when no longer needed.

Copyright Matters Index

This index is used as an investigative aid in the Los Angeles field office for copyright matters. It consists of index cards listing individuals who are motion-picture collectors, producers, or major distributors. It also contains film titles.

Disposition Schedule HQ: NA. FIELD: All records—Destroy when no longer needed.

Criminal Intelligence Index

This index is maintained at two field offices as an administrative aid when searching for reports relating to individuals who have become the subject of antiracketeering investigations. Originally on cards (and since computerized), the index is generally used as a quick reference tool to ascertain case-file numbers and the correct spelling of names.

Disposition Schedule HQ: NA. FIELD: All records—Destroy when no longer needed.

Criminal Informant Index

This index is maintained at headquarters to provide information on all active and inactive criminal informants. Originally on index cards (and since computerized), it contains identity information and some background data on informants who have furnished information to the Bureau in the criminal area. It is cumulative.

Disposition Schedule HQ: All records—Permanent. FIELD: NA

Drug Enforcement Agency (DEA) Class I Narcotics Violators Listing

This listing, maintained at headquarters and at all fifty-nine field offices, consists of a computer listing of narcotics violators—persons known to manufacture, supply, or distribute large quantities of illicit drugs. It is used by the Bureau in assisting the DEA in disseminating intelligence data concerning illicit drug trafficking.

Disposition Schedule HQ: All records—Destroy when no longer needed. FIELD: All records—Destroy when no longer needed.

Deserter Index

This index is maintained in four field offices and contains the names and military service of known military deserters. It is not cumulative.

Disposition Schedule HQ: NA. FIELD: All records—Destroy when no longer needed.

Electronic Surveillance (ELSUR) Index

This is an important index maintained at headquarters and at all fifty-nine field offices. It consists of the names of individuals who have been the target of direct FBI electronic surveillance, who have participated in conversations monitored by the Bureau, or who have owned, leased, or licensed premises on which the Bureau conducted ELSUR activities. The index goes back to 1960 and is maintained primarily to enable the Bureau to respond quickly and efficiently to judicial inquiries concerning electronic surveillance coverage of witnesses, defendants, or attorneys involved in Federal court proceedings. The majority of the names in the index are simply those overheard or mentioned in the monitoring of a conversation. They are generally spelled phonetically. The main subject cards record clearly identifiable individuals who were or are the subject of an FBI investigation.

Disposition Schedule HQ: "Principal" cards—Permanent; "proprietary interest" cards—Destroy; "overhear" or "mention" cards—Destroy. FIELD: All records—Destroy when no longer needed.

Evidence Control Index

This is a computerized index used by the FBI laboratory to control and track evidence submitted to it for analysis.

Disposition Schedule HQ: Destroy when no longer needed. FIELD: NA

Extremist Informant Index

This index was maintained at headquarters and consisted of identity information and background data on extremist informants. The Bureau used it as a quick reference aid in the supervision of its informant program primarily during the 1960s and 1970s. The Bureau discontinued its use in November 1976.

Disposition Schedule HQ: All records—Permanent. FIELD: NA

Extremist Photo Albums

These albums were maintained at headquarters and in at least twenty field offices. They consisted of photographs, physical descriptions, and other background information on individuals the Bureau considered extremists. All persons in the Key Extremists Program, for example, were represented in the albums, as were some of the Bureau's informants. The Bureau discontinued the albums in January 1977.

Disposition Schedule HQ: All materials—Permanent. FIELD: All materials— Destroy when no longer needed.

False Identities Index

This index has been maintained by the FBI laboratory as an administrative aid in organizing its examinations of the identification papers of deceased persons. It consists of index cards with the names of deceased individuals whose birth certificates were obtained by suspects for possible use in producing false identifications. The cards (since computerized) also record all laboratory work completed on the materials.

Disposition Schedule HQ: All records—Destroy when no longer needed. FIELD: NA

False Identities Program List

Maintained in thirty-one field offices as an investigative aid, this index is a part of the FBI's program to identify and locate persons using false identities for illegal purposes. It consists of a listing of names of deceased individuals whose birth certificates were obtained after the person's death and whose names, therefore, were possibly being used to create false identification papers.

Disposition Schedule HQ: NA. FIELD: All records—Destroy when no longer needed.

False Identity Photo Albums

Maintained in two field offices as an investigative aid, the albums consist of names and photographs of individuals positively identified as possessing false identification papers.

Disposition Schedule HQ: NA. FIELD: All materials—Destroy when no longer needed.

FBI/Inspector General Case Pointer System

This is a computerized listing of the names of organizations that are the subjects of active or inactive fraud investigations. The listing also provides the name of the agency conducting the investigation and is used to prevent duplication of investigative activity.

Disposition Schedule HQ: Destroy when no longer needed. FIELD: NA

FBI Wanted Persons Index

Used at headquarters as a ready reference tool, this index consists of index cards (since computerized) on persons sought on Federal warrants as fugitives under investigation by the FBI. It is not cumulative.

Disposition Schedule HQ: All records—Destroy when no longer needed. FIELD: NA

Foreign Counterintelligence (FCI) Asset Index

Maintained at headquarters, this index contains identification information and background data on all active and inactive FBI assets in the foreign counterintelligence field. It is used in conjunction with the FCI Asset Program.

Disposition Schedule HQ: All records—Permanent. FIELD: NA

Foreign Police Cooperation Index

Maintained at headquarters as an administrative aid, this index consists of the names of fugitives whom foreign police agencies have requested FBI assistance in apprehending.

Disposition Schedule HQ: All records—Destroy when no longer needed. FIELD: NA

Fraud against the Government Index

Maintained only at the Washington field office, this index is used as an investigative aid. It consists of names of individuals who have been the subject of a "Fraud against the Government" investigation.

Disposition Schedule HQ: NA. FIELD: All records—Destroy when no longer needed.

Fugitive Bank Robbers File

This file is maintained at headquarters and forty-three field offices and consists of printed fliers picturing bank robbery fugitives. It is essentially a wanted-poster file on bank robbers who have been fugitives for fifteen or more days. Headquarters distributes these fliers to the field for identification purposes.

Disposition Schedule HQ: All materials—Destroy when no longer needed. FIELD: All materials—Destroy when no longer needed.

General Security Index

This index is an administrative aid maintained at the Washington field office to assist it in making background investigations. It contains the names of all persons who have been the subject of a security classification investigation in the Washington area.

Disposition Schedule HQ: NA. FIELD: All records—Destroy when no longer needed.

Hoodlum License Plate Index

Maintained by three field offices, this index is used for quick identification of known criminals and their automobiles as well as vehicles observed in the vicinity of the criminals' homes. It contains the names of the individuals, their license plate number, the make and model of the vehicle, and, often, descriptive data on the individual.

Disposition Schedule HQ: NA. FIELD: All records—Destroy when no longer needed.

Identification Order Fugitive Flier File

Maintained at headquarters and forty-three field offices, this file consists of printed fliers filed numerically in a control file and is essentially a wanted-poster file for fugitive investigations stretching back to 1919. The fliers are given wide circulation among state and local law enforcement agencies throughout the United States and are displayed in post offices across the country. The fliers contain the fugitive's photograph, fingerprints, and physical description, as well as the crime for which the individual is wanted.

Disposition Schedule HQ: All materials—Permanent. FIELD: All materials— Destroy when no longer needed.

Informant Index

Each field office maintains an index of informants currently and previously operated by that office. The indexes themselves consist of the name, symbol number, and background information on the following types of active and inactive informants: Top Echelon Criminal Informants, Security Informants, Operational and Informational Assets, Extremist Informants (discontinued), Defense Plant and Military Bases Informants (discontinued), and potential Criminal Informants.

Disposition Schedule HQ: NA. FIELD: All records—Destroy when no longer needed. (Informant indexes at headquarters duplicate these field office indexes.)

Informants in Other Field Offices, Index of

Maintained at fifteen field offices, this index provides a quick reference to names and/or symbol numbers of informants in other field offices.

Disposition Schedule HQ: NA. FIELD: All records—Destroy when no longer needed.

Interstate Transportation of Stolen Aircraft Photo Album

Maintained by the Miami field office, this album consists of photographs and physical descriptions of individuals suspected or known to be involved in the interstate transportation of stolen aircraft. The album has become increasingly important as an investigative aid in attempts to intercede in the drug trade, as these small planes are often used to transport narcotics into the United States.

Disposition Schedule HQ: NA. FIELD: All materials—Destroy when no longer needed.

Internal Revenue Service (IRS) Wanted List

Maintained in eleven field offices, this list is used in the identification of persons wanted by the IRS. The list consists of one-page printed fliers from the IRS on individuals wanted for tax evasion.

Disposition Schedule   HQ: NA. FIELD: All materials—Destroy when no longer needed.

Key Activist Program Albums

Maintained at headquarters and forty-seven field offices, these albums were used to aid in identifying and tracking individuals the Bureau identified as advocating civil disobedience and violent disruptive acts against the government. They consist of photographs of individuals mounted on pages with physical descriptions and other information relating to the individual, such as their affiliations with known radical groups. The Bureau discontinued the albums in February 1975.

Disposition Schedule   HQ: All materials—Permanent. FIELD: All materials— Destroy when no longer needed.

Key Extremist Program Listing

Maintained at headquarters, the Key Extremist Program Listing gathered the names of individuals the Bureau suspected of extremist activities, including civil disobedience and violent acts against the government. Most individuals on the list were investigated intensively by the Bureau. The Bureau discontinued the listing in February 1975.

Disposition Schedule   HQ: All records—Permanent. FIELD: All records— Destroy when no longer needed.

Kidnapping Book

Maintained at headquarters, the Kidnapping Book is used as a reference tool when attempting to match prior methods of operation in unsolved kidnapping cases. The book consists of the victim's name, the suspects, if known, and a brief description of the circumstances surrounding the kidnapping. It goes back to cases in the early 1950s.

Disposition Schedule   HQ: All materials—Destroy when no longer needed. FIELD: NA

Known Check Passers Albums

Maintained in four field offices, these albums are used as an investigative aid in identifying known check forgers and counterfeiters. They consist of photographs and physical descriptions of the individuals.

Disposition Schedule HQ: NA. FIELD: All materials—Destroy when no longer needed.

Known Gambler Index

Maintained as an investigative aid in five field offices, the index is used to help identify known bookmakers and gamblers. The index contains the name, physical description, known address, and, sometimes, a photograph of the individual. It also notes any organized crime connection.

Disposition Schedule HQ: NA. FIELD: All materials—Destroy when no longer needed.

La Cosa Nostra (LCN) Membership Index

Maintained at headquarters and fifty-five field offices, the index is used by FBI agents to help identify individuals suspected to be or known to be members of LCN. The index consists of names, physical descriptions, addresses, license plate numbers, and photographs of the individuals.

Disposition Schedule HQ: All materials—Permanent. FIELD: All materials— Destroy when no longer needed.

Leased Line Letter Request Index

Maintained at headquarters as an administrative and statistical aid, this index contains the names of individuals and organizations who are or have been the subject of electronic surveillance investigations relating to national security concerns where a leased-line letter (a grant of authorization by the telephone company) was necessary in order to institute the investigation.

Disposition Schedule HQ: All records—Destroy when no longer needed. FIELD: NA

Mail Cover Index

A mail cover is the examination of the information, such as a name, address, postmark, and return address, carried on the outside of an envelope. It is in contrast to a "mail opening," which is the actual opening of a letter for intelligence purposes.

Maintained at headquarters, this index contains information on all FBI mail covers conducted on individuals and groups since January 1973 and includes some mail covers as early as 1960. It is often used for reference purposes in preparing new mail-cover requests for the Department of Justice and the courts.

Disposition Schedule   HQ: All records—Permanent. FIELD: All records— Destroy when no longer needed.

Mail Cover Statistics Index

Maintained at headquarters, this index provides statistical information on mail covers in criminal, fugitive, and national security matters.

Disposition Schedule   HQ: All records—Destroy when no longer needed. FIELD: NA

Military Deserter Index

This index consists of 3" x 5" cards containing the names of all military deserters in whose cases the various military services have requested FBI assistance.

Disposition Schedule HQ: Destroy when no longer needed. FIELD: NA

National Bank Robbery Albums

Maintained at headquarters as a control file and in forty-two field offices, the albums consist of printed fliers describing bank-robbery suspects. Most of the fliers have a bank-camera photograph of the suspected robber. Headquarters sends the fliers to the field offices to aid in the identification of suspects.

Disposition Schedule   HQ: All materials—Destroy when no longer needed. FIELD: All materials—Destroy when no longer needed.

National Fraudulent Check File

Maintained at headquarters, this file contains photographs of the signatures found on stolen or counterfeit checks. The index is used as a control file in helping to solve stolen check or counterfeit check cases by comparing signatures in new cases against the index. Files are arranged alphabetically by surname. The Bureau, however, in most cases has no way of knowing whether or not the name is real.

Disposition Schedule HQ: All materials—Destroy when no longer needed. FIELD: NA

National Security Electronic Surveillance (ELSUR) Card File

Maintained at headquarters, this ELSUR file covers FBI activities in this field back to 1941. It contains information relating to all previously authorized electronic surveillance cases and a historical, inactive section believed to contain information on nonconsensual physical entries in national security cases ("black bag" jobs), previous toll billings, mail covers, and leased lines. It also contains information relating to attorney general approvals and denials for warrantless ELSUR cases in the national security area.

Disposition Schedule HQ: All records—Permanent. FIELD: NA

National Security Electronic Surveillance (ELSUR) Statistics File

Maintained at headquarters, this index provides a daily statistical summary of ELSUR activities in place and ongoing.

Disposition Schedule HQ: All records—Destroy when no longer needed. FIELD: NA

National Security Electronic Surveillance File

Maintained at headquarters, this file contains a chronological list of all individuals and organizations since 1940 who have been the target of national security electronic surveillance.

Disposition Schedule HQ: All records—Permanent. FIELD: NA

Night Depository Trap Index

Maintained at headquarters, this index is used by the FBI laboratory in the analysis of evidence from bank thefts. Specifically, the index contains information on individuals previously involved in the theft of bank deposits made in bank night-depository boxes. The laboratory attempts to match similar methods of operation to possible suspects.

Disposition Schedule HQ: All records—Destroy when no longer needed. FIELD: NA

Organized Crime Photo Albums

Maintained in thirteen field offices, these albums are used to aid agents in the identification of organized crime figures within the field office's jurisdiction. They consist of photographs, physical descriptions, and other identifying information concerning individuals involved in organized crime activities.

Disposition Schedule   HQ: NA. FIELD: All materials—Destroy when no longer needed.

Photospread Identification Elimination File

Maintained in fourteen field offices, this is essentially a mug shot file used by Bureau agents to assist witnesses in identifying suspects. It consists of photographs and physical descriptions of individuals. The photos are from Bureau files and from state and local law enforcement agencies.

Disposition Schedule   HQ: NA. FIELD: All materials—Destroy when no longer needed.

Prostitute Photo Albums

Maintained in four field offices, these albums are used to identify prostitutes in connection with Bureau investigations under the Mann Act (White Slave Traffic Act). They consist of photographs, with physical descriptions and background data, of individuals who have prior local or Federal arrest records for prostitution.

Disposition Schedule   HQ: NA. FIELD: All materials—Destroy when no longer needed.

Rabble-Rouser Index

Maintained at headquarters, the Bureau created this index in 1968 when it renamed its Agitator Index of "extremist subjects" and ordered the field offices to obtain photographs of each person listed within it. It has focused on New Left, anti-Vietnam War protestors, and black militants.

Disposition Schedule   HQ: No information available. FIELD: No information available.

Reserve Index

Maintained at headquarters, this index was created by the Bureau in 1960 when it renamed its Security Index and expanded it to include potential subversives in addition to Communists.

Disposition Schedule HQ: No information available. FIELD: No information available.

Royal Canadian Mounted Police (RCMP) Wanted Circular File

This is a control file listing individuals wanted by the RCMP. It contains biographical information and tells the crime for which the person is wanted. It is used by headquarters to notify the RCMP if an individual listed in it is located in the United States.

Disposition Schedule HQ: Destroy when no longer needed. FIELD: NA

Security Index

Maintained at headquarters, this index was a joint FBI-Department of Justice program originally based on department plans for the emergency detention of Nazi and Fascist sympathizers during World War II. With the end of the war it evolved into a listing of suspected Communists. In the 1960s the Bureau expanded it to include "influential" persons deemed likely to "aid subversive elements." In the late 1960s and early 1970s it came to include persons listed on the Key Activist Program: members of the Students for a Democratic Society, the anti-Vietnam War groups, the New Left, and black nationalist groups.

Disposition Schedule HQ: No information available. FIELD: No information available.

Security Informant Index

Maintained at headquarters, this is the main control index for all active and inactive informants providing the Bureau information on criminal activities. It consists of names, code numbers, physical descriptions, and background data.

Disposition Schedule HQ: All records—Permanent. FIELD: NA

Security Subjects Control Index

This index consists of 3" x 5" cards containing the names and case-file numbers of individuals who have been the subject of a security investigation check.

Disposition Schedule HQ: Disposal not authorized. FIELD: NA

Security Telephone Number Index

Maintained at the Washington field office, this index contains telephone subscriber information subpoenaed from the telephone company in any security investigation. It is used as a reference aid as part of the Bureau's electronic surveillance coverage in security investigations.

Disposition Schedule HQ: NA. FIELD: All records—Destroy when no longer needed.

Selective Service Violators Index

Maintained at headquarters as a noncumulative administrative aid, this index contains the names of individuals being sought on the basis of Federal warrants for violation of the Selective Service Act.

Disposition Schedule HQ: All records—Destroy. FIELD: NA

Skyjack Fugitive Albums

Maintained at headquarters and five field offices, these albums contain photographs with physical descriptions and other descriptive data relating to fugitives wanted for skyjacking.

Disposition Schedule HQ: All materials—Destroy when no longer needed. FIELD: All materials—Destroy when no longer needed.

Sources of Information Index

Maintained at ten field offices, this index contains information on individuals and organizations such as banks, motels, and local government officials that are willing to furnish information to the FBI with sufficient frequency to justify a listing in the index.

Disposition Schedule HQ: NA. FIELD: All records—Destroy when no longer needed.

Special Services Index

Maintained in several field offices, this is a 3" x 5" card index listing prominent individuals who are in a position to furnish assistance in connection with FBI investigations.

Disposition Schedule HQ: NA. FIELD: Destroy when no longer needed.

Stolen Checks and Fraud-by-Wire Index

Maintained as an investigative aid in one field office, this index consists of information on individuals involved in check fraud and fraud-by-wire violations.

Disposition Schedule HQ: NA. FIELD: All records—Destroy when no longer needed.

Stop Notices Index

This index is maintained by forty-three field offices as a reference aid. It consists of the names of subjects and the descriptions of property items upon which the field office has placed a stop notice at other law enforcement agencies or private businesses, such as pawnshops, in the event the person or item shows up. It is used to assist the agent in locating subjects or items connected with an ongoing investigation.

Disposition Schedule HQ: NA. FIELD: All records—Destroy when no longer needed.

Surveillance Locator Index

Maintained in two field offices, this index contains information relating to individuals or businesses that have come under physical surveillance by the field-office agents. It is used primarily for general reference purposes with regard to antiracketeering figures.

Disposition Schedule HQ: NA. FIELD: All records—Destroy when no longer needed.

Symbionese Liberation Army (SLA) Index

The SLA kidnapping of Patricia Hearst in 1974 prompted headquarters and two of the field offices in California to establish a quick reference aid on the individuals identified as being part of this radical terrorist group. The entries list individuals, weapons, vehicles, and houses thought to be connected with the SLA.

Disposition Schedule HQ: All records—Permanent. FIELD: All records— Destroy when no longer needed.

Telephone Number Index—Gamblers

Maintained in two field offices, this index contains information on persons identified, usually as a result of a subpoena for the names of subscribers to particular telephone numbers or toll call records, as suspected gamblers or bookmakers.

Disposition Schedule HQ: NA. FIELD: All records—Destroy when no longer needed.

Telephone Subscribers and Toll Record Check Index

Maintained by one field office as an administrative aid, this is a check list with information on persons identified, as the result of a formal request or subpoena to the phone company, as subscribers to particular telephone numbers. The index, filed by telephone number, includes the identity of the subscriber, billing parties, subscriber's address, the date of the Bureau request to the phone company, and a file number.

Disposition Schedule HQ: NA. FIELD: All records—Destroy when no longer needed.

Thieves, Couriers, and Fences Photo Index

Maintained in four field offices as an investigative aid, this index consists of photos and background information on individuals who have been convicted of or are suspected of being thieves, couriers, or fences based on their past activity in the interstate transportation of stolen property.

Disposition Schedule HQ: NA. FIELD: All materials—Destroy when no longer needed.

Toll Records Request Index

Maintained as an administrative aid at headquarters, this index contains the names of individuals and organizations for which the Bureau prepared an official request letter to the Department of Justice, the courts, or the telephone company. It relates to national security cases and involves requests from the Bureau for long-distance call records and toll records.

Disposition Schedule HQ: All records—Destroy when no longer needed. FIELD: NA

Top Burglar Albums

Maintained at four field offices as an investigative aid, these albums consist of photos and background data on known and suspected burglars involved in the interstate transportation of stolen property.

Disposition Schedule HQ: NA. FIELD: All materials—Destroy when no longer needed.

Top Echelon Criminal Informant Program Index

Maintained at headquarters, this index contains identity and background information on persons who are either furnishing high-level information on organized crime activities or are under development to furnish such information. The index is used primarily to evaluate, collaborate, and coordinate informant information and to develop prosecution data against racketeer figures under Federal, state, and local statutes.

Disposition Schedule HQ: All records—Permanent. FIELD: NA

Top Ten Program File

Maintained at headquarters and forty-four field offices, this index is in reality a file of printed fliers on fugitives considered by the FBI to be the ten most wanted. The "most wanted" posters date from 1951 when the program was established.

Disposition Schedule HQ: All materials—Permanent. FIELD: All materials—Destroy when no longer needed.

Top Thief Program Index

Maintained at twenty-seven field offices as an investigative aid, this index consists of names of individuals who are professional burglars, robbers, or fences dealing in items likely to be passed in interstate commerce or who travel across state lines to commit a crime. The index entries usually contain a photograph, physical description, and some background information on the individual.

Disposition Schedule HQ: NA. FIELD: All materials—Destroy when no longer needed.

Truck Hijack Photo Albums

Maintained at four field offices as an investigative aid, these albums contain photos and descriptive data on individuals who are suspected of truck hijacking. It is often shown to witnesses and/or victims to help identify unknown subjects in hijacking cases.

Disposition Schedule HQ: NA. FIELD: All materials—Destroy when no longer needed.

Truck Thief Suspect Photo Album

Maintained by one field office as an investigative aid, this album consists of photos and background data on individuals previously arrested or currently suspected in truck thefts.

Disposition Schedule HQ: NA. FIELD: All materials—Destroy when no longer needed.

Traveling Criminal Photo Album

Maintained by one field office as an investigative aid, this album consists of photographs, with identifying data, of individuals convicted of a variety of criminal offenses and suspected in other crimes.

Disposition Schedule HQ: NA. FIELD: All materials—Destroy when no longer needed.

Veterans Administration (VA)/Federal Housing Administration (FHA) Matters Index

Used at the Washington field office as an aid in VA and FHA investigations, this index consists of names of individuals who have been the subject of an investigation relating to the VA or FHA.

Disposition Schedule HQ: NA. FIELD: All records—Destroy when no longer needed.

Wanted Fliers File

Maintained at headquarters and at forty-six field offices, this is a serial set of printed fliers, dating from 1934, listing fugitives wanted by the Bureau. The flier contains the name, a photograph, aliases, previous convictions, the crime the person is wanted for, and a caution note on how dangerous the person is.

Disposition Schedule HQ: All materials—Permanent. FIELD: All materials— Destroy when no longer needed.

Weathermen Photo Album

Maintained at headquarters and several field offices, these albums were used during the 1960s and 1970s to track persons believed to be members of or closely associated with the radical Weathermen. The index consists of photographs and descriptions of individuals and location possibilities.

Disposition Schedule HQ: All materials—Permanent. FIELD: All materials— Destroy when no longer needed.

Wheeldex

Maintained in the New York field office, this index relates to organized crime figures. It contains the names, nicknames, and case file numbers of organized crime members.

Disposition Schedule HQ: NA. FIELD: All records—Destroy when no longer needed.

White House Special Index

Maintained at headquarters, this index contains information on all potential White House appointees, staff members, guests, and visitors referred to the FBI by the White House security office for a security check. The index was used to expedite such checks in view of the time frame usually involved. The index is currently sealed under a court order (*Howard S. Abramson v. the Federal Bureau of Investigation*) and will be destroyed upon completion of the case.

Disposition Schedule HQ: All records—Destroy when no longer needed.
FIELD: NA

Witness Protection Program Index

Maintained by headquarters, this index relates information concerning those persons enrolled in the Witness Protection and Maintenance Program. Individuals in the program are provided new identities by the Department of Justice because of their testimony in organized crime trials. It is used primarily by the Bureau to notify the U.S. Marshals when information related to the safety of a protected witness comes to the Bureau's attention.

Disposition Schedule HQ: All records—Destroy when no longer needed.
FIELD: NA

SPECIAL FILES

J. Edgar Hoover's Official and Confidential (O&C) File and the Nichols File

On October 1, 1941, J. Edgar Hoover established a series of files separate from the central files of the Bureau. It was Hoover's desire that "a confidential file be maintained in the office of Mr. [Louis B.] Nichols, under his direction and supervision" to gather "items believed inadvisable to be included in the general files of the Bureau."[1] Upon Hoover's death in 1972, these files consisted of 139 file folders arranged alphabetically by the name of the individual or subject. Most pertain to specific individuals, such as John F. Kennedy, Robert Kennedy, Joseph Kennedy, Lyndon Johnson, Dwight D. Eisenhower, Martin Luther King, Jr., Richard Nixon, Adlai Stevenson, Francis Biddle, Elizabeth Bentley, Harry Bridges, Clinton P. Anderson, Martin Dies, Judith Coplon, Thomas Dewey, Felix Frankfurter, Harry Hopkins, Drew Pearson, Henry Wallace, Sumner Welles, Wendell Willkie, and Walter Winchell.[2] Although there is some "gossip" type information in these files (concerning alleged homosexual activities on the part of Sumner Welles, for example), in general they do not live up to their reputation as a cache of intimate information maintained by Hoover.

The files do reflect Hoover's interest in promoting a desired FBI image. He took personal interest in everything written about the Bureau and paid close attention to the media and how FBI activities were portrayed by them. For example, there are folders on the movie *The FBI Story* and the television series

---

[1] See the text of Hoover's memorandum, in U.S. Congress, House Committee on Government Operations, Subcommittee on Government and Individual Rights, *Hearings on Inquiry into the Destruction of Former FBI Director Hoover's Files and FBI Recordkeeping*, 94th Cong., 1st Sess., 1972.

[2] For a complete list of persons and subjects as well as the FBI records released under FOIA from the O&C File see *Guide to the Scholarly Resources Microfilm Edition: The Official and Confidential File of FBI Director J. Edgar Hoover* (Wilmington, DE, 1988).

"The FBI." Moreover, there are folders on sensitive Bureau operations, such as counterintelligence activities and technical surveillance, and background information for the FBI's Special Intelligence Operations, the Office of Strategic Services, and "black bag" jobs.

With the exception of folders that pertain to special investigations, the files are fragmentary and are not the FBI's primary source of information concerning their subject. For example, the folders in the O&C File that relate to Alger Hiss consist primarily of materials brought together in the 1950s to indicate that Hoover had warned the Department of State about Hiss before the case ever became public.[3] At present, the O&C File consists of 164 folders and the Nichols File of an additional 86 folders.

Hoover's October 1, 1941, memorandum also created a confidential file "in Miss Gandy's Office." (Helen Gandy was Hoover's longtime private secretary.) This file was for "restricted or confidential items of a more or less personal nature of the Director's." They were, according to Hoover's memorandum, "items which [he] might have occasion to call for from time to time, such as memoranda to the Department on the Dies Committee, etc." This is the file that Gandy destroyed as "personal records" upon Hoover's death.[4]

---

[3] See the NARA/FBI Task Force write-up on the O&C Files, NARA/FBI Task Force Records, NARA.

[4] Ibid.

W. Mark Felt Files

There is some confusion over what actually constituted the Felt Files. W. Mark Felt was a longtime deputy director under Hoover. After the latter's death in 1972, Hoover's close companion and confidant, Clyde Tolson, transferred Hoover's Official and Confidential File to Felt's office along with six volumes of official memorandums from Hoover to Tolson. Many people have referred to these records as the Felt Files. Felt himself, however, referred to taking charge of certain sensitive files from Louis B. Nichols upon Nichols's retirement in 1957. According to Felt, he ordered these sensitive materials, which included information on Martin Luther King, Jr., returned to the Special File Room when he placed Hoover's O&C File there. According to the NARA/FBI Task Force report, most of the files referred to as the Felt Files have either been returned to Hoover's O&C File in the Special File Room or found to be reintegrated into the Central Records System.[1]

[1] See W. Mark Felt, *The FBI Pyramid from the Inside* (New York: Putnam's, 1979) pp. 231–32, and NARA/FBI Task Force report.

Electronic Surveillance Files

FBI records concerning the establishment of Bureau policies, procedures, and methods relating to electronic surveillance are found in four major FBI files: (1) Technical Surveillance 66-8160, (2) Wiretapping 62-12114, (3) June Mail 66-1372, and (4) ELSUR 62-3181. These files are enormous and record in detail changing FBI policies with regard to the use of electronic surveillance techniques by the Bureau.[1]

Technical Surveillance

Initially this file, and the term "technical surveillance," related to telephone wiretaps. By the 1950s, however, it came to encompass microphone surveillance techniques as well. In August 1940, Hoover issued instructions to all special agents in charge with regard to establishing a uniform method of transmitting and maintaining records relating to telephone surveillance. According to Hoover, purely personal information obtained from technical surveillance methods was not to be forwarded to headquarters, but the field offices were to maintain a complete log or summary showing all the information obtained. The pertinent information relating to a particular case was to be transmitted to the Bureau with a cover letter titled "CONFILE" which would indicate that the information came from a confidential source without revealing what the source actually was.

From the 1940s the file contains numerous documents relating to Attorney General Robert Jackson's March 1940 prohibition of electronic surveillance and President Franklin D. Roosevelt's partial lifting of the ban, in May of that year, for national defense cases. In 1941 the FBI installed a number of surveillance taps on embassies and individuals despite the reluctance of recently appointed Attorney General Francis Biddle to grant such authorization. Even after December 7, 1941, Biddle continued to refuse FBI requests for authority to wiretap

---

[1] The discussion of FBI ELSUR files is based on the studies of these files by Dr. Timothy Nenninger of the NARA/FBI Task Force. See his reports in NARA/FBI Task Force records, in the National Archives.

individuals and ordered several surveillance operations relating to national security cases to be discontinued.

During the late 1940s the Bureau continued to have legal problems with electronic surveillance cases. In 1949, for example, in response to judicial setbacks in the Judith Coplon espionage case, Associate Director Clyde Tolson recommended, and Hoover approved, that the FBI avoid using technical surveillance in criminal cases or in any espionage cases likely to go to trial. Coplon, an employee of the Foreign Agents Registration Section of the Department of Justice, handled "internal security" documents, including sensitive FBI reports, in the course of her work. Legal blunders on the part of the Bureau during her trial on espionage charges compromised classified FBI materials that showed the Department of Justice had been penetrated by the Soviet intelligence network. Nevertheless, the Bureau continued to use technical surveillance to accumulate information for general intelligence purposes while recognizing that such information was not admissible in court.

In the same memorandum, Tolson established new record-keeping procedures for technical surveillance information within the Bureau. Henceforth, logs and other documentation relating to technical surveillance were to be maintained separately from other records. In response to a request from the attorney general in 1949, Hoover reported that following FDR's guidelines the Bureau had instituted approximately two hundred technical surveillance operations during the 1940s. He further claimed they were of "inestimable assistance" in obtaining information on persons suspected of subversive activity.

During the 1950s and 1960s tension between the Department of Justice and the Bureau over the use of electronic surveillance techniques continued to increase as the Bureau increasingly sought their use not only in espionage cases but in criminal cases as well. In 1966, Hoover and Attorney General Ramsey Clark exchanged conflicting views on the issue. Hoover claimed that with the passage of the Safe Streets and Crime Act, if no trespass was involved the Bureau could obtain Department of Justice and court authority for wiretaps and bugs and that such information was admissible as evidence. Clark declared this was not the case. According to the attorney general, "Obviously, evidence derived in such a manner cannot be used at trial." Moreover, for Clark, microphone coverage, if installed by unauthorized entry, was a Fourth Amendment violation. Clark ignored FBI requests for authority to use electronic surveillance in organized crime cases.

In addition to reflecting the tension between the Bureau and the Department of Justice over this issue, the file also provides a look at the number of publicly reported FBI electronic surveillance operations. On June 14, 1972, for example, the Bureau reported twenty-eight telephone and six microphone monitoring installations in national security cases then in place. In February 1972, in preparation for testimony before a senate committee, however, the Bureau informed the Department of Justice in open testimony that it did not consider electronic surveillance conducted at the behest of another Federal agency an FBI surveillance. Accordingly, any request from the Department of State for such assistance would not be counted. The Bureau deliberately undercounted its incidents of surveillance in order to show its "restraint" in electronic surveillance matters.

Finally, the file reflects the enormous amount of paper and man-hours involved in technical surveillance. An internal Bureau memorandum, for example, reported that one Washington field office warrantless wiretap produced five reels of 1,800 feet of tape per day, amounting to ten hours of conversation, much of it in a foreign language. The average five-day workweek produced more than four hundred pages of logs alone.

Wiretapping

Early records in this file relate to FBI investigations of possible violations of state and local laws by law enforcement officials who tapped telephone lines. While other Federal agencies during the 1920s and 1930s, especially the Prohibition Unit of the Treasury Department, tapped telephone lines, Hoover prohibited Bureau agents from engaging in such practices. Even after a Supreme Court decision (*Olmsted v. United States*) declared wiretap information admissible court evidence, Hoover remained adamant that FBI agents not engage in such activities. According to Hoover, "While it may not be illegal I think it is unethical." By 1931, however, the Bureau began to reconsider its policy. In February 1931, Attorney General James Dewitt Mitchell specially authorized the FBI to institute wiretaps if the director and the appropriate assistant attorney general approved. As a result, Hoover changed the *FBI Manual of Rules and Regulations* to permit wiretapping.

From early 1931 to mid-1933 the file consists largely of copies of newspaper editorials and excerpts from congressional hearings on the ethics and efficiency of wiretapping as a law enforcement tool. Despite the 1931 change in policy the FBI appears not to have engaged in wiretapping during this time. The Prohibition Unit, however, now a part of the Department of Justice, continued to operate wiretaps.

On June 22, 1933, the Chicago field office requested authority to place a wiretap in connection with an investigation of the murder of an FBI agent, and Hoover granted the request. This was the first documented Bureau authorization for such a tap. Subsequently, headquarters received numerous requests from its field offices for authority to institute wiretaps. Hoover continually insisted that the field offices obtain prior approval for such taps (from the records this request seems to have been routinely ignored). In a January 1934 letter to the special agents in charge, for example, Hoover reiterates this policy. Three months later, however, he admitted, "I suspect this practice [requesting authorization after the tap was already in place] was being indulged in rather freely by our field offices."

In addition, during 1934, Hoover's attitude and Bureau policy regarding wiretapping dramatically changed, as the Director became firmly convinced of its utility in kidnapping, extortion, and other serious felony cases. By 1936 field offices were receiving instructions in wiretapping, and Hoover ordered wiretap equipment for each field office.

Responding to Supreme Court decisions in 1937 and 1939, which again called into question the legality of wiretapping by Federal officials, Attorney General Jackson prohibited all wiretaps by the FBI. Hoover complied by banning any new taps and discontinuing those then in place, but he vigorously protested the prohibition—especially in espionage and kidnapping cases. On May 21, 1940, President Roosevelt directed Jackson to authorize wiretaps in espionage, sabotage, assassination, or other "grave matters involving the defense of the nation." Despite the president's approval, Hoover remained cautious concerning the Bureau's use of such wiretaps. He requested specific legislation authorizing their use and recommended that the attorney general exercise authority over all wiretaps initiated by any executive department. On February 1, 1941, Hoover wrote to Attorney General Biddle that taps should be used only in kidnapping, extortion, narrowly defined national defense, and possibly narcotics cases. He warned that to extend the use of taps to other felonies and to allow other executive departments to authorize their use would inevitably result in abuse and public resentment and opposition.

During the 1950s, in the wake of the Coplon case, Hoover and the Bureau again became concerned about the admissibility of wiretap and microphone surveillance evidence in court. Hoover carefully instructed the field offices on what they could or could not use in court. Despite such warnings and the rather narrow use of surveillance information in court cases, Hoover's attitude toward using electronic surveillance techniques had clearly changed by the 1950s: he was now much more willing to allow Bureau agents to engage in such techniques.

By the late 1960s and early 1970s the character of the file became quite different. No longer an important policy file reflecting Bureau attitudes, it became instead a public relations file. It does, however, recount the Bureau's continuing battle with Attorney General Clark over the effect of wiretaps and its claim that they were essential in solving several gambling cases in Las Vegas involving La Cosa Nostra.

June Mail

This file is a curious amalgam, gathering not only the basic documentation on June Mail procedures but also documents on general technical surveillance procedures and policy. In June 1949, Hoover established the separate June Mail filing procedures for information received from or relating to the Bureau's "most secretive sources," including governors, secretaries to high officials, extremely confidential informants, and "highly confidential or unusual investigative techniques." Later in 1949, Hoover included records relating to electronic surveillance under the June Mail procedures. In 1952 the Bureau authorized the placing of an asterisk (*) behind the symbol number on administrative pages to distinguish a technical or microphone surveillance from a live informant. On April 24, 1952, it extended the use of an asterisk to denote a few of the most highly placed live confidential informants.

From its origins, most June Mail related to information gathered in security cases. In 1964 some information relating to criminal intelligence, such as La Cosa Nostra and the Top Echelon Criminal Informants, was authorized to be handled under the June Mail procedures. In 1970 the June Mail categorization was further broadened when Hoover authorized each special agent in charge to determine what should be considered June Mail regardless of its case origins. On November 7, 1978, the Bureau discontinued the June Mail designation but continued to require special handling and separate filing of sensitive materials.

ELSUR

The Bureau established the ELSUR file in 1966 in response to a Department of Justice Tax Division inquiry regarding Bureau use of electronic surveillance in specific organized crime cases. The Department of Justice officials needed to know whether the subject of court proceedings had ever been monitored electronically by the FBI. They believed that the nature of the surveillance and the information derived from it could affect the government's ability to prosecute such cases successfully. Initially the Department of Justice wanted to know if an individual was the subject of a surveillance. Almost immediately it broadened its request to include individuals mentioned in monitored conversations but not necessarily participants. In response, the Bureau established a centralized, separate ELSUR index to facilitate retrieval of such information.

Department of Justice inquiries in this area usually involved numerous individuals. The initial request contained 151 names. By 1970 such requests were so frequent that the Bureau designed a printed form letter to respond. In the beginning the overwhelming majority of names submitted by the Department of Justice were individuals involved in organized crime cases. There is a good deal of information relating to Jimmy Hoffa and Teamster associates, for example. In the mid-1960s there were several inquiries concerning individuals involved in civil rights investigations in the South (addressing, in part, the bombing of the Sixteenth Street Baptist Church in Birmingham, Alabama, in September 1963, in which four young girls were killed), and the 1964 murders of civil rights workers Lemuel A. Penn and Viola Gregg Liuzzo. During the late 1960s and early 1970s political activists, antiwar demonstrators, Black Panther party members, and members of the Students for a Democratic Society and the Weathermen accounted for a significant portion of the inquiries. By the late 1970s organized crime figures returned to prominence. Because the inquiries are limited to individuals involved in court proceedings, there is little in the file relating to espionage or national security cases.

Most of the documentation in the file pertains to routine confirmations or denials of ELSUR coverage on individuals. In fact, only a small minority of the people about whom the Department of Justice requested information show up in the ELSUR index. There is some documentation, however, on the types of surveillance equipment used, the methods of installation, and other surveillance techniques. The file contains little information about basic ELSUR policy.

The FBI Interesting Case Program

J. Edgar Hoover instituted the Interesting Case Program in 1927 to provide the press and public with interesting and factual data concerning the accomplishments of the Bureau. In the beginning, such cases only involved fingerprint comparisons. By 1932, however, cases were drawn from a variety of Bureau classifications. Eventually the program served as a public-relations source for FBI personnel in preparing the budget and the annual report to Congress, as well as a source for television, radio, and film producers.[1]

Initially, headquarters personnel prepared the cases based on recommendations received from either headquarters or the field. Beginning in 1944, Hoover, who took a direct interest in the program, required each field office to submit drafts of the cases, which were then edited by the Crimes Record Section and later by the Research Section of the External Affairs Division. According to Hoover's guidelines, cases selected for the program "should demonstrate the FBI at its best." In general, the write-ups include the facts relating to a specific violation, the steps taken by the Bureau to identify and apprehend the subject, details of the investigation, and the results of the prosecution "with appropriate protection afforded to confidential investigative techniques and informants." The Bureau discontinued the program in 1972 in the face of concerns raised by the Privacy and the Freedom of Information acts. By this time, there were more than two thousand cases from thirty-three different classifications included in the program. In 1974 the Bureau resumed the program, only to terminate it again in 1977.

The first eight sections of Classification 62-23346 consist of a numbered collection of Interesting Case write-ups, numbered 1 to 307 and dating from 1927 to 1932. After 1932 the Interesting Cases were not numbered consecu-

---

[1] This section is based primarily on the special study completed by Dr. Gregory Bradsher as a part of the NARA/FBI Task Force. See the records of the NARA/FBI Task Force in the National Archives.

tively. Instead, each bears the same number as its related case file number. The Bureau's Research Section maintains a complete set of Interesting Cases arranged within each classification numerically by case number.

FBI Budget Records

Bureau budget-related records maintained outside of the FBI's Central Records System span from 1939 to the present. The files between 1939 and 1979 contain records relating to budget formulation as well as budget execution, reflecting the fact that until 1979 both activities were performed by a single organizational unit of the Bureau. In 1979, however, Bureau officials established a Budget Formulation and Presentation Unit to handle budget formulation, while budget execution was left to the Accounting and Budget Analysis Unit. Each unit maintained its records separately. Files accumulated between 1939 and 1979 are arranged chronologically by year and thereunder by subject. Current records are maintained in three-year blocks, which are arranged alphabetically by subject and thereunder chronologically by year.[1]

Records relating to FBI budget preparation document the initial formulation of the Bureau's budget and its revisions as it is reviewed by the Department of Justice, the Office of Management and Budget, and finally the U.S. Congress. Included in these files are memorandums prepared by the various units of the Bureau outlining their programs and budgetary needs for the coming year, memorandums of high-ranking Bureau officials concerning budget questions, and records connected with budget hearings, such as copies of appropriation bills, internal FBI memorandums concerning the status of the FBI appropriations, and copies of formal FBI budget requests and justifications. Since 1979 the Budget Formulation and Presentation Unit has filed most of its records under Congressional Affairs and Estimates, Office of Management and Budget, and Spring Planning Estimates.

Records relating to budget execution are a mass of fiscal accounting-type documents, such as ledgers, vouchers, apportionment and reapportionment schedules, reports on the status of obligations, reconciliations, and similar materials.

---

[1] This section is based primarily on the special study prepared by Dr. Jerome Nashorn of the NARA/FBI Task Force on Bureau Records Maintained Outside of the FBI Central Records System, NARA/FBI Task Force Records in the National Archives.

They are all used to document the allocation and disbursement of appropriated funds.

According to the NARA/FBI Task Force report on Bureau budget records, the Bureau insisted that all budget records could be found in the Central Records System. The NARA/FBI Task Force examination of these records tended to confirm this contention. The older record materials, however, according to the Task Force report, contained a high proportion of original material, including documents and exhibits prepared for Hoover in connection with his appearances before congressional committees. Moreover, the records maintained by the individual budget units were easier to use for research purposes. In addition to the records of the Bureau's budget units, a researcher needs to consult FBI Classifications 62-40772 House Appropriations Committee, 62-18217 Bureau of the Budget/Office of Management and Budget, 66 Appropriations, and 66-18000 FBI Budget and Accounting Procedures.

Japanese Activities in the United States

Because of the wide interest in the internment of Japanese Americans during World War II and the legal cases that resulted from it, the NARA/FBI Task Force carefully reviewed Bureau records relating to this issue. This section is a summary of its findings.[1]

The Bureau files found in the Los Angeles field office relating to Japanese activities in the United States during the 1940s are extensive and are the best source of information in the Bureau's records on the Japanese internment and subsequent problems. In response to a request from Hoover for information on Japanese activities, the Los Angeles office established a special Japanese squad and proceeded to survey all Japanese associations and organizations in the metropolitan area considered dangerous to the internal security of the United States. The squad also monitored the Japanese intelligence situation in the area. In 1941, for example, the field office opened more than one hundred cases on the Japanese Navy League alone. The major file concerning Japanese espionage activities is 65-4370 (numbering 5 volumes). This file contains brief descriptions of Japanese organizations such as the Japanese Tourist Information Bureau, the Japanese American Citizens League, the Japanese American Association, suspected Japanese espionage agents and Japanese intelligence groups, and the Japanese Foreign Trade Bureau. The FBI did not have jurisdictional authority in this area, and therefore there is no one central file relating to the camps or the program (see the Records of the War Relocation Authority, Record Group 210, and the Records of the Immigration and Naturalization Service, who ran the camps, Record Group 85, both in the National Archives). In the Los Angeles field office, however, are numerous files relating to conditions within the camps (see cases 100-1478, 100-10294, 105-00-11, 66-0, 66-2042, 100-17513, and 100-19832 for examples).

---

[1] This section is based primarily on the special study prepared by Dr. Gerald K. Haines as a member of the NARA/FBI Task Force. See the Task Force records in the National Archives.

After the war the Bureau developed a close working relationship with the Japanese intelligence services concerning Communist activities and the Japanese Red Army (see 105-22772 and 105-39351). The indexes in the Los Angeles field office are extensive concerning Japanese activities in the United States for the war and the postwar period. Most cases are in Classifications 65, 66, 100, and 105. The Index to Japanese Organizations and the Index of Japanese Organizations in the United States have been destroyed. Nevertheless, the Los Angeles field office remains a rich source of information for research on Japanese activities in the United States during the 1940s and the early Cold War period and has not yet been exploited. The researcher also should consult FBI Headquarters files 129 Evacuation Claims and 97 Foreign Agents Registration Act.

APPENDIXES

I. Standard FBI Abbreviations

ACDA	U.S. Arms Control and Disarmament Agency
ACMN	Altered Confidential Motor Number
ACSI	Assistant Chief of Staff for Intelligence, U.S. Army
ACSI	Assistant Chief of Staff, Intelligence, U.S. Air Force
ACSN	Altered Confidential Serial Number
ACVIN	Altered Confidential Vehicle Identification Number
ADM	Administrative Matters
ADW	Assault with a Dangerous Weapon
AEA	Atomic Energy Act
AFA	Ascertaining Financial Ability
AFO	Assaulting a Federal Officer
AFSN	Air Force Serial Number
AG	Attorney General of the United States
AGO	Adjutant General's Office
AI	Administrative Inquiry
AID	Agency for International Development
AIDA	Automobile Information Disclosure Act
AKA	Also Known As
ALF	Anonymous Letter File
AMN	Altered Motor Number
AMSD	Airmail Special Delivery
AP	Aircraft Piracy
APACS	Application for Pardon after Completion of Sentence
APCM	Alien Property Custodian Matter
APLI	Applicant (General)
APMN	Altered Public Motor Number
APRCR	Application for Pardon to Restore Civil Rights
APSN	Altered Public Serial Number
APVIN	Altered Public Vehicle Identification Number
AR	Anti-Racketeering

AR-IGCS	Anti-Racketeering—Interference with Government Communications System
ARINC	Aeronautical Radio Inc.
ARL	Antiriot Laws
ARRFP	Authority Requested to Release Facts to the Press
ASAC	Assistant Special Agent in Charge
ASD	Administrative Services Division
ASIO	Australian Security Intelligence Office
ASN	Altered Serial Number (ITSMV cases)
ASN	Army Serial Number
ATA	Air Transportation Association
ATF	Bureau of Alcohol, Tobacco, and Firearms
ATSFO	Air Transportation Security Field Office
AUSA	Assistant United States Attorney
AVIN	Altered Vehicle Identification Number
BATF	Bureau of Alcohol, Tobacco, and Firearms
BATSI	Bilateral Air Transportation Security Information Officer (Department of State)
BB	Bank Burglary
BDC	Bomb Data Center
BEP	Bureau of Engraving and Printing
BF&E	Bank Fraud and Embezzlement (abbreviations approved for use in these cases: FCU—Federal Credit Union; SLA—Savings and Loan Association)
BKTCY	Bankruptcy
BL	Bank Larceny
BOL	Broadcasting Obscene Language
BR	Bank Robbery
BT	Bomb Threats
BUAP	Bureau Applicant
BUCAR	Bureau Car
BUDED	Bureau Deadline
BULF	Black United Liberation Front
CAA	Crime Aboard Aircraft
CAS	Congressional Assassination Statute
CFTC	Commodity Futures Trading Commission
CGR	Crime on Government Reservation
CHS	Crime on High Seas
CIA	Central Intelligence Agency
CID	Criminal Investigation Division
CIR	Crime on Indian Reservation
CMN	Confidential Motor Number
CO	Conscientious Objector
COB	Close of Business

COC	Contempt of Court
CODD	Central Office Dispatch Drop
COI	Conflict of Interest
COPMAT	Copyright Matter
CP	Communist Party
CPUSA	Communist Party of the USA
CR	Civil Rights
CRA-64	Civil Rights Act of 1964
CSA	Community Services Administration
CSN	Confidential Serial Number
CTCL	Court of Claims
CVIN	Confidential Vehicle Identification Number
CVR	Cockpit Voice Recorder
CWAA	Carrying Weapons Aboard Aircraft
DAA-50	Dependents Assistance Act of 1950
DAMV	Destruction of Aircraft or Motor Vehicles
DAPLI	Departmental Applicant
DBA	Doing Business As
DCA	Defense Communications Agency
DCII	Defense Central Index of Investigations
DEA	Drug Enforcement Administration
DESECO	Program for Development of Selected Contacts (terminated 1974)
DEPT	Department or Departmental
DGP	Destruction of Government Property
DIA	Defense Intelligence Agency
DIH	Discrimination in Housing
DIP	Destruction of Interstate Property
DIS	Defense Investigative Service
DMP	Damaging Property
DNA	Defense Nuclear Agency
DOB	Date of Birth
DOE	Department of Energy
DOE-A	Department of Energy—Applicant
DOE-CSC	Department of Energy—Civil Service Commission
DOE-E	Department of Energy—Employee
DOF	Desecration of the Flag
DOJ	Department of Justice
DOKEX	Document Examiner
DOT	Department of Transportation
DP	Disorderly Person
DPOB	Date and Place of Birth
DUPREQ	Duplicate Request
EAR	Escape and Rescue

ECT	Extortionate Credit Transaction
EEOA-72	Equal Employment Opportunity Act of 1972
EFP	Escaped Federal Prisoner
EFTO	Encrypted for Transmission Only
EGP	Embezzlement of Government Property
EID	Explosives and Incendiary Devices
EL	Election Laws
ELSUR	Electronic Surveillance
EOD	Entry on Duty
EPA	Environmental Protection Agency
EPOW	Escaped Prisoner of War
ERISA	Employee Retirement Income Security Act
ESP	Espionage
EXT	Extortion
FAA	Federal Aviation Administration
FAG	Fraud against the Government
FAMNIFA	False Advertising or Misuse of Names to Indicate Federal Agency
FBI	Federal Bureau of Investigation
FBIHQ	Federal Bureau of Investigation Headquarters
FCA	Farm Credit Administration
FCC	Falsely Claiming U.S. Citizenship
FCI	Foreign Counterintelligence
FCLAA	Federal Cigarette Labeling and Advertising Act
FCU	Federal Credit Union
FDIC	Federal Deposit Insurance Corporation
FEA	Federal Energy Administration
FERIC	False Entries in Records of Interstate Carriers
FHA	Federal Housing Administration
FI	False Information
FISUR	Physical Surveillance
FJDM	Federal Juvenile Delinquency Matters
FLIA	Federal Lending and Insurance Agencies
FNU	First Name Unknown
FOIA	Freedom of Information Act
FPC	Foreign Police Cooperation
FR	False Report
FRLA	Federal Regulation of Lobbying Act
FTCA	Federal Tort Claims Act
FTWS	Federal Train Wreck Statute
FUDE	Fugitive-Deserter
FUG	Fugitive
G-2	Office of the Assistant Chief of Staff, G-2 (applies to some major Army commands)

GAO	General Accounting Office
GOVT	Government or Governmental
GSA	General Services Administration
HA	Hatch Act
HEW	Department of Health, Education, and Welfare
HILEV	High Level Intelligence Program (1970s)
HUD	Department of Housing and Urban Development
HUDM	Department of Housing and Urban Development Matters
IC	Intelligence Community
IGA	Interstate Gambling Activities
IGB	Illegal Gambling Business
IGB-F	Illegal Gambling Business—Forfeiture
IGB-O	Illegal Gambling Business—Obstruction
ILO	International Labor Organization
IMP	Impersonation
INC	Incorporated
INS	Immigration and Naturalization Service
INTD	Intelligence Division
IO	Identification Number or Intelligence Officer
IOC	Interception of Communications
IOHTC	Interstate Obscene or Harassing Telephone Calls
IPGP	Illegal Possession of Government Property
IRS	Internal Revenue Service
ISS	Involuntary Servitude or Slavery
ITAR	Interstate Transportation in Aid of Racketeering
ITF	Interstate Transportation of Fireworks
ITGD	Interstate Transportation of Gambling Devices
ITLT	Interstate Transportation of Lottery Tickets
ITOM	Interstate Transportation of Obscene Matter
ITPMG	Interstate Transportation of Prison-Made Goods
ITSA	Interstate Transportation of Stolen Aircraft
ITSB	Interstate Transportation of Strikebreakers
ITSC	Interstate Transportation of Stolen Cattle
ITSMV	Interstate Transportation of Stolen Motor Vehicle (abbreviations approved for use in these cases: VIN—Vehicle Identification Number; MN—Motor Number; SN—Serial Number. Prefixes for use of the above: A—Altered; C—Confidential)
P	Public
ITSP	Interstate Transportation of Stolen Property
ITSP-CT	Interstate Transportation of Stolen Property—Commercial Theft
ITSP-MT	Interstate Transportation of Stolen Property—Major Theft
ITUR	Interstate Transportation of Unsafe Refrigerators

ITWP	Interstate Transportation of Wagering Paraphernalia
IWFC	Interference with Flight Crew
IWU	Illegal Wearing of Uniform
JCS	Joint Chiefs of Staff
JDA	Juvenile Delinquency Act
KFO	Killing of Federal Officer
KID	Kidnapping
KRA	Kickback Racket Act
K&S	Known and Suspected
LDB	Local Draft Board
LEGAT	Legal Attaché
LEUN	Loyalty of Employees of the United Nations and Other Public International Organizations
LFPS	Latent Fingerprint Section
LHM	Letterhead Memorandum
LMRA	Labor-Management Relations Act
LMRA-IM	Labor-Management Reporting and Disclosure Act of 1959—Investigative Matter
LNU	Last Name Unknown
MAOP	Manual of Administrative Operations and Procedures
MCRP	Main Card Repair Project
MEMO	Memorandum
MEMOS	Memorandums
MF	Mail Fraud
MIG	Military Intelligence Group, U.S. Army
MIOG	Manual of Investigative Operations and Guidelines
MISC	Miscellaneous
MISUR	Microphone Surveillance
MN	Motor Number
MO	Modus Operandi
MP	Missing Person
MPD	Metropolitan Police Department
MRV	Mandatory Release Violator
MSN	Marine Serial Number
NA	National Academy
NAANF	National Automobile Altered Numbers File
NAC	National Agency Check
NACC	National Agency Check Center, Department of the Army
NASA	National Aeronautics and Space Administration
NBA	National Bankruptcy Act
NCIC	National Crime Information Center
NFA	National Firearms Act
NFCF	National Fraudulent Check File
NFIP	National Foreign Intelligence Program

NIC	Naval Intelligence Command
NIS	Naval Investigative Service (Headquarters)
NISO	Naval Investigative Service (Field Installations)
NLRB	National Labor Relations Board
NMCC	National Military Command Center
NMI	No Middle Initial
NMN	No Middle Name
NO	Number
NRC	Nuclear Regulatory Commission
NRC-A	Nuclear Regulatory Commission—Applicant
NRC-E	Nuclear Regulatory Commission—Employee
NRC-OPM	Nuclear Regulatory Commission (Office of Personnel Management)
NSA	National Security Agency
NSF	National Science Foundation
NSN	Navy Serial Number
NSP	National Stolen Property
NTSB	National Transportation Safety Board
OCAF	Open Case Ammunition File
OCI	Obstruction of Criminal Investigations
OCO	Obstruction of Court Orders
OMB	Office of Management and Budget
OO	Office of Origin
OOJ	Obstruction of Justice
OPM	Office of Personnel Management
OSD	Office of Secretary of Defense
OSIAF	Office of Special Investigations, Air Force
PA	Public Accommodations
PAREN	Parenthesis
PBV	Probation Violator
PC	Peace Corps
PCI	Priority Case Indicator
PD	Police Department
PE	Public Education
PERJ	Perjury
PF	Public Facilities
PFO	Protection of Foreign Officials
PHS	Public Health Service
PMN	Public Motor Number
POB	Place of Birth
PSN	Public Serial Number
PV	Parole Violator
PVIN	Public Vehicle Identification Number
RA	Registration Act

RCA	Red Cross Act
RCMP	Royal Canadian Mounted Police
REAIRTEL	Reference Is Made to Airtel
REBUAIRTEL	Reference Is Made to Bureau Airtel
REBUCAL	Reference Is Made to Bureau Call
REBUFAC	Reference Is Made to Bureau Facsimile
REBULET	Reference Is Made to Bureau Letter
REBURS	Reference Is Made to Bureau Routing Slip
REBUTEL	Reference Is Made to Bureau Teletype or Telegram
RECAL	Reference Is Made to Call
REFAC	Reference Is Made to Facsimile
RELET	Reference Is Made to Letter
REMEMO	Reference Is Made to Memorandum
REMEMOS	Reference Is Made to Memorandums
REMYMEMO	Reference Is Made to My Memorandum
REMYMEMOS	Reference Is Made to My Memorandums
REREP	Reference Is Made to Report
RERS	Reference Is Made to Routing Slip
RETEL	Reference Is Made to Teletype or Telegram
REURAIRTEL	Reference Is Made to Your Airtel
REURCAL	Reference Is Made to Your Call
REURFAC	Reference Is Made to Your Facsimile
REURMEMO	Reference Is Made to Your Memorandum
REURMEMOS	Reference Is Made to Your Memorandums
REUREP	Reference Is Made to Your Report
REURLET	Reference Is Made to Your Letter
REURS	Reference Is Made to Your Routing Slip
REURTEL	Reference Is Made to Your Teletype or Telegram
RICO	Racketeer Influenced and Corrupt Organizations
RUC	Referred upon Completion to Office of Origin
RMIS	Resource Management Information System
SA	Special Agent
SAA	Special Agent Accountant
SAB	Sabotage
SAC	Special Agent in Charge
SAIS	Satellite Intelligence Service
SB	Sports Bribery
SBA	Small Business Administration
SC	Special Clerk
SE	Special Employee
SED	Sedition
SFCAA	State Firearms Control Assistance Act
SGE	Security of Government Employees
SI	Security Informant

SIS	Special Intelligence Service
SISS	Senate Internal Security Subcommittee
SKA	Switchblade Knife Act
SLA	Savings and Loan Association
SM	Subversive Matter
SN	Serial Number
SNIF	Serial Not in File
SO	Sheriff's Office
SPEN	State Penitentiary
SPI	Special Inquiry
SPIN	Conduct Thorough Background Investigation (including character, loyalty, and ability of presidential appointees)
SPJF	Stolen Personalized Jewelry File
SPOL	State Police
SPR	State Prison
SS	Secret Service
SSA	Selective Service Act
SSAN	Social Security Account Number
SSCO	Selective Service Conscientious Objector
SSN	Social Security Number
SSN	Selective Service Number
SUAIRTEL	Submit Airtel
SUCOP	Submit Copy
SULET	Submit Letter
SUREP	Submit Report
SUTEL	Submit Teletype Summary
TECIP	Top Echelon Criminal Informant Program
TENFUG	Ten Most Wanted Fugitives
TESUR	Technical Surveillance
TFIS	Theft from Interstate Shipment
TGP	Theft of Government Property
TOPLEV	Top Level Intelligence Program (in mid-1950s directed toward Communists; later used in investigations of racial matters)
TR	Treason and Related Statutes
TURK	Time Utilization Record-keeping
TWEA	Trading with the Enemy Act
UACB	Unless Advised to the Contrary by Bureau
UFAC	Unlawful Flight to Avoid Custody or Confinement
UFAP	Unlawful Flight to Avoid Prosecution
UFAT	Unlawful Flight to Avoid Testimony
UISC	Unreported Interstate Shipment of Cigarettes
UMTD	Use of Mails to Defraud
UNSUBS	Unknown Subjects

UPRF	Unlawful Possession or Receipt of Firearms
US	United States
USA	United States Attorney
USAF	United States Air Force
USAIRR	United States Army Investigative Records Repository
USCAPLI	United States Courts—Applicant
USCG	United States Coast Guard
USDC	United States District Court
USDJ	United States District Judge
USIA	United States Information Agency
USM	United States Marshal
USMAGIS	United States Magistrate
USMC	United States Marine Corps
USPS	United States Postal Service
USSS	United States Secret Service
VA	Veterans Administration
VAM	Veterans Administration Matters
VIKEX	Victim Extortion
VIKID	Victim Kidnapping
VIN	Vehicle Identification Number
VRA-65	Voting Rights Act of 1965
WF	Wanted Flier
WH	White House
WHO	World Health Organization
WSTA	White Slave Traffic Act

II. Abbreviations Used in Espionage and Foreign Counterintelligence Cases

Country

Albania	AL
Bulgaria	BU
China	CH
Cuba	CU
Czechoslovakia	CZ
East Germany	EG
Hungary	HU
Poland	PO
Romania	RO
Soviet Union	USSR
Yugoslavia	YU

III. Abbreviations of Field Office Locations

City			City	
Albany	AL		Knoxville	KX
Albuquerque	AQ		Las Vegas	LV
Alexandria	AX		Little Rock	LR
Anchorage	AN		Los Angeles	LA
Atlanta	AT		Louisville	LS
Baltimore	BA		Memphis	ME
Birmingham	BH		Miami	MM
Boston	BS		Milwaukee	MI
Brooklyn-Queens	BQ		Minneapolis	MP
Buffalo	BU		Mobile	MO
Butte	BT		Newark	NK
Charlotte	CE		New Haven	NH
Chicago	CG		New Orleans	NO
Cincinnati	CI		New Rochelle	NR
Cleveland	CV		New York City	NY
Columbia	CO		Norfolk	NF
Dallas	DL		Oklahoma City	OC
Denver	DN		Omaha	OM
Detroit	DE		Philadelphia	PH
El Paso	EP		Phoenix	PX
Honolulu	HN		Pittsburgh	PG
Houston	HO		Portland	PD
Indianapolis	IP		Richmond	RH
Jackson	JN		Sacramento	SC
Jacksonville	JK		Saint Louis	SL
Kansas City	KC		Salt Lake City	SU

San Antonio	SA	Seattle	SE
San Diego	SD	Springfield	SI
San Francisco	SF	Tampa	TP
San Juan	SJ	Washington Field	
Savannah	SV	Office	WFO

IV. Abbreviations of Foreign Office Locations

Foreign Office

Bern	BER
Bogota	BOG
Bonn	BON
Hong Kong	HON
London	LON
Manila	MAN
Mexico City	MEX
Ottawa	OTT
Panama	PAN
Paris	PAR
Rome	ROM
Tokyo	TOK

V. FBI Records Released under the Freedom of Information Act

(Files are available in the FBI Reading Room, Washington, DC.)

Subject	Pages Released	Classification(s)
Adamic, Louis	632	100
Addams, Jane	188	61
Algren, Nelson	687	100
Ali, Noble Drew (*See* Moorish Science Temple of America)		
Alscher, Ruth		65, 100, 101, 165
Amerasia	12,853	100
America First Committee	2,939	
American Friends Service Committee	3,498	
American Indian Movement	17,722	100, 105, 157, 176
American Legion Contact Program		
Ananda Marga	1,510	
Arendt, Hannah		40, 105
Atlanta Child Murders (ATKID)	2,825	7
Ball, Lucille	46	94, 100
Barker, Arthur	252	7, 76
Barker, Fred	16	
Barker, Herman	190	26
Barker, Lloyd	11	62
Barker, Kate (Ma)	5	7, 62
Barker/Karpis Gang	76,159	
Hamm Kidnapping	5,249	7
Edward Bremer Kidnapping	70,910	7
Barrow, Clyde, and Bonnie Parker	461	26, 52
Black Extremists		100, 105, 157

VI. Classification 80: Standard Files and Reference Collections

80-8	Uniformity of Write-ups of White Slave Cases
80-11	Criminal Laboratory—General
80-12	Fingerprint Analysis
80-15	Handwriting Analysis
80-87	Collection of News Type
80-94	Moot Court
80-95	Fingerprint Analysis
80-97	Glass File
80-98	Outside Experts
80-99	Handwriting Analysis
80-176	Multi-Line Recorder Circuit
80-600	Checks
80-601	Tape (adhesive, surgical)
80-606	Crime Laboratories throughout the United States
80-610	Watermarks and Paper
80-611	Fake Titles and Bills of Sale
80-612	Cryptography
80-613	Rubber Stamp Exhibits
80-619	Rubber Shoe Heel File
80-620	Fuses and Commercial Explosives
80-621	Wood Specimens
80-624	Hair and Fiber Reference File
80-625	Handwriting Sample—Domestic
80-630	Laundry Marks
80-637	Interdepartmental Radio Advisory Committee
80-638	FBI Radio Transmitting Station
80-643	Radio Direction Finding Systems
80-644	Forged Suicide Notes
80-646	CW Radio Transmitter Project

80-648	FM Radio Station
80-657	Microwave Apparatus—Radar
80-661	Sound and the Transmission of Secret Messages
80-669	Radio Crystal Project
80-670	Radio Monitoring
80-671	Battery and Radio Tube Survey of Bureau Equipment
80-675	Bankruptcy Documents Reference File
80-676	Selective Service Registration Card Standards
80-677	Sound Playback
80-679	Cryptography
80-682	Cryptography
80-684	Cryptography
80-691	Anonymous Letter File
80-692	Safety Paper Standards
80-693	Cryptography
80-696	National Security File (handwriting specimen of key activists)
80-698	File of Passport and Identity Papers
80-703	Radio Monitoring Logs
80-716	Radio Monitoring Logs
80-717	Preamplifiers
80-719	Radio Monitoring Logs
80-720	Radio Monitoring Logs
80-722	Radio Monitoring Logs
80-723	Radio Monitoring Logs
80-727	Radio Monitoring Logs
80-728	Cryptography
80-731	Cryptography
80-733	Standard File of Gummed Paper Tape
80-735	Federal Impersonators Handwriting File
80-738	Standard Ammunition File
80-742	Cryptography
80-743	Firearms Reference Collection
80-744	Open Case Ammunition File
80-748	Cryptography
80-749	Cryptography
80-750	Mobile Radio Equipment
80-751	Administrative—Monitoring
80-752	Administrative—Radio
80-753	Administrative—Sound
80-755	Portable FM Radio Equipment
80-759	Police Radios in Bureau Cars
80-760	Ultrasonic Listening Devices
80-762	Seals

80-763	Cryptography
80-764	Cryptography
80-765	Cryptography
80-768	Magnetic Tape
80-769	Deal Recorder
80-770	30x Sound Recorder
80-772	Single Pair Telephone Microphone Units
80-773	Identification Passes
80-780	110-Volt AC Power Line Microphones
80-781	Confidence Microphones
80-784	Motion-Activated Surveillance Transmitter
80-787	Resonant Microphones
80-788	Radio-Controlled Microphones
80-789	Tracing Telephone Calls
80-791	Transistorized Preamplifier
80-792	Handwriting Analysis
80-795	Administrative—Monitoring
80-796	Administrative—Monitoring
80-797	Administrative—Monitoring
80-798	Administrative—Monitoring
80-802	Amplifiers Detectaphone
80-808	Miniature Radio Equipment
80-810	Russian Radio Receiver Radiation
80-821	Automatic Gain-Adjusting Amplifier
80-825	Radio—Maintenance
80-833	Video Recorders
80-844	Specialized Scientific Aid and Training for Police
80-848	Handwriting Analysis
80-851	American Society of Crime Laboratory Directors
80-859	Forensic Sciences Foundation
80-868	Motion-Controlled Transmitter
80-87	Collection of News Type
80-870	Computer Printouts

VII. Symbols Used by the FBI on Documents

Blue Circle indicates subject of mail

Red X indicates *See* reference

Red Underlining indicates pertinent information to be entered on "See" card

Dotted Circle indicates main card found in index

Blue Zip in Circle indicates main card not found

Green Line through Blue Zip indicates main card has been entered

X in Circle over the name indicates not necessary to make a main card. It also means no indexing by the field office. This should be in the lower right-hand corner of mail.

Blue Flag indicates cards in index on same name buildup, breakdown, or variation of name, but not necessarily identical to subject

Blue N before file number indicates new case has been opened

Green X or **Green Underlining** indicates agent wants additional indexing

Blue Underlining indicates pertinent information to be entered on main card

Blue Numbers after Subject indicate page number(s) for pertinent data to be entered on main card

Red Numbers in Upper Left Margin indicate page number(s) for "See" cards to be entered

VIII. The Freedom of Information Act (FOIA)

Purpose

A. The Freedom of Information Act (FOIA) mandates that all agencies provide any person who submits a request under the act responsive information maintained in agency records, unless it is exempted by the act.

B. Definition of "agency" within the act excludes Congress, the personal staff of the president, the Office of the Counsel to the President, and units within the Executive Office of the President whose sole function is to advise and assist the president.

C. Term "records" is very broad, but does not include tangible evidentiary objects. One of the factors that determines whether documents are agency records is whether the agency has possession and control.

D. Term "any person" encompasses individuals (including foreign nationals), partnerships, corporations, associations, and foreign or local governments, but not fugitives from justice.

Administrative Process

A. Requester must (1) submit an FOIA request pursuant to the Federal agency's published regulations and (2) reasonably describe the records sought.

    1. Description of the records is sufficient if it enables a professional agency employee familiar with the subject area to locate the record with a reasonable amount of effort.

    2. Requests not submitted in accordance with published agency regulations are not considered received and there is no obligation on the part of the agency to search or release records.

    3. Each agency must publish a description of its system of records and its rules of procedures for submitting FOIA requests in the *Federal Register*.

B. Upon receipt of a request made pursuant to an agency's regulations, the Federal agency must:

1. Inform the requester of its decision to grant or deny access to the requested records within *ten* working days.

2. This time period may be extended for an additional ten working days for one of three specified reasons: (1) the need to search for and collect records from separate offices; (2) the need to examine a voluminous amount of records required by the requester; and (3) the need to consult with another agency or agency component.

3. Requester is deemed to have exhausted administrative remedies by failure of the Federal agency to respond within these time limits. Recent cases from the Circuit Court of the District of Columbia have held that if a requester has received the initial response from the agency, even an untimely one, prior to filing a lawsuit, the requester *must* seek an administrative appeal and exhaust administrative remedies.

4. Agencies must make determination on administrative appeals within *twenty* working days.

C. A Federal agency must conduct a reasonable, good-faith search. Standard of reasonableness criteria include: (1) whether the agency conducted a search; and (2) whether the search was reasonably calculated to uncover all relevant documents.

1. Certain "operational" files of the CIA are exempt from search under the CIA Information Act.

2. An agency need not search when it "glomars" an FOIA request by refusing to confirm or deny the existence of records whenever the existence or nonexistence of requested information is itself classified under Executive Order 12356. (Such information must fall within the substantive definitions of classified material authorized to be kept secret in the interest of national security under EO 12356, as information relating to intelligence sources or methods and intelligence activities and properly classified in accordance with the requirements of the executive order.)

D. An agency must release nonexempt, segregable information.

E. An agency must categorize the requester for purposes of fee assessment. Requesters may ask that fees be waived or reduced.

F. An agency may not require advance payment of fees unless the requester has failed to pay fees for previous FOIA requests or the agency has determined that the cost of the search will exceed $250.

Information Exempt from Release under FOIA

A. Nine categories of information are exempt from release under FOIA (listed in subsections of Title 5, U.S. Code, section 552).

(b)(1) Information specially authorized under criteria established by an executive order to be kept secret in the interest of national defense or foreign policy which is in fact properly classified pursuant to such an executive order.

(b)(2) Information relating solely to the internal personnel rules and practices of an agency.

(b)(3) Information exempted from disclosure by statute provided that such statute requires that the matters be withheld from the public in such a manner as to leave no discretion on the issue or establishes particular types of matters to be withheld.

(b)(4) Information on trade secrets and commercial or financial information obtained from a person and privileged or confidential.

(b)(5) Interagency or intra-agency memorandums or letters which would not be available by law to a party other than an agency in litigation with the agency.

(b)(6) Personnel, medical, and similar files the disclosure of which would constitute a clearly unwarranted invasion of personal privacy.

(b)(7) Information or records compiled for law enforcement purposes if certain enumerated adverse conditions could be reasonably expected to result from disclosure of the information.

(b)(8) Information contained in or related to examination, operating or condition reports prepared by, on behalf of, or for the use of an agency responsible for the regulation or supervision of financial institutions.

(b)(9) Geological or geophysical information and data, including maps, concerning wells.

Judicial Review

A. Jurisdiction over FOIA lawsuits is vested in the U.S. district courts.
B. A plaintiff must show that an agency has improperly withheld agency records. (Under the concept of "Open America" the courts usually grant the agencies additional time necessary to complete the administrative processing of a request.)
C. An agency must file its answer to an appeal within thirty days from the date of the origin of the service request.
D. Federal agencies bear the burden of justifying withholding information.
E. The district court conducts de novo review. On the issue of fee waivers the review is also de novo; however, it is limited to the administrative record before the agency.

F. Although the court at its discretion may review agency records withheld from the requester in camera to determine the propriety of the withholdings, substantial weight is to be accorded to the agency's affidavit.

G. Discovery in FOIA cases is limited and can be allowed, if at all, only after the government has moved for summary judgment and submitted its supporting affidavits. (Discovery is not permitted to enable a plaintiff to obtain the contents of withheld agency records.)

H. FOIA exemptions not invoked when responding to a requester during the administrative process are not waived for purposes of litigation.

I. Failure to raise an exemption at the outset of litigation may result in a waiver.

J. There are no damages available under FOIA. The court may only order production of any agency record improperly withheld and assess against the United States reasonable attorney fees and other litigation costs incurred when the plaintiff has substantially prevailed. (The mere filing of a lawsuit and the subsequent release of the records do not necessarily mean that the plaintiff substantially prevailed.)

Sample FOIA Letter

Name and address of the government agency
Washington, DC

Dear Sir or Madam:

Pursuant to the Freedom of Information Act, 5 USC 552, I hereby request access to (or a copy of) [describe the documents containing the information that you desire in as much detail as possible].

As you are aware, the FOIA as amended provides that if some parts of these files are exempt from release, "reasonable segregable" portions shall be provided. If you withhold some information I would also like to be advised as to which exemptions you are applying.

If any expenses in excess of $[   ] are incurred in connection with this request, please inform me of all such charges, prior to their being incurred, for my approval. I believe, however, since this research will be used in producing a book on the FBI, my request qualifies for a waiver of any search and reproduction fees according to the FOIA, which states that fees shall be waived if the request "is in the public interest because furnishing the information can be considered as primarily benefiting the public."

If this request is denied either in whole or in part, please inform me as to your agency's appeal procedures. If you do not grant my request within ten working days, I will deem my request denied.

Thank you for your prompt attention to this matter.

Sincerely,

Judge William H. Webster's Memorandum
Regarding FBI Searching Procedures

UNITED STATES DEPARTMENT OF JUSTICE   7-79

FEDERAL BUREAU OF INVESTIGATION

WASHINGTON, D.C. 20535

September 6, 1979

MEMORANDUM TO ALL BUREAU OFFICIALS AND SUPERVISORS

RE: REQUEST FOR INDICES SEARCH - SEARCHING PROCEDURES

  The General Index of the Central Records System has been divided into two separate sections (active and inactive) in order to facilitate the future conversion of the General Index to an automated mode. Recent surveys determined that most searches of the index are satisfied with index cards generated within the last 5 years for criminal matters and within the last 20 years for applicant- and security-related matters. The Active Index will contain cards generated since 1973 for criminal matters and since 1958 for applicant- and security-related matters. The Inactive Index will contain cards generated earlier than 1973 for criminal matters and 1958 for applicant- and security-related matters.

  Henceforth, a request for a Restricted Index Search will be limited to the Active Index, resulting in a check of criminal matters since 1973 and a search of cards for applicant- and security-related matters since 1958. A request for an Unrestricted Index Search will include both the Active and Inactive Index. A revised search slip will enable a requester to indicate variations of a search by making a proper check under the caption of Special Instructions.

  Special instructions requesting a subversive or nonsubversive index search remain basically the same, except for the limits established as a result of the separation of the General Index. For example, a request for an Unrestricted Search (Active and Inactive Index) with a check under special instructions for all references (subversive and nonsubversive) would result in a listing of all information in FBIHQ index.

ALL INFORMATION CONTAINED
HEREIN IS UNCLASSIFIED
DATE 6-1-81/ BY 4383 V67/

NOT RECORDED
167 SEP 12 1979

ORIGINAL FILED IN

MEMORANDUM TO ALL BUREAU OFFICIALS AND SUPERVISORS
RE: REQUEST FOR INDICES SEARCH - SEARCHING PROCEDURES

Classifications listed in the subversive search are
set forth below and those classifications underlined,
although criminal, will also be searched upon request or
special instructions asking for a subversive search. All
remaining classifications, including those criminal matters
underlined, would be included in a request for a
nonsubversive search.

1,	2,	3,	14,	19,	25,	39,	40,	44,
51,	54,	57,	61,	62,	64,	65,	67,	74,
77,	89,	94,	96,	97,	98,	100,	101,	102,
105,	106,	107,	108,	109,	110,	111,	112,	113,
114,	116,	117,	118,	121,	122,	123,	124,	126,
127,	128,	130,	132,	133,	134,	135,	136,	137,
138,	140,	151,	155,	157,	158,	161,	163,	170,
173,	174,	175,	176,	180,	184,	185,	191,	199,
200,	201	202,	203.					

A request identified as a Freedom of Information/
Privacy Act matter will receive a total search of both the
active and inactive indices of the General Indices. Requests
from outside agencies will be limited to their needs by
agreement with the requesting agency. It should be noted
that some of the above classifications are no longer in use,
however, they are listed for searching purposes in order to
provide the requester with all available information in FBI
files.

As previously stated, based on survey findings,
most searches of the index are satisfied with index cards
generated and segregated in the active section of the index.
Supervisory personnel should be aware of the index searching
procedure to insure that responses to their requests will
meet their needs.

William H. Webster
Director

-2-

IX. Department of Justice Classification System

1   Insecticide and Fungicide
2   Plant Quarantine Act
3   Weeks Forestry Act
4   Prisons Matters
5   Tax—Income and Inheritance
6   Stamping Act
7   Virus Act
8   Migratory Bird Act
9   European War Matters
10 Red Cross
11 War Tax—Amusement and Cigarette
12 Narcotic Act
13 National Defense Act
14 Cotton Future Act
15 Theft from Interstate Commerce
16 Strikes
17 War Risk Insurance
18 Standard Container Act
19 Opinions of the Attorney General
20 Standard Grain Act
21 Food and Drug (Prosecution)
22 Food and Drug (Seizure)
23 Liquor
24 High Cost of Living
25 Military Draft
26 Dyer Act (Automobile theft)
27 Patents
28 Copyrights
29 National Banking Act

30	Quarantine
31	White Slave Act (Mann Act)
32	Federal Building (Space)
33	Federal Building (Site)
34	Lacy Act (Game)
35	Civil Service Act
36	Mails to Defraud
37	Bonus Overpayment—World War I
38	Naturalization
39	Immigration
40	Passport and Visa
41	Explosives
42	Desertion from Armed Forces of United States, Harboring Such Deserters
43	Illegal Wearing of Uniform
44	Department of Justice (Closed)
45	Crime on the High Seas
46	Fraud against the Government
47	Impersonation of a Federal Officer
48	Postal Violations (Not otherwise classified)
49	Bankruptcy
50	Peonage
51	Offenses against Public Justice/Bribery and Perjury
52	Theft of Government Property
53	Excess Wool Profits (Closed)
54	Customs Violations
55	Counterfeit and Forgery
56	Future Trading Act, Commodity Exchange Act
57	Seed Grain Loans
58	Stockyards and Packers Act
59	Railroads, Transportation, and ICC Acts
60	Antitrust Violations
61	Admiralty Act
62	Obstruction to Navigation and Pollution of Streams
63	Warehouse Act
64	Lottery
65	Motorboat Act
66	Rentals and Leases
67	Bail Bonds and Forfeitures
68	Federal Farm Loan Act
69	Filled Milk Act
70	War Transaction—World War I
71	Neutrality
72	Election Frauds—Hatch Act

73	Oleomargarine Act
74	Title Registration
75	Eight-Hour Law
76	Opinions of the Courts
77	Claims in Favor of the U.S.
78	Tucker Act (Claims against the U.S.)
79	Tick Eradication
80	Firearms Act, Permits to Carry Arms
81	Prize Fight Films
82	Communications Act
83	Federal Employees' Compensation and Longshoremen's Act
84	Extortion and Blackmail
85	Produce Agency Act—Illegal Dumping
86	Federal Seed Act (Misbranding)
87	Franking Act
88	Air Traffic Act—Civil Aeronautics
89	Federal Aid Highway Fraud
90	Lands
91	Federal Conservation and Regulation of Resources
92	Naval Stores Act
93	Habeas Corpus (Federal prisoners)
94	Census
95	Miscellaneous Criminal Cases
96	Tobacco Stocks and Standards Act
97	Obscene Literature
98	Meat Inspection and Horsemeat Act
99	Federal Escape Act
100	Miscellaneous Correspondence
101	Mortgage and Lien Foreclosure Act
102	Federal Trade Commission Act
103	Wills, Bequests, Gifts
104	Caustic Poison Act
105	Reconstruction Finance Corporation
106	Agriculture Marketing Act, Agricultural Adjustment Act, Federal Supplies Commodity Act, Federal Crop Insurance Act
107	Perishable Commodity Act (Apple and Pear Export Act)
108	Misuse of Official Insignia
109	Kidnapping—Lindbergh Act
110	Honeybees Act
111	Federal Home Loan Bank
112	Gold Reserve Act
113	Federal Securities Act, Securities, and Exchange Commission
114	National Recovery Act
115	Tennessee Valley Authority

116	Farm Credit Administration (Closed)
117	Public Works Administration, Puerto Rican Reconstruction Loans, Rural Electrification
118	Emergency Conservation Works
119	Federal Emergency Relief Administration
120	Commodity Credit Corporation, International Wheat Agreement
121	Kickback from Public Works Employees
122	National Stolen Property Act
123	Anti-Racketeering Act
124	Railroad Labor Act
125	Killing or Assaulting a Federal Officer
126	Fugitive Felon Act
127	Harboring Felons (Except deserters)
128	Connolly Hot Oil Act
129	Offenses against the President
130	Federal Housing Act
131	Interstate Transportation of Prison-Made Goods
132	Bituminous Coal Conservation Act
133	Public Utility Holding Company Act
134	Labor (Wagner Act)
135	Halibut Act
136	Farm Security, Rural Rehabilitation, and Soil Conservation Loans (Farmers Home Administration)
137	Social Security Act
138	Black Bass Act
139	Interstate Transportation of Strikebreakers
140	Tobacco Inspection Act
141	Merchant Seamen
142	Eviction and Delinquent Rentals
143	Fair Labor Standards Act
144	Civil Rights
145	Federal Service
146	World War II (Subversive activities and other matters)
147	Food Stamp Act
148	War Policy Classification
149	Foreign Agents Registration Act
150	Knock for Knock (International maritime accidents)
151	World War II Veterans Matters
152	Tax Court Cases—Renegotiation of Contracts
153	Federal-State Relations
154	Court of Claims
155	Rules of Criminal Procedure
156	Labor Management Relations
157	Federal Tort Claims Act

X. Department of Justice
Old Classification System

80094	Traffic and Motor Safety
84381	Witness Immunity
118982	Diplomatic Immunity
219715	Walsh-Healy Act
223076	Occupational Safety
233279	Subpoenas
235033	Jurisdiction
235460	Railroad Retirement
235981	Alcohol Administration Act
236380	Administrative Procedures
236452	Mine Safety
236517	Tax Assessments
236702	Lucas Act

XI. FBI Central Records Classification System

1	National Academy Matters
2	Neutrality Matters
3	Destruction or Overthrow of the Government
4	National Firearms Act
5	Income Tax
6	Interstate Transportation of Strikebreakers
7	Kidnapping
8	Migratory Bird Act
9	Extortion
10	Red Cross Act
11	Tax (Other than income)
12	Narcotics
13	National Defense Act, Prostitution, Selling Whiskey within Army Camps, 1920 only (Obsolete)
14	Sedition
15	Theft from Interstate Shipment
16	Violation of Federal Injunction
17	Fraud against the Government—Veterans Administration
18	May Act
19	Censorship Matters (Obsolete)
20	Federal Grain Standards Act, 1920–21 (Obsolete)
21	Food and Drugs
22	National Motor Vehicle Traffic Act, 1922–1927 (Obsolete)
23	Prohibition (Obsolete)
24	Profiteering, 1920–1943 (Obsolete)
25	Selective Service Act
26	Interstate Transportation of Stolen Motor Vehicles and Stolen Aircraft
27	Patent Matters

28   Copyright Matters
29   Bank Fraud and Embezzlement
30   Interstate Quarantine Law (Obsolete)
31   White Slave Traffic Act
32   Fingerprint Matters
33   Uniform Crime Reporting
34   Violation of Lacy Act (Obsolete)
35   Civil Service
36   Mail Fraud
37   False Claim against the Government, 1921–1928 (Obsolete)
38   Application for Pardon to Restore Civil Rights,
         1924–1938 (Obsolete)
39   Falsely Claiming Citizenship
40   Passport and Visa Matters
41   Explosives (Obsolete)
42   Deserter
43   Illegal Wearing of Uniform
44   Civil Rights
45   Crime on the High Seas
46   Fraud against the Government
47   Impersonation
48   Postal Violations (Except mail fraud)
49   National Bankruptcy Act
50   Involuntary Servitude and Slavery
51   Jury Panel Investigations
52   Theft or Destruction of Government Property
53   Excess Profits on Wool, 1918–1925 (Obsolete)
54   Customs Laws and Smuggling
55   Counterfeiting
56   Election Laws
57   War Labor Dispute Act (Obsolete)
58   Bribery, Conflict of Interest
59   World War Adjusted Compensation Act, 1924–1944 (Obsolete)
60   Anti-Trust
61   Treason
62   Administrative Inquiry
63   Miscellaneous—Nonsubversive
64   Foreign Miscellaneous
65   Espionage
66   Administrative Matters
67   Personnel Matters
68   Alaskan Matters (Obsolete)
69   Contempt of Court
70   Crime on Government Reservation

71	Bills of Lading Act
72	Obstruction of Criminal Investigations
73	Application for Pardon
74	Perjury
75	Bondsmen and Sureties
76	Escaped Federal Prisoners
77	Applicants (Special inquiry, departmental, other government agencies)
78	Illegal Use of Government Transportation Requests
79	Missing Persons
80	Laboratory Research Matters—Headquarters
81	Gold Hoarding, 1933–1945 (Obsolete)
82	War Risk Insurance (Obsolete)
83	Claims Court
84	Reconstruction Finance Corporation Act (Obsolete)
85	Home Owners Loan Corporation (Obsolete)
86	Fraud against the Government—Small Business Administration
87	Interstate Transportation of Stolen Property
88	Unlawful Flight to Avoid Prosecution
89	Assaulting or Killing a Federal Officer
90	Irregularities in Federal Penal Institutions
91	Bank Robbery
92	Racketeering Enterprise Investigations
93	Ascertaining Financial Ability
94	Research Matters
95	Laboratory Examinations
96	Alien Applicants (Obsolete)
97	Foreign Agents Registration Act
98	Sabotage
99	Plant Survey (Obsolete)
100	Domestic Security
101	Hatch Act (Obsolete)
102	Voorhis Act
103	Interstate Transportation of Stolen Cattle
104	Servicemen's Dependents Allowance Act of 1942 (Obsolete)
105	Foreign Counterintelligence
106	Alien Enemy Control
107	Denaturalization Proceedings (Obsolete)
108	Foreign Travel Control
109	Foreign Political Matters
110	Foreign Economic Matters
111	Foreign Social Conditions
112	Foreign Funds
113	Foreign Military and Naval Matters

114	Alien Property Custodian Matters (Obsolete)
115	Bond Default
116	Department of Energy, Applicant
117	Atomic Energy Act
118	Applicant, Central Intelligence Group (Obsolete)
119	Federal Regulation of Lobbying Act
120	Federal Tort Claims Act
121	Loyalty of Government Employees (Obsolete)
122	Labor Management Relations Act
123	Special Inquiry—Department of State, Voice of America (Obsolete)
124	European Recovery Program (Obsolete)
125	Railway Labor Act
126	National Security Resources Board (Obsolete)
127	Sensitive Positions in the United States Government (Obsolete)
128	International Development Program (Obsolete)
129	Evacuation Claims (Obsolete)
130	Special Inquiry—Armed Forces Security Act (Obsolete)
131	Admiralty Matters
132	Special Inquiry—Office of Defense Mobilization (Obsolete)
133	National Science Foundation Act Applicant (Obsolete)
134	Foreign Counterintelligence Assets
135	Protection of Strategic Air Command Bases of the U.S. Air Force (PROSAB) (Obsolete)
136	American Legion Contact (Obsolete)
137	Informants
138	Loyalty of Employees of International Organizations
139	Interception of Communications
140	Security of Government Employees
141	False Entries in Records of Interstate Carriers
142	Illegal Use of Railroad Pass
143	Interstate Transportation of Gambling Devices
144	Interstate Transportation of Lottery Tickets
145	Interstate Transportation of Obscene Matter
146	Interstate Transportation of Prison-Made Goods
147	Fraud against the Government—Department of Housing and Urban Development
148	Interstate Transportation of Fireworks
149	Destruction of Aircraft or Motor Vehicles
150	Harboring of Federal Fugitives, Statistics (Obsolete)
151	Referral Cases from Office of Personnel Management— Applicant Loyalty
152	Switchblade Knife Act
153	Automobile Information Disclosure Act
154	Interstate Transportation of Unsafe Refrigerators

155 National Aeronautics and Space Act of 1958
156 Employee Retirement Income Security Act
157 Civil Unrest
158 Labor-Management Reporting and Disclosure Act of
    1959 (Obsolete)
159 Labor-Management Reporting and Disclosure Act of 1959
160 Federal Train Wreck Statute
161 Special Inquiries for the White House, Congressional Committees,
    and Other Governmental Agencies
162 Interstate Gambling Activities
163 Foreign Police Cooperation
164 Crime Aboard Aircraft
165 Interstate Transmission of Wagering Information
166 Interstate Transportation in Aid of Racketeering
167 Destruction of Interstate Property
168 Interstate Transportation of Wagering Paraphernalia
169 Hydraulic Brake Fluid Act (Obsolete)
170 Extremist Informants (Obsolete)
171 Motor Vehicle Seat Belt Act (Obsolete)
172 Sports Bribery
173 Civil Rights Act of 1964
174 Explosives and Incendiary Devices
175 Assaulting, Kidnapping, or Killing the President
176 Antiriot Laws
177 Discrimination in Housing
178 Interstate Obscene or Harassing Telephone Calls
179 Extortionate Credit Transactions
180 Desecration of the Flag
181 Consumer Credit Protection Act
182 Illegal Gambling Business
183 Racketeer-Influenced and Corrupt Organizations
184 Police Killings
185 Protection of Foreign Officials and Official Guests
186 Real Estate Settlement Procedure Act of 1974
187 Privacy Act of 1974
188 Crime Resistance
189 Equal Credit Opportunity Act
190 Freedom of Information/Privacy Acts
191 False Identity Matters (Obsolete)
192 Hobbs Act—Financial Institutions, Commercial Institutions
193 Hobbs Act—Commercial Institutions
194 Hobbs Act—Corruption of Public Officials
195 Hobbs Act—Labor Related
196 Fraud by Wire

197	Civil Actions or Claims against the Government
198	Crime on Indian Reservation
199	Foreign Counterintelligence—Terrorism
200	Foreign Counterintelligence—People's Republic of China
201	Foreign Counterintelligence—Satellites
202	Foreign Counterintelligence—Cuba
203	Foreign Counterintelligence—All Other Countries
204	Federal Revenue Sharing
205	Foreign Corrupt Practices Act of 1977
206	Fraud against the Government—Department of Defense
207	Fraud against the Government—Environmental Protection Agency, Department of Energy, National Aeronautics and Space Administration, and the Department of Transportation
208	Fraud against the Government—General Services Administration
209	Fraud against the Government—Department of Health and Human Services
210	Fraud against the Government—Department of Labor
211	Ethics in Government Act 1978
212	Foreign Counterintelligence—Intelligence Community Support
213	Fraud against the Government—Department of Education
214	Civil Rights of Institutionalized Persons Act
215–229	Foreign Counterintelligence Matters
230	Training Received—Foreign Counterintelligence
231	Training Received—Organized Crime
232	Training Received—White-Collar Crime
233	Training Received—Antitrust and Civil Matters
234	Training Received—Civil Rights
235	Training Received—Fugitives
236	Training Received—General Government Crime
237	Training Received—General Property Crime
238	Training Received—Personal Crime
239	Training Received—Terrorism
240	Training
241	DEA Applicant Investigations
242	Automation Matters
243	Intelligence Identities Protection Act of 1982
244	Hostage Rescue Team
245	Drug Investigative Task Force
246–248	Foreign Counterintelligence Matters
249	Toxic Waste Matters
250	Tampering with Consumer Products
251	Controlled Substances
252	National Center for the Analysis of Violent Crime/Violent Criminal Apprehension Program

253   Fraud and Related Activity in Connection with Identification
        Documents
254   Destruction of Energy Facilities
255   Counterfeiting of State and Corporate Securities
256   Hostage Taking—Terrorism
257   Trademark Counterfeiting Act of 1984
258   Credit and/or Debit Card Fraud
259   Security Clearance Investigation Program
260   Industrial Security Program
261   Security Officer Matters
262   Overseas Homicide/Attempted Homicide—International Terrorism
263   Office of Professional Responsibility Matters
264   Computer Fraud and Abuse Act of 1986 and Electronic
        Communications Privacy Act of 1986
265   Acts of Terrorism in the United States—International Terrorist
266   Acts of Terrorism in the United States—Domestic Terrorist
267   Drug-Related Homicide
268   Engineering Technical Matters—Foreign Counterintelligence
269   Engineering Technical Matters—Non-Foreign Counterintelligence
270   Cooperative Witnesses
271   Arms Control Treaty Matters
272   Money Laundering
273   Adoptive Forfeiture Matter—Drug
274   Adoptive Forfeiture Matter—Organized Crime
275   Adoptive Forfeiture Matter—White-Collar Crime
276   Adoptive Forfeiture Matter—Violent Crime/Major Offenders
        Program
277   Adoptive Forfeiture Matter—Counterterrorism Program
278   President's Intelligence Oversight Board

XII. FBI Records Turned over to NARA in 1992

The following lists investigative case files pertaining to various organizations and persons relating to the U.S. involvement in World War II. Some of these records remain classified.

Jane Anderson, Classification 65-36240, Sections 1–5, 1 cubic foot

Axis Sally (Mildred Gillars), Classification 100-232559, Sections 1–6 with Enclosures behind file, 2.5 cubic feet

Charles Bedeaux, Classification 100-49901, Sections 1–5 with Enclosures behind file, 1.5 cubic feet

Robert Best/8 Nazi Saboteurs, Classification 100-103780, Sections 1–4, 1 cubic foot

Niels Bohr, Classification 40-569222, Section 1, 2 cubic feet, and Classification 117–784, Section 1, 2 cubic feet

Douglas Chandler, Classification 100-32785, Sections 1–5, 1 cubic foot

George Dasch (George John Davis)/8 Nazi Saboteurs, Classification 98-10288, Sections 1–45 with Enclosures behind file and Bulkies, 18 cubic feet

Donald Day, Classification 62-11729, Sections 1–3, 2 cubic feet

Tyler G. Kent, Classification 65-27850, Sections 1–2, 1 cubic foot

Bernard Julius Kuehn, Classification 65-1574, Sections 1–7 with Enclosures behind file, 1 cubic foot

National German-American Alliance, Classification 62-1151, Section 1, 2 cubic feet

Louis B. Nichols (Official and Confidential) File, Classification 62-116607, 2 cubic feet

Dusko Popov, Classification 65-36994, Sections 1–19 with Enclosures behind file, 2.5 cubic feet

Steffi Richter, Fritz Weidmann, Franz Hohenlohe, and Kalman Szepessy, Classification 65-1649, Sections 1–29 with Enclosures behind file, 3 cubic feet

Paul Schulte, Classification 65-1627, Sections 1–5 with Enclosures behind file, 1.5 cubic feet

Otto Skorzeny, Classification 98-37716, Sections 1–2, 1 cubic foot

Special Intelligence Service, Classification 64-4104, Sections 1–11 with Enclosures behind file, 1 cubic foot

Admiral Graf Spee, Classification 65-16112, Sections 1–5, 2 cubic feet

War Relocation Authority, Classification 62-69030, Sections 1–16, 1 cubic foot

FBI ORGANIZATIONAL CHARTS, 1941–1990

1941

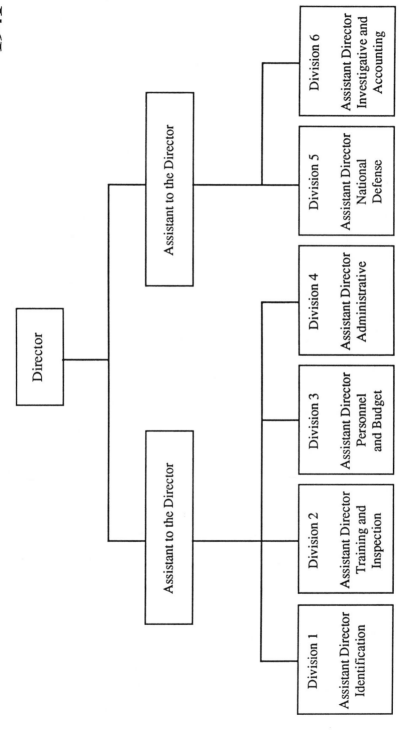

1943

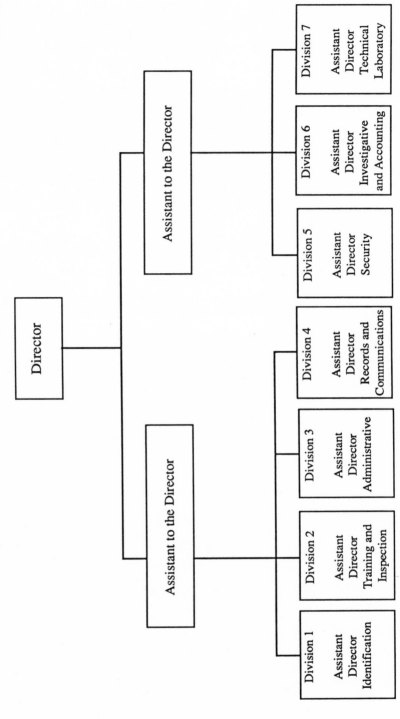

Director

Assistant to the Director

Assistant to the Director

Division 1	Division 2	Division 3	Division 4	Division 5	Division 6	Division 7
Assistant Director Identification	Assistant Director Training and Inspection	Assistant Director Administrative	Assistant Director Records and Communications	Assistant Director Security	Assistant Director Investigative and Accounting	Assistant Director Technical Laboratory

1958

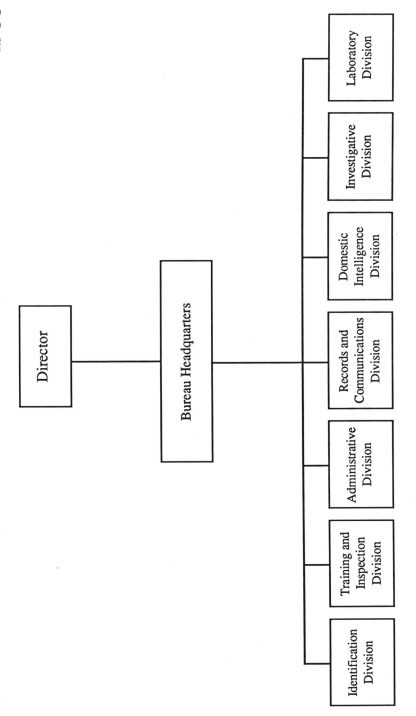

Director

Bureau Headquarters

Identification Division

Training and Inspection Division

Administrative Division

Records and Communications Division

Domestic Intelligence Division

Investigative Division

Laboratory Division

1965

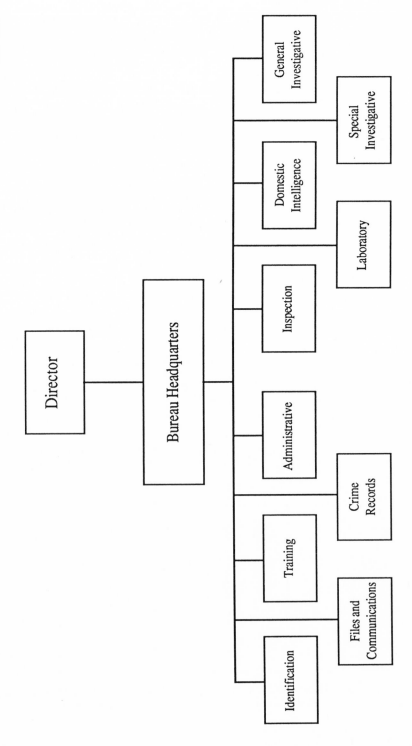

1976

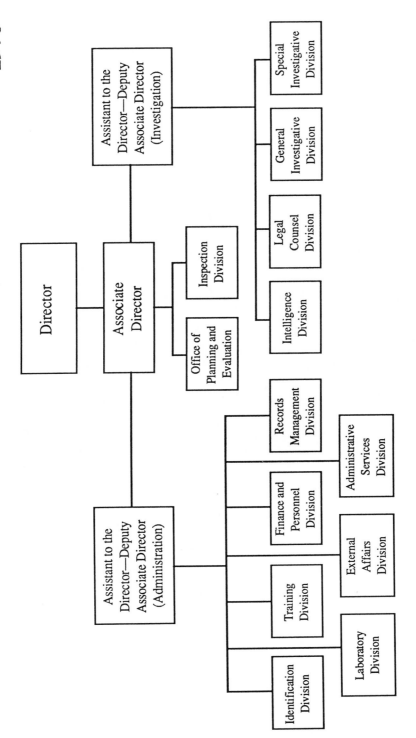

1986

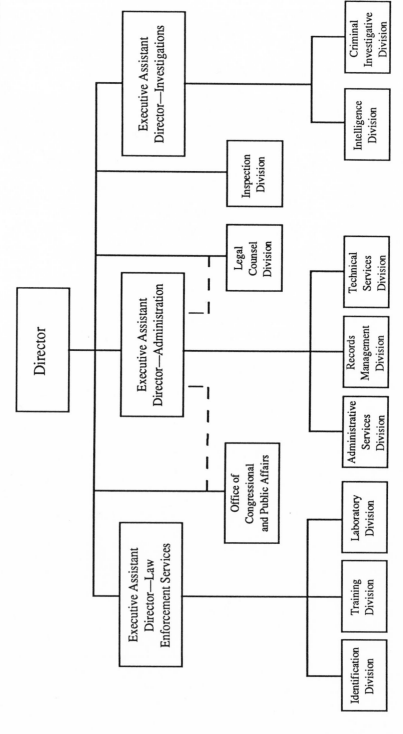

1990

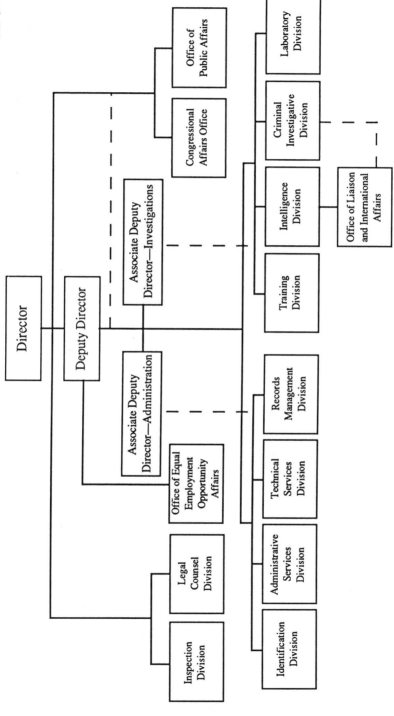

Director

Deputy Director

Office of Public Affairs

Congressional Affairs Office

Associate Deputy Director—Investigations

Associate Deputy Director—Administration

Office of Equal Employment Opportunity Affairs

Inspection Division

Legal Counsel Division

Identification Division

Administrative Services Division

Technical Services Division

Records Management Division

Training Division

Intelligence Division

Criminal Investigative Division

Laboratory Division

Office of Liaison and International Affairs

Index